ENDORSEMENTS

A thought-provoking, perspective-broadening, heart-expanding spiritual adventure story that shows the power and potential of God's touch on every human heart.

Savannah Guthrie
Author, *Mostly What God Does*

You asked the impossible, Teri. I meant to speed-read your book but couldn't. From the beginning it captured my attention and demanded I put away other things I was working on. I marvel at what a believer in Christ can accomplish—and endure! Such courage and tenacity. I'm hoping there'll be a Volume 2, picking up the story where this one leaves off.

Dr. E. LeRoy Lawson
Former President of Hope International University, CA
Christian Missionary Fellowship board member
20 years Senior Pastor of Central Christian Church, AZ
Author of over 30 books

This is a dangerous book. Justino's story relieves us of all the excuses we've ever made for lacking money or for our family troubles. They pale in comparison with Justino's. He was powered by purpose and joy. His story encourages us to live by faith in the Living Lord Jesus and to follow him without reserve. I want you to take a risk and read this book. You won't be the same by the end.

Dr. D. C. Kean
Frontiers, Consultant to Sending Int.
Author, *Uncharted Mission: Going to the Final Frontiers*

This book is not just a read; it's an inspiring journey into challenging locations, into Stone Age living in the Amazon and into civil war in Argentina. As you travel alongside Justino Rosa you will witness how his connection with God empowers him to transcend his limitations, conquer fear, and embrace his calling with unwavering faith. That kind of faith transforms the ordinary into the extraordinary, inspiring all of us to listen to God's voice and step into our own remarkable destinies.

Bryan Yeager
COO of Samaritan Aviation
Former Director of Events at Promise Keepers
Missionary to Kenya, Lead Pastor

Going blindly into the Amazon, without any skills to speak of and only his faith to protect him, speaks volumes to Justino's stubborn conviction in his belief. I couldn't help but continually compare our lives—different countries, socioeconomic opportunities, and diverse cultures. It was hard to grasp how different our lives could be. I am in awe of people with that deep belief system and the courage to follow through on their calling. I would like to meet this man of faith, Justino.

Commander Robert A. Dorman
USN, Retired

Ann Stauffer's book, *You Should Have Died,* is a compelling account of faith and sacrifice. It is rich in its portrayal of spiritual warfare and offers a unique perspective on the concept of discipleship, emphasizing the importance of listening to and following God's voice, even when it leads to the unknown or the seemingly impossible. This story is not just a narrative of one man's journey; it is a reflection on the universal themes of trust, transformation and divine guidance that resonate with anyone who seeks a deeper experience with God.

Dr. Jorge Henrique Barro
General Director and Professor, Faculdade Teologica
Sul Americana, Londrina, Brasil

YOU SHOULD HAVE DIED

The True Adventures of a Young Man
Who Followed the Voice of God

ANN T. STAUFFER

In loving memory of Alcione Rosa

CONTENTS

FOREWORD

Dearest reader of frequently-forgotten forewords, I'll keep it short. As an editor, I often feel privileged not to be the one carrying the heaviest responsibility. I only have to take what's offered and ensure the author's conveying just the right tone and feel, saying only what needs to be said, and then get out of the way to let readers make up their own minds about things and enjoy themselves. It's not a bad gig reading for a living, and I do highly recommend it. While it has its challenges, when it's good, which it frequently is, for me editing is right up there next to being an explorer or traveling for a living.

And working on this book was really something. After my second read, I suggested the title *Just Justino* because our subject and main character here is so incredibly humble, and I felt compelled to highlight that quality for the rarity it is. It's a primary reason I agreed to help, or indeed why I ever agree to help on a book, because there's no shortage of people wanting to publish, after all. It was reading that first introduction to him in the following pages that convinced me I too wanted to understand what made this man so powerfully meek.

One has to wonder what could make someone so willing to be starved, endangered, maligned, and even used the way he was. And through Teri's persistent, insightful storytelling, we're invited along to hear what she found as she continued threading the details out of him and following the longing in herself to know the answer to that single burning question.

Though, of course, there were many other questions as well. How did he survive? How did he forgive? And how did he recover from what would have surely been enough for most people to be quickly disabused of their notion of serving God, without visible reward or adequate recompense?

I was immediately struck by how different and foreign and altogether strange his story felt to my own prototypical, American-suburban existence. Coming up on fifty now, I'm increasingly grateful for any chance to compare my life with another's. And Justino's is certainly a unique one. I can promise if you read it, you will agree. It might actually change you as well, like it did me, leaving me with the afterglow of having experienced a truly meaningful encounter.

I've worked on a lot of books for big publishers, but few have impacted me as much as this one. It's one of those once-in-a-lifetime stories that introduces you to an amazing experience and leaves you a bit breathless. Myself, I was left feeling hopeful that living with God could really be just like this—freaky, for sure, but also a bit fantastic and exciting. I've never tried ayahuasca, or been attacked by piranhas, but now I feel like I have. And I'm better for it.

Now you want to come along, right?

Mick Silva
Editor & Author Coach
November 2023

...shuffling, tired
willing, brave, bruised
resolute, planted
stretched, hurting
tripping, climbing
blistered, muddied...
beautiful
are the feet of those who bring good news,
who announce peace,
who bring good tidings,
who proclaim rescue...

-Isaiah 52:7 (author's paraphrase)

PREFACE

In 1989, after finally purchasing a car in the midst of Brazil's hyperinflation, we were ready to travel, thrilled not to have to squeeze our family into a crowded omnibus to get around every day. Our Christian Missionary Fellowship team of five families caravanned together to meet for a few days at a beautiful *sítio*, farm, surrounded by coffee plantations. We met there for the weekend and hosted a well-respected Brazilian church planter in order to learn from him.

For the past year, we had been cramming Portuguese and meeting strangers, asking them dumb questions, and trying to figure out what they said. Our family was a bit numb from so much language study and culture change when we arrived at the small ranch. Our busy, noisy city of Campinas, São Paulo, had primed our senses to adore this countryside escape. Our own three kids had adjusted more easily to Brazilian life than my husband Chip and me, but they needed a break too. As soon as we arrived, they promptly disappeared to explore the farm on horseback with the other kids.

Our team gathered for typical Brazilian-style refreshments. We sipped the rich *café com leite* brewed with beans grown and roasted nearby, the fragrance making the air *gostoso*, delicious. A pitcher of local, creamy raw milk had been heated to pour liberally into our mugs of coffee for lattes. We chose treats from a tray laden with *salgados* and *doces* and *pãozinhos*—cheese, meat, or sweet-filled pastries and little loaves of bread—just baked in the kitchen while noisy cattle and tropical birds called to us from outside.

This was the first time Chip and I met Justino Rosa, a man in his mid-thirties (like us) and the key speaker at the retreat. Listening to him talk was like hearing straight from the book of Acts. This humble, passionate man obviously heard things from God and had made it his practice to go where God directed him. And he had traveled twelve hours by omnibus to talk with us about just that—God's direction.

I'm not sure I can capture all the feelings that flooded my mind and heart as I sat with the team and heard him speak. We had been anticipating leveling up our preparedness for this missionary life, something close to the training that we acquired in the United States, only in Portuguese. But Justino was talking about more than practical considerations and earthly concerns. The light in his calm eyes ignited a fire in me as he spoke of a present-day resistance, and an unmistakable spiritual warfare we hadn't yet identified but had definitely experienced, as surely as gravity.

As I listened with rapt attention, my heart pounded with misgivings about our own readiness for this work he described. I was wondering how much our culture study and demographic strategies had prepared us for what God had in store for us here. This man's approach to creating Christian community was based on simply listening to God and trusting. *Could that really be enough? And how would you do that?* This no-nonsense Brazilian pastor had said God alone was the one with the plan and the method and the power to accomplish it, with or without us. I blinked and gulped my coffee, trying to take it all in as my heart began to swell at the thoughts he was inspiring. I realized that what he so plainly stated was so biblical, so simple, and ironically, such good news.

Pastor Justino didn't hold back. We understood from his tone that our bold American self-confidence was of concern to him. He had sparred with dark powers he suspected we could miss seeing because of our naïveté and our unconscious sense of privilege. We were from a different world—a world that greatly undervalued anything that wasn't American, including the people.

Having been in Brazil a year now, as hard as we'd tried to become embedded missionaries, our Christian culture of measurable goals and certainty caused us to underestimate the people we came to live among and work with. They'd continually surprised us with their capacity for joy, their forgiveness of our mistakes, their openness, their generosity, their humility, and their sincere love for us. They'd surprised us with the power of their great faith, their hard work in the community, and their eagerness to pray and worship, sometimes throughout the night. Gently but firmly Justino helped us see that we were the brash, numbers-driven people who had come to show Brazil what needed to be done. We thought we knew how to meet these people's needs and tackle the forces and influences that surrounded them. We did not.

Our team left that retreat challenged by the fact that we had a lot to learn—but we also felt refreshed and inspired. And we jointly shared the belief that God's kingdom is near, that the gospel is for today, and that we are called to spread its regenerating power to the people in our midst. As we parted, Justino expressed his eagerness for our help in his country, and we were appreciative of his counsel.

A few years later, our team would reach out to Justino to lead our young Campinas church plant, believing the people should have a Brazilian pastor. Justino accepted our invitation and brought his family of five down to Campinas from Goiânia to lead and grow that church. They would eventually stay there, working and helping the people of that metropolitan city in southeastern Brazil for more than thirty years.

Working closely with Justino in Brazil for a few months, Chip and I quickly came to appreciate his way of serving the beloved people our team had gathered. And, as we got time to hear more of his story, we came to learn Justino had spent time in the Amazon basin, living for some years among an undiscovered tribe of indigenous people. Astounded, we had to know more. And so he began to recount some of his adventures and tales of his early life. The more he talked, the more we marveled at how he had survived to tell us about it. As Chip says it, it was as if he were serving us the most amazing meal we'd ever eaten, but to him it was just an ordinary snack. To Justino, following God anywhere and everywhere was simply a matter of fact; it was truly no big deal to him. Justino's wife, Alcione, became the prayer minister for our church women, and I learned from her how to pray in a way that transformed my restless nights into peaceful sleep, even as we transitioned back into life in the United States.

Our friendship continued between continents, and I never forgot the stories Justino told us of his earlier life and time spent in the Amazon territory. I revisited Brazil ten years later and told Justino that his stories raised my hopes and expectations of God, and I felt compelled to write them all down. That very week his whole family assembled in the Rosa living room and the recordings began, all of us full of emotion as we interviewed him together. I continued to videotape many more of those stories every few years, in Brazil and in the United States, whenever Justino visited in person.

During the past decade and a half, I have unwrapped and translated the many taped sessions with Justino as if they were divine gifts because each speaks of God's presence and power in everyday life. Knowing and contemplating Justino's deep experience with God has helped me to try to journey into a deeper faith in God myself as well. I only hope I've done his story justice.

CHAPTER 1

OBSESSION

My grandfather, who gave me his name, Justino Pereira Rosa, was brought up in Campos, in the state of Rio de Janeiro, Brazil, in the late 1800s. At the time, the German community controlled most of the sugarcane plantations in the region. As a Negro and child of slaves, my grandfather lived and worked on such a plantation. His humble position in life did not prevent the German plantation owner's daughter from admiring his gentle strength and falling in love with him. He and my grandmother, Maria Braulia Heringer, ignored the rules of society of the era and married. Fair-skinned Maria marrying a black man was too much for this German family. Because of their elopement, the newlyweds were expelled from the Heringer property and family.

Maria's German Lutheran and Presbyterian background greatly influenced the Rosa family. Maria taught my grandfather the Bible, and he became a believer in Jesus Cristo. After a few years, Maria tragically died, leaving five little ones for Justino to raise alone. The Heringer family then softened and grieved the hard line they had taken against their daughter and Justino. Maria's sisters helped him care for the children after their mother's death, taking the littlest children into their own homes. As soon as it was possible, young Samuel Moacir, João, Hercilia, Erondina, and Julieta were all brought back under one roof together and raised by their own *Papai*, Justino. He did his best to bring them up in the way Maria had requested, as followers of Jesus.

The youngest, Samuel Moacir Rosa, became my father. He married Almerindadias Azevedo, also born of European parents—José Azevedo from Portugal, and Maria Euvia Dias Donierego from Italy. This is how my three brothers and seven sisters and I all came to be Brazilian sons and daughters of Africa, Germany, Portugal, and Italy. Our names are Cidalia, Celia, Gerci, Maura, Jesus, Elza, Justino, Selma, Adamario, Neida, and Luzineide. I am number seven of eleven.

The visible racial diversity of our family was not something that we children discussed at home. This is an ambiguous part of our ethnic identity that we didn't try to understand or define. We knew we were poor, though. Growing up in rural Brazil meant that we were part of a two-class society of rich landowners and poor plantation laborers. Our parents dreamed of having their own land to farm, and we were all part of their wish. We learned from our parents that the vulnerability and hardship of the poor were part of life's injustice. Yet there was that hallowed hope that hard work and resourcefulness would bring us opportunity.

I was born in 1951, about five hundred kilometers north of Rio de Janeiro, in a little town called Chalé. My father, like his father, was a very honest man, a *muito trabalhador*, very hard worker, who was committed to taking good care of his family no matter what the sacrifice. My father brought us up knowing the Bible, following Jesus, going to church regularly, and reading the Scriptures every morning at home. When my *irmãos*, siblings, and I were old enough to go to school, we were each given a *Bíblia*, Bible, as a present. I don't have mine anymore, but I do have my sister Elza's Bible. Later, Selma gave me her first Bible too. The three of us wrote daily verses sitting together to practice some of the writing of our rather difficult language, *Português*. We missed school because of our chores, but this ritual of opening our Bibles every day we did not miss. To give Pai credit, we might have been illiterate without his religion.

The church we attended was planted by my father on the *fazenda*, farm, where we lived and worked. It was the only one of its kind in the area, as most of Brazil was Catholic, and my father was raised in a kind of Lutheran Presbyterian tradition. At first it was just us: just Pai, Mamãe, and their children. Others in the community watched as he built the church and we attended the worship that he led every Sunday. Then Papai began to tell everyone in the surrounding area about the Lord Jesus and invited them to worship with us in the church he built.

As time passed, the little church grew with many families coming to know of life with Jesus. Pai said we had won the Família Maulais, the Família Correia, and even the Família Paixão to faith in Jesus Cristo. The Paixão clan were reputed to be notorious bandits, even believed to kill people for money. All in each of the families were called to new life in Jesus. And so, I was raised with this practice of sharing our life with Jesus with others and seeing their transformation. My father received this way of gathering a community to follow Jesus from his father, for whom I was named, just as my grandfather received it from his dying wife.

When I was born, my family says, my little face was the exact image of *Avô*, Grandfather. Grandfather Justino said that when he looked at me, it was like looking in the mirror. So Avô gave me his name, not knowing the burden it would be for me to wear it. I never personally knew my avô, but his name was used by our father to tell stories, to set the bar high, to give us an example of everything upright, and to call me, Justino, to account. There wasn't anyone like this self-educated black man who had raised five children and taught them from the Scriptures when it was still forbidden to read the Bible without a priest.

Papai also was a very good man, a *brincalhão* like his father, loveable, with a gregarious nature. Pai would often sit down with our big family and tell us stories about each one of us. When we had visitors, his stories became theater. Pai learned *capoeira* from his father, a master of that martial art. It's a popular sport today but was originally the slaves' way of defending themselves. People loved to watch Pai and others perform capoeira, and sometimes our church family brought their music, friends, and food, and we had a night of fun after working hard all week.

When I was still just a boy, our family lost everything, and my father decided to move us to another state. I haven't been back to my hometown of Chalé since then, and I let most of the memories of that place we left behind evaporate. But I remember moving away.

The evening before we left, some of the *irmãos*, brothers and sisters of the church, came to our house for a farewell blessing, *culto de despedida*. They prayed for us, and I remember the sharp ache of *tristeza* when they sang the old folk songs and hymns we all knew by heart. I knew I would never see these people again, share food with them, or sing with them around the fire outside. Papai said it was time to put the fire out. So, I extinguished all their faces and watched them turn to smoke and drift up into the night clouds. Mamãe wiped her face, but I *segurei as lagrimas*, held back the tears. I began to learn how to block out my losses at a young age. I observed that this was the way of my older brothers and Papai.

When morning came, we set off with all our belongings in a truck with Mãe and Papai and little Selma in the front with them. I rode in the back on top of everything we had packed, along with the older Rosa brothers and sisters. We were on our way to the state of Paraná to start a new life in the *sul*, south, of Brazil. From the top of the truck, I looked out beyond the highway and saw a train pass by. It was the first train I had ever seen. I asked my older brothers what it was, but they didn't know. That sight, that *trem de ferro*, left a mark on my life. I felt it, but I wouldn't know what it was or what it meant until I was a young man.

After driving all day, we finally crossed the Rio Doce, River Sweet, at twilight on a ferry. Still in the state of Minas Gerais, we had come to a place called Resplendor. When it was dark, we were all exhausted and grateful to stop at a little inn called Pensão. All we really wanted to do was sleep, but there were so many *pernilongos*, long-legged mosquitoes, flying around us we couldn't sleep at all, not that entire night.

After a few days of traveling south, in the middle of our journey, Elza slipped and struck her head on the edge of the truck bed. She was bleeding everywhere, and we were many days of travel away from any kind of medical help. We children agonized over our sister, sure she would die. She was only a little girl, a year older than I was. She survived that long journey, but for days we were very afraid she wouldn't. That was a terrible, helpless time for our family. We desperately clung to the hope of a safe arrival in our beautiful new land.

We did arrive safely, but we soon found our new home in Paraná to be a brutal change for us. We were accustomed to the warmth of Minas Gerais, which lies closer to the equator. *Que saudades!* What homesickness! We had arrived in Paraná in December on a surprisingly cold Christmas Eve during *verão*, summer, in Brazil. Our family was completely unprepared for the approaching autumn and frigid winter cold coming. My brothers and sisters reminisced, but I wrapped myself in amnesia that Christmas. My father had bought our piece of land in Paraná along with the truck, and that was the extent of his resources. With just one field to plant, and no yield yet, we had barely a roof over our heads before winter arrived. In our crude shelter we had no furniture, no warm clothing, no blankets, and no money to buy the most basic necessities. We put anything we found on the land that would burn into a large basin that we fashioned into a fireplace, and we slept on the floor near it to save ourselves from freezing. We had never before seen frost or ice outdoors, and we suffered so much from this harsh cold that we thought we would die.

My father pawned his beloved watch to buy food for us. He had nothing else of value. As soon as he had enough money, he bought it back. But before long he had to pawn it again. And again. My father's uncle helped us by selling some of his land to lend us money. But like my father with his watch, he didn't want to let go of the land, and we forever owed him money so that he could buy back his piece of land. So Papai was always selling his watch and buying it back to pay *Tio*, Uncle, who was always selling his piece of land and sooner or later buying it back. Papai and Tio could not get off their merry-go-round.

"Por que não ficamos em Chalé? Why didn't we stay in Chalé where we were warm and happy?" asked my older brothers and sisters. I knew it was a very difficult time for our family, but for me, it was worse. I did not have the spirit or *facilidade*, easiness to adapt, the way they did. I could no longer remember *ever* being warm or happy. Something in me went dark, and I rejected their offers of help and their pretended good cheer. To me, this was our unalterable bitter reality. Papai had said that Jesus turns curses into blessings, and I had tried to believe this as long as I could. But now I was *tomando nota*, taking note, every day that many things did not change for the better. And I was not growing up to be what Avô or Papai expected me to be. I was not the little brother or the big brother my family wanted or what my mother hoped I could become. I was a disappointment because I could not live up to my name. This had a major effect on my childhood and probably altered the course of my adolescent life.

Within a few years I grew certain that I wanted a different life from what my father had chosen for our family. I didn't want to go to church anymore. In fact, I hated church. I didn't read my Bible anymore. I tried to smoke, but I didn't like it. I tried to drink, but I didn't like drinking. The only thing I did like to do was work. It was my only escape from life.

And so, I began to work, day and night, and that's how I passed the time. I was a *trabalhador muito duro*, workaholic. I worked in the fields and saw only my parents and my brothers and sisters in my own house. The vibration of the tractor, the smell of earth and clouds, the rhythm of the seasons with my sickle—this was the methadone I needed to numb my sadness. I worked so much that I didn't have any time to develop any relationships with people, not even with my family.

I'm not sure how this happened, but I persisted for many years in declining to enter the house of anyone. I didn't go to the houses of my married brothers and sisters. I didn't go to the houses of friends of the family. I don't think I had a single childhood friend. Until I was eighteen years old, I refused to join any gathering in the house of anyone.

During this *epoca* of my life I was not only *sem amigos*, friendless, but also at odds with all of my brothers and sisters. I had no love for them, and they had none for me. I was *muito estranho, sim*, very strange, yes. I picked fights with my brother Jesus, who was five years older than I was. I struck Elza, my slightly older sister, more than once. I think I beat on all my brothers and sisters. They all despised me because I was *horrível*, horrible! And I despised them too. I didn't care that my words and actions were vile toward the only people I knew.

Our little old tractor was used to farm in the *roça*, countryside, where we planted our crops. Papai loved his fine field of *mandioca*, a root Brazilians grind for flour and fry like potatoes. One day while in a rage against my father, I took that tractor and plowed up his crop of mandioca until there was nothing left of it. I wanted to kill my father. Once we had such a violent fight that I took a *foice*, scythe, from the farm tools and tried to cut his throat with it. Somehow, he got free of me, *graças a Deus*, thank God! I was strong, but he was fast and skilled at martial arts. In a breath he had the pole and the long, curved blade out of my hand. I had little remorse at the time. Not an empathetic thought for Pai. He expected me to be similar or even equal to his father and demanded perfection from me for having Avô's name and for wanting me to honor the name. How could I be anything but myself, Justino? How could I be like Avô Justino when I didn't even know him?

Pai was very conscious of his image in the community wherever we lived and, as a black man, this was no easy image to care for. He had to somehow overcome the prejudices against his race as well as those against his religion. My father was the grandson of a slave and the pastor of his own Protestant church when most of the country confessed themselves to be Catholic. Papai needed to prove that his family knew how to be as faithful to God as any Catholic family. I was living proof he was a failure because he could not make me obedient. If I was a threat to his success in life, then so be it. He was a threat to mine. I could not exist under the harshness of my father's authority, and early on I chose to be independent of it. And yet, if someone had asked me if I loved my father, my mother, and all of my brothers and sisters at this time, I would have said yes. I didn't know I was like my father and my grandfather in my obstinance and my independence. I didn't know why I was so angry and unhappy. No one did.

Something very dark and hateful warred within me, you see. I was hostile and without compassion. I walked with no one, related to no one. I only worked; night and day I worked. I arose before dawn and labored until very late out in the roça, farming. Nights filled with moonlight, and I stayed in the roça working as long and as late as I could. In the daytime I plowed, planted, or picked cotton. At night, I sorted, separated, bundled, and packed cotton. Hands bleeding, back throbbing, I gutted through the hours. Whatever the season, whatever the crop, I kept to the task. I was obsessed and consumed.

Sometimes I knew my mother wanted to talk with me, but I didn't want to see anyone and I ignored her. I rarely stopped to eat. Any type of feeling only increased my grief. It was better to feel nothing. Brazilian families gather to eat together at midday, even in the city, and this is a very important part of our national culture. But I was only content to eat while working, which isolated me further from the company of my family. I had only one goal, one dream, one intention in this period of my life in Paraná—to become a great *fazendeiro*, plantation owner. I imagined having the power to possess things that no one else had. It wasn't enough to be a rich fazendeiro; I wanted to have more than anyone. With my drive and my ambition, I believed that I would indeed come to a point where I would succeed in this in spite of the drought in my soul. I worked for Papai on the farm during regular hours, but during all my "free" hours I worked for myself.

As much as I worked, I found no fulfillment. During all of my *adolescencia* I was impenetrable and dark of heart and mind. I thought that my whole childhood was devoid of affection and affirmation because I had made it that way. Not my father. I blamed no one, not even myself. I did not know that I was *muito triste*, very sad. I did not know I was *deprimido*, depressed. *Todo o trabalho e nenhuma brincadeira faz um menino chato.* This is the "all work and no play makes a dull boy" saying. I had no idea that my personal compulsion to better myself with hard work was a common, impious way of hollowing me out, and it was not improving me in any way. It was not a new invention. I wasn't bucking the system. No one was impressed.

Some days the intense weight of my fatigued body forced me to rest after working all day. I went to the *praça*, little village square, in the middle of our town. As night fell, I would sit there alone on a bench. I watched the villagers as creatures, not as people, walking and talking in the marketplace and around the park. My little sister Selma sometimes found me there. She would try to befriend me with a smile. She would come and sit by me on the park bench. This pierced me, though. I moved down away from her. I didn't want anyone close to me.

I remember I wanted to learn to shoot and so I bought a gun. For target practice, I used my father's banana orchard. The bananas grew high up in great bunches linked to the tree canopies by vine-like cords. The bananas were inhabited by a host of birds and mice and insects that I interrupted when I tried to sever the cords with my well-aimed shots. The great kisskadees, camouflaged in their yellow-green feathers and black-and-white war paint, scolded me for my meanness. The toucan eyed me in judgment. I mostly split the bananas with the bullets rather than hit the cords. Later I tried throwing knives at the bananas, and this is the diversion I allowed myself after work. I pretty much ruined my father's banana groves improving my aim. A malevolent period of my life, I know. I shake my head in wonder.

One of those nights it was very cold, and I arrived home especially downhearted. That day I was painfully bad off. I had worked hard all day, and then I had gone to the *praça da villa,* central park of the town, to do who knows what because I had nothing to do. I sat on the bench and watched without seeing. When I got home, the pounding in my ears and the ache inside me was unbearable. I felt confused and there was a profound *desânimo,* despondency, weighing me down. I felt beaten and weak and agitated at the same time, and I didn't know why. I knew I didn't like anything in this bleak life and least of all, myself. It was late when I arrived home, but I didn't want to sleep. I couldn't be still.

I thought of the Bible that my father had given me as a boy and remembered it was on top of the wardrobe. I reached up and found it. For a long while I just held it in my hand. I thought about my mother and how good she was and felt a stab in my heart. She always knew the things her eleven children liked best. Whether she cooked or sewed, she made our favorite things for us. All of us. When she did this for me, even though I liked it, I said nothing and only left the house to return to work. The way I treated her was my greatest sorrow. Restless, I finally opened that Bible, which I had not done in a long time. I was immediately affected by what it said, right where I first read: "*porque nem quente nem frio,* because you are...neither hot nor cold" (Revelation 3:16a NIV).

These words were for me. I was missing out on any awareness, any progress, any high or low, utterly uncaring, unfeeling, deaf and tasteless to life. My sense of loss was so great that the burden of grief was unbearable.

That spoke to me. That was me. I was neither hot nor cold, nem quente nem frio. Inside I was dark and empty. From that moment, a change began in my life. I would not sleep that night, no. I lay down but I was unable to sleep, not all night. That phrase stayed with me—nem quente nem frio, neither hot nor cold—repeating those words. I knew that I was broken and helpless. Finally, I had been called out. I was relieved and thankful to be called out by Jesus, the voice of love.

It was finally morning, four o'clock in the morning, and time for me to get up. I got ready to go to work and went to the kitchen. Mamãe had made breakfast as she always did, and I stood near her as she poured my coffee. I lay my hand on her back and patted her, something I hadn't done for years. She looked up at her son and I smiled at her.

Like always, I ate my breakfast silently and went out to work, but something had happened inside me. I felt different. I could feel again! Without even knowing what it would mean, I had let someone in. I had opened the door and allowed the Lord Jesus to begin cultivating the soil of my life. He had reattached me. I worked all that day and didn't stop for lunch at all. That night I came directly home and went to bed early. I was *verdadeiramente*, truly, exhausted.

CHAPTER 2

GOD SPEAKS

On Saturdays, it was part of the Brazilian way to have a large family midday meal and then enjoy the afternoon. I usually came home to eat and immediately returned to work. That morning I went to work, returned home, took my bath, had lunch, and instead of going back to work I went to the praça. The shops were closed now, and people were visiting with family and friends. There was nothing to look at. The village square was empty. I remember looking down at my mud-caked field boots, shivering alone in the cold on that park bench in the praça.

About four o'clock in the afternoon my little sister Selma and some of her friends passed by. They were on their way to church to rehearse their singing for worship and to pray together. Selma was very involved with the other young people of the church, a nice group of adolescents whose parents lived and worked on the local farms. When Selma and her friends saw me, they called out to me.

"*Vamos pra igreja—venha conosco, Justino!* Come go to church with us! Come with us!" they said.

"*O que vou fazer na igreja?* What am I going to do at church? *Não tem nada ai para mim!* There's nothing there for me!" I called back.

My eyes followed them and then went safely back to my boots, as if they were finishing a story. There were two new young ladies in the group, as well as a cousin of mine and another boy I didn't know. I looked out at them again, considering them each by name—a little group of kids of maybe eleven to fourteen years of age. It really was a very cold afternoon, and they looked *tão jovem*, so young, in their huddle taking the *avenida* near me to shorten their walk. I felt sorry for them, and I even had a pang of conscience for having so coolly rejected their invitation.

"I am so much older at sixteen. I should be looking after them or, at least, supporting their activities," I chided myself.

Now, this was a new *jeito de pensar*, perspective, for me, you see! So, I got up and ran after them. When we got to the church, I saw they didn't waste any time but began to pray right away. I installed myself over in a corner, but they really had my attention. Almost holding my breath, I was inert, listening, watching. *Foi muito bom!* It was so very good! *Sinceramente*, sincerely, it moved me to hear them pray! They were endearing, all kneeling at the simple, rustic church benches. Rosali had been leaning so close to the back of the pew in front of her that she had slipped her head through the separation of the wooden planks. Now she couldn't get her head back out.

"*Gente, estou presa aqui do banco!* Friends, I'm stuck here in the bench!" she cried.

The kids tried different ways to free her but without success. They moved the position of her neck and her head. They tugged on her. They tried everything. Suddenly I realized why I was there. They needed *my* help. I found a kind of lever to pry the wooden planks apart so that Rosali could pull out her head without hurting herself. When all this was done and she was free, they all thanked me.

With enthusiasm, they said, "*Podemos orar por você?* Could we pray for you?"

I felt *meio sem graça*, awkward and embarrassed. They wanted to pray for me to thank me, to help me in return. I didn't know how to receive it. But what could I say? I let them pray for me as if I were doing a favor for them. And when they prayed for me, *algo saiu de mim!* Something went out of me! *Naquele dia, eu mudei.* That day, I changed. Before that day, it had never occurred to me that I should, or could. Something powerful happened to me. On that day, I myself knew I was made different inside. I felt as if a new heart had been placed inside of me, very like the day Jesus had called out my condition and rooted me in so that I could feel again.

At that time, we had a little jeep at our house. It was very old, but it had great value to me because I used it for my work. The next morning was Sunday, and I normally would have gotten into that jeep and driven to the fields to work while Pai walked to church.

That morning, I said to my father, "*Pai, eu vou na igreja hoje.* Dad, I'm going to church today."

"You're going?" asked my father in disbelief.

That day I took the jeep to church, instead of to work. My father rode with me, along with some of the family. It was the first time in my life I remember really considering the people around me. I simply had not seen them before. I had never had any interest in anybody until that time. I noticed that Sonia, who was the sister of the girl who was stuck in the prayer bench, was very pretty. Sonia and Rosali were the daughters of an officer of the bank in the city.

I gazed at the people in the congregation and thought, "It's time for me to start going to church. *Tem meninas na igreja!* There are girls at church!"

I began to go often to church and to take part in the activities of the group *de adolescentes*, of young people. I joined them in visiting the surrounding farms to talk to people about Jesus. It was a satisfying time of my life as I began to learn and grow and change on the inside.

Some changes didn't come quickly or easily. I was so very behind. I was resistant, even impervious, to change. I still would not enter the house of anyone; not anybody. If I was invited, I brusquely declined. And then Sonia asked me to come to dinner at her house one day. We had gotten to know each other better and had developed an affinity between us. Sonia was a lovely light that shone onto my shadowy path.

"No, I don't go to the houses of others," was my idiotic response. "I have a house," I said as if it explained everything. She smiled and nodded, as if it did, indeed.

One day Sonia introduced me to her father when we suddenly encountered him walking down the street. She did this in the most natural way, as if her father would want to know me and I would want to know him too.

"Papai, this is Justino," she said, serenely, grinning. Her pai reached out to shake my hand, smiling just like his daughter.

"What a *prazer*, pleasure, to know you, Justino!"

"Prazer, Senhor," was my shy reply.

His hand was as big as mine, but as soft as hers. My next day in town, I made a brave visit to his place of work at O Banco Nacional to say hello. He brought me in like I had an appointment. I remember how *muito simpatico*, very nice, he was to me.

"Justino, I want you to come to my house," Senhor Nivaldo said insistently.

"*Não, Senhor. Não vou nas casas dos outros; eu tenho a minha casa,*" was my reply. "No, Senhor, I don't go to the houses of others; I have my own house."

I laugh at myself to think of it. Though I was mingling with others, in many ways I continued as that same Justino—immature and antisocial. I didn't yet know how to relate well. But I was unearthing my way. I began to pray with the young people in our church and joined in during our youth group visits to other churches with their prayer circles. Learning to pray was life-changing for me. It was a way of sharing life with God. I had not known how to share life before.

We were identified with the youth of an Evangelical Presbyterian congregation, a sister church of the larger mother church in the *sul*, south, of Brazil. Other sister churches were forming in our state of Paraná, and we visited many of them for worship and fellowship outside of our own community. We asked God to teach and lead us, and we prayed for each other wherever we gathered. We told one another what we were learning about God and about His love. One cold holiday, probably in June, our little group of five or six planned a prayer retreat. We traveled to a wooded area and fasted and prayed all day, reading our Bibles together in a quiet place near a little stream. It was *muito bom*, very good! It was beautiful being away from the noise and in the *natureza*, nature, all around, its mysterious silence interrupted only by birdsong.

When I was kneeling by a fallen log, I had an astonishing experience during my prayers. I found myself listening to God's voice. I heard His voice speak to me in my mind and show me things that were to be His plan for my life! This was an experience set apart, not explainable in terms I presently knew. This was beyond anything I had ever experienced. After this indescribable time with God, I looked around and noticed that the others were nowhere near me. I had heard the voice of God, speaking to my very soul, and I believed this without question. I knew it was God who had spoken. I wanted to tell someone.

The first person I wanted to talk to was my little sister Selma. Going to *igreja juntos*, church together, we had become close. For months we had been singing, praying, and discovering fellowship with Jesus together. As soon as I found her, I told her about the voice of God I had heard within me.

"*Eu tenho certeza que foi Deus que falou comigo.* I know it was God who spoke to me."

"Tininho," said Selma, using my family nickname in her gentlest reproach. *"Cuidado viu? Deus não fala assim, não.* Tininho, be careful, okay? God doesn't speak like that, no."

"Mas ouvi! Deus falou comigo! But I heard him! God spoke to me!" I insisted.

I was certain of what I heard, and I had a deep conviction that it was the voice of our Lord God.

Our forest retreat ended, and we returned to our homes in the late afternoon. I was really looking forward to talking to Papai. He had been a Christian for many years. He taught the Bible and he knew the ways of God. He would certainly understand! I was excited to finally have a reason to go to him and talk to him about something important. For years we had nothing between us holding us together. I so wanted my Papai to be close to me, proud of me, not disappointed in me. I had never been able to honor Avô's name with my life. I could honor my Papai now. I had stopped being a sour, sullen, unresponsive teenager. Yes, I had found a way to make life difficult for him as payback for his rigid, demanding parenting. Here was a way back to him. Now I had a destiny for my life, a gift from heaven. Since Papai understood well the Christian life, he would identify with me now, and this would bring us together. Besides, he had probably heard God's voice too.

"Pai, I went to pray with the other *jovens*, young people, and while I was kneeling God spoke to me. I heard God speak to me."

"*Que isso, menino!* What's wrong with you, boy? You've always been strange. God doesn't speak like that. Forget this!" said my father.

My father's words stung badly. I had convinced myself that the two of us would be brought closer, that Papai and I could finally agree completely on something that was important to both of us. I hadn't taken into account that my father was *muito bravo*, very tough, very authoritarian. He was a strict disciplinarian; he had whipped us severely and often while we were growing up. Especially me. I had fought back bitterly, and this had perpetually alienated us from one other. Why was I surprised he didn't believe God had spoken to me? I was taken aback with the idea that Papai may not know everything about faith in Jesus! How could Papai not know that our God speaks? In this case, he was clearly the one who was wrong!

I appealed to my mother.

"Mamãe," I said, "I was in the woods praying, kneeling on the ground, and I heard God's voice and saw amazing things. *Ouvi Deus falar comigo!* I heard God speak to me!"

"Forget this, son. Your father told you that God doesn't speak. Your father knows the Bible, knows the Christian experience, has lived his whole life in the church. *Esquece isso.* Forget this!" I knew she would side with Pai. She thought she had to. I suspected she knew she would regret it, and I forgave her. But it made me sad for her.

I grew more frustrated because I had this unyielding conviction within me, this certainty that I had heard something real. This was not a dream, but an audible voice. And my own family thought that *estava louco*, I was crazy! I had no doubt that I had received something from God, and I was sure this was the voice of God. I went to the church to talk to a leader whom my father had known for many years.

"I need to talk to you," I said to José Carreiro. I told him about the prayer retreat and my experience. He patted my shoulder shaking his head.

"God doesn't speak like that," he said. "God used to speak this way to the prophets and others like Moses and Abraham. But now God doesn't speak aloud anymore. Today we have the Bible, and God speaks to us through the Bible only. You didn't hear God's voice, Justino. *Deus não fala assim.* God doesn't speak like that."

There was no pretense in me. I had no habits of persuasion or invention. I was *absolutamente sincero!* I was sure that it was God. I was sure that He had spoken directly to me. And so, completely frustrated, I decided to meet with Pastor Jonatan of the Igreja Cianorte, the mother church of the congregation I attended. He would surely understand and advise me, I assured myself. Pastor Jonatan had something a little different to say to me.

"Be careful, Justino. We must use great caution with things like this. I can't confirm that it was the voice of God speaking to you, no. Neither can you. It isn't only God who speaks."

Pastor Jonatan's response surprised and comforted me a little bit. This wasn't really what I wanted to hear, but at least his caution was easier to accept.

Understand, this was in the sixties, when Christian churches in Brazil were experiencing spiritual change and renewal, and there was talk of a new charismatic experience even in traditional congregations. But I knew nothing of this. I didn't know the practices of my own Presbyterian church. I certainly was not part of any religious movement. I only knew that something real and extraordinary had occurred in my life with God. I understood I was on a journey of faith that meant putting my relationship with God first. Even if it was apparently contrary to the beliefs of my family and my church, I believed God expected me to trust Him in this.

There was a huge gathering of the youth of all the Presbyterian churches being planned in the city of Umuarama, only a couple hours away by *ônibus*. It was called *Presbiteriana Retiro de Jovens*, Retreat for Youth. I had wanted to attend, but now I didn't know if I should. I was sixteen years old, feeling wounded and disconnected from my youth group. It seemed I would never fit in, that no one understood me and I understood no one. People were a mystery to me. As much as I tried, I didn't seem to belong to the human race. I never had.

As a bitter and isolated youth, working day and night, mistreating my own family, fighting with the only people I knew, my feelings were mostly wounded, selfish, and pessimistic about everything. I assumed that I had changed now that I had begun this process of inner growth, learning that God loves me even though no one else does. But here I was, stuck with my same incomprehensible self. In open confidence and sincerity, I had told others what had happened at the prayer retreat, ignoring my family's warning for discretion. I stubbornly believed that my hearing God's voice would and should be accepted as a good thing, not just for me, but for anyone. Wouldn't people want to know that God speaks? When people distanced themselves from me over this truth, I was crushed.

"Something is very wrong with me; I must be a sick person. My life is no good to anyone," I thought.

The happiness that I had just begun to taste, I lost. This setback threw me into a dejected, lonely existence all over again. This relapse was very painful, even traumatic. *Era muito triste para mim, aquilo.* It was a very sad time for me, indeed. I felt like I had fallen out of my tractor while plowing and had broken something crucial, and now I was incapacitated, made useless at something I knew all about. Sonia sought me out like a shepherding Brazilian collie, nudging me back towards the fold, relentlessly checking on me, taking responsibility for me. This girl God must have sent to dog my steps was relentless.

"They say Presbiteriana Retiro de Jovens will be at the high school! We will meet kids from everywhere!" she said gayly. Of course, this sounded terrifying!

Our July winter school break was approaching. Churches everywhere were making preparations for their youth groups to attend. I didn't fit in with my youth group anymore, but I still attended church. I was very *nervoso*, nervous, about going on a retreat. But I had that one, lone supporter who accepted and respected me even if she may have had her doubts about my experience with God. She still kept her mind open and trusted my sincerity. Sonia, the banker's daughter, kept me focused on hope. She was of the opinion that I had just gotten hurt but could get back in stride if she stayed after me.

"*Fique firme!* Stay strong!" she said.

What an encourager and coach she was to me. She wanted one thing from me, she said—that I would try to prove her right. I could endure the activities, go home afterward, and return to my life of working in the fields around the clock. I didn't want to disappoint my one friend, so I agreed to attend the retreat.

True to my old self, I stayed in my corner in the shadows, marginalizing myself as always. Head down, I was in my apprehensive frame of mind, the outsider, detached from what was going on around me. I simply couldn't connect with people. I felt like a fish out of water because I was one.

At the mid-morning *café* break, the high school loudspeaker announced that a missionary was there to recruit young people to join him on a project in the Amazonas. The missionary was looking for jovens to train for missionary service in the densely forested region of northern Brazil. This struck a chord with me!

When I heard this announcement over the public address system, I felt a richness in my heart that was just like the day I heard God's voice. The strong stirring inside me I recognized as having the same origin as the voice. There was surely a connection between these two things! I watched as young people got up and went to the classroom where the missionary would be talking about missions.

I joined them, sitting safely in the back in a middle desk, pondering this refreshed state of mind I had. I felt good, strong. I was excited, relieved of my anxiety. The missionary began to talk about his own call to Brazil to work in the Amazonas. Soon I heard him saying many, many things I had heard from God the day I kneeled in prayer and heard His voice—the same words, as if echoing, quoting, underlining them for me!

Then came the moment when he stopped writing on the chalkboard and spun around. Down the aisle he walked, until he stood right in front of me.

"*Deus,* God, led me to tell you this," he said, tapping his finger on my desk. "*Que foi Ele mesmo que falou com você.* That it was He, Himself, who spoke to you. *Aquela palavra é Dele para sua vida.* The word you received is *His* for your life."

My insides began to flood with joy. This man believed me, and I had never even talked to him. There was a murmur from the people around me in the room.

"Afterwards, I want to hear what God told you," said the missionary before he returned to his message.

I was trembling with excitement. This man said he wanted to hear what God said! My father didn't want to know. My mother didn't want to know. My sister didn't want to know. The pastors didn't want to know. No one asked me and no one wanted to know until this kind missionary asked. I will never forget that happy moment. I wasn't crazy. I wasn't stupid. I wasn't sick. *Deus fala!* And God speaks! He must have spoken to the missionary too! In this way, using a man who would become a mentor to me, God confirmed His word and His will for me.

When the missions class was dismissed, it was the hour of *almoço,* luncheon. The class dispersed quickly, and I entered the stream of people approaching Pastor Arthur, the missionary. He placed his hand on my arm and ushered me to an uncrowded place for just the two of us outside on the lawn. As we sat there on the grass, I realized it was the first time in all my life that someone had sat down with me to speak only with me, intending to hear my story.

CHAPTER 3

PASTOR ARTHUR

Pastor Arthur wanted to know who I was. He asked what it was like growing up on our farm, surrounded by riparian forest. He was impressed that I knew how to take care of the fields of manioc, corn, fruit trees, rice, beans, and coffee with great care. He got me to talk about what vegetables needed a greenhouse to survive and how to maintain the springs so a drought couldn't steal our whole crop.

"You have learned so much about God by learning patience, Justino. You have had to wait for rain and have endured many storms that could have harmed your harvest. Stay steady and strong in what God has already taught you."

Arthur quickly recognized the sense of disadvantage I had internalized because of the years of elementary and high school I missed taking care of my father's fields. He considered my farming a strength! He said that God would make strengths of my weaknesses and give me all the knowledge I needed. I was abruptly conscious that I spoke very badly and told him I feared the classroom. My four years of schooling had barely taught me to read and write. Pastor Arthur said he wouldn't have guessed that I struggled to express myself. This encouraged me greatly, for speaking out loud caused me an upwelling of embarrassment and shame.

Being a foreigner, Pastor Arthur didn't flinch hearing my bad grammar. He was Canadian, and his wife, Irmã Meire, Sister Mary, was American. He appreciated the obstacles to learning Português.

"Obstacles are just hurdles to jump when you are running the path God has given you," he said.

I didn't know what hurdles were, but I was a pretty good runner. This man was fascinated with what I had to say and took extra pains to learn everything he could about me and God's call on my life. He actually believed he was sent to help me to obey it. We completely missed the *almoço*, generally the most important meal of the day to us Brasileiros. I was *tão animado*, so delighted, to have been sought out by this man, I couldn't have eaten anyway. *Imagina*, to sit down with someone who was interested in me as a person! Almoço was the last thing on my mind! Pastor Arthur was interested in the kingdom of God and finding out what God was doing in the world. He told me of his own call to missionary service in Brazil. He described his missionary initiative to take the good news of the love of Jesus Christ to the indigenous people of the Amazonas.

He was not surprised when I told him that I heard God speak to me, saying that I would go to a faraway place. That I would be His servant. That I would not be a *fazendeiro rico*, a rich plantation owner, as I had envisioned. I would *conhecer o mundo*, see the world, one day. And countless others would accompany me as fellow servants in the kingdom of God. I told Arthur everything I had heard from God because he listened to me. He was the first person who had asked to hear what God had said. I told him how God had shown me *andando de avião*, traveling by jet. I had never even seen a large airplane, much less a jet. God had also shown me *andando de navío*, traveling by ship, of which I knew nothing at all. It seemed God had shown me my future and now used this man to validate and illuminate the things I had seen in that time of prayer at the youth retreat. These were things I had not yet known by experience. I didn't have to convince Arthur that I had heard God. He already knew this before we talked. That day, Pastor Arthur's acknowledgment of my testimony placed a new frame of reference around my experience with God and my inner identity. God had called me, Justino, into ministry. His plan for my life was His destiny for me. I returned home greatly encouraged and in a new, secure, and peaceful state of mind. My soul was restored. I was in God's hands, and my future was up to Him.

One day a few weeks later, I saw a car maneuver up the dirt road turnoff to our farm. True to his word, it was Pastor Arthur coming for a visit. We did not have a telephone, so he had come in person to talk with me and my family about my future. Pastor Arthur came into the house and visited with my family over a meal my mother cooked. Arthur was glad to stay for supper and thankful to stay the night, as well, since our meal was at sundown. His trip home would take him close to three hours. He smiled at my parents and my family and spoke openly to me by name during our meal at the table.

"Senhor e Senhora Rosa, I'm training our young missionaries at the Presbyterian Institute in Cianorte. Justino, I want to invite you to register to take part in the seminary. *Rapaz*, young man, you were not ready to join the first team we formed, but fortunately, you could join the second team."

This was the first time my parents had heard about the seminary at Cianorte. They nodded politely, certain their son would not be a candidate. My heart galloped as Pastor Arthur explained that there were young people registered for the second seminary training from cities all over Brazil—Rio de Janeiro, São Paulo, Belo Horizonte, and even nearby Londrina and Maringá, to name a few.

"These young people live together in dormitories and study the Bible," he said. "They take ministry and fieldwork courses morning, noon, and evening, preparing for missionary service. At the end of a year of training they are sent to regions in the Amazonas, far north of us."

I wondered if my Papai and Mamãe had ever even thought about the Amazonas. Rubber trees, native to the wet rainforests, grew there supplying us with boots and tires for our farm vehicles. I knew from common knowledge that Amazonas was a state, like our Paraná, in the south. In the Território Amazônico, the Amazon Territory, flowed the mighty Amazon River with a floating capital city called Manaus. Manaus was named after a river tribe of índios. We didn't know anyone who lived in the state of Amazonas—ten thousand kilometers away near Colombia, Peru, Bolivia, and Venezuela. It was not where you would move or go for a visit unless you were a miner or an adventurer. I had heard there was an airport and a famous new university in Manaus for research on Amazonian ecology. Manaus and Belém were important port cities on the Amazon River, the second largest river in the world. I would have liked to show off what I knew, but I preferred to stay quiet at supper, heartened to have my own friend as a guest in my home for the first time in my life.

Early the next morning, Arthur talked with me privately about the demands and trials of seminary training as we walked about my father's farm. The harder he made it sound, the more I wanted to go. I told Pastor Arthur I would join his team of young people. I would become part of his second team, following the path God was preparing for us into the

Amazonas to reach indigenous tribes there with the love of Jesus. The next morning, this teacher, friend, and missionary drove away with my answer.

I worked very hard all that day, feeling in my bones that much had already transpired. Like a very short season of crops that I had only just begun to appreciate, I realized I was ready for the harvest. I had not yet discussed anything with my parents, who would naturally assume Pastor Arthur's ideas were out of the question because I had not even completed primary school. I had not really put my decision into words for anyone except Arthur—not even my friend Sonia or my sister Selma. It was the beginning of August 1969, and it was time to begin my seminary training. The morning after Pastor Arthur left, I looked for my father and found him in the pasture not far from the house.

"*Pai, eu preciso falar com o Senhor.* Dad, I need to speak to you."

"*Falar comigo? O que você tem para falar comigo, filho?* What do you have to talk to me about, son?"

We walked over to a log in the meadow near us where we could sit down. As we gazed out at the fields we had plowed and planted, I told Papai that I was leaving. I told him of the decision I had made to attend seminary for a year to study the Bible. I told him that the seminary was to train me to become a missionary in the Amazonas, ten thousand kilometers to the north of us.

I had never seen my father cry. In my seventeen years, this was the first time. He put his head in his weathered hands and wept, his shoulders shook, and tears streamed down his cheeks. To see my Papai, a man so serious, so systematic, strict, and tough, now sobbing uncontrollably was bewildering. It hurt to see him simply fall apart like this, knowing I was the cause of his pain. He was not ashamed of his emotion. When he could speak, he looked at me.

"*Eu sempre soube disso, filho.* I always knew this, son. I knew you would leave me. As soon as you learned to pull up your trousers, I knew you would be off on your own. This I will say, son. You want to leave; you can go. You won't have my help. I have no part in this. From now on, you can do what you want. *É a sua vida.* It's your life."

I looked at him. I wanted to embrace him, but he did not want a hug from me. My father's disappointment in me was not new to me, but this was something much worse. I didn't know what to think or do. So, I got up and went to talk to my mother.

When I told Mamãe of my decision, she was quiet. She didn't say a single word. Her only response was a slight change in the coloring of her face, and she put her head down. I backed away. She was like Papai usually was, not demonstrative or affectionate. They had never shown much emotion around us children. But I had made my decision, and now I had told them I was leaving within a few days. I knew I could not make things okay with them. I knew I could not convince them that this was not just my decision. They had not believed that God would speak to me. I thought if God would speak to me, maybe He would eventually tell them why He gave them such a strange son.

I packed a small bag and bought a bus ticket. Very early in the morning on August 7, I walked the long path from our fazenda up to the shoulder of the highway where I waited for the ônibus. From where I stood, I could see the smoke cascading from our chimney. The day had already begun without me on my family's farm. I was off to Cianorte in northwest Paraná, the first time I had ever been away from my family.

Away at seminary in Cianorte, I immediately discovered I was way behind in school. How could I study the Bible when I could hardly read Portuguese? School opened my eyes to the fact that I could barely communicate in my mother tongue. I had been such a loner that conversations and relationships had not taught me my own language. Grade school would have helped me, but I had quit school very young to help on the farm. Since I had spent so little time in community with others in my life, both dormitory living and schoolwork were battlefields. Little by little I began to surrender my failures and let God school me. The Bible became a frustrating conversation with God. I did not know how hard and how rich this conversation would be. I did not know how much God would help me with my battles. *He* wasn't frustrated with me.

Every day continued to be like the marathon of the first day until Arthur's wife took me under her wing. Sister Mary had a very deep walk with Jesus, and in compassion, she confronted me like a Roman centurion with my need to study. Chained to her tutoring, I eventually became part of the team as we all prepared together for our calling. I had learned of my need for help and how to humbly accept it. Sister Mary said that one day I would find out that my solitary life had given me attributes that I could appreciate in myself. For now, I must daily trust God for whatever I didn't have.

Each of us on the team was to raise his or her own financial support for the journey to the Amazon basin. Most of the students had parents or relatives with good jobs, church support, or a more privileged background with connections to people with the means to help support their endeavors. Few others were like Sergio, Isalino, and me, with no means to raise our support. These new friends and I were the poor, isolated, ignorant, country boys with humble backgrounds! We were from tiny churches with no financial means to support seminary training. We had no associations with people who had money to finance the expensive journey all the way to the Amazonas.

I was simply unable to raise any support during my year in seminary in Cianorte, and so I continually feared I would be held back. Eventually I discovered this was true for Sergio, Isalino, and some of the others as well. Raising support for ourselves seemed impossible, and our apprehension increased as most of our more affluent fellow students raised their support with success. We were not informed until the end of the year that we would not be held back for our lack of funds. Suddenly it was decided that our support-raising would be done along the way. They would not leave us behind! *Que alívio!* What a relief! In our hearts, we were already on our way north to the Amazon region!

Before leaving for the Amazonas, all of us returned to our hometowns to say goodbye to our families. After having been away a year, most of us reported that our folks were glad to see us, but they had obviously gotten used to our absence. Our families were excited for our adventure to begin. My brothers and sisters were happy for me. My parents were hard to read.

Our seminary and missionary training class was assembled into teams, and we were all to meet with our designated team members in different cities according to our travel arrangements. My home base was now Jussara, in the state of Paraná. There I met my companions and assigned fellow missionaries, Mario, Sergio, and Isalino. From Jussara in southwest Brazil, the four of us traveled north by ônibus, passing through first São Paulo and then Brasília in the interior of Brazil. In Brasília, we stopped to spend a few days with the church called Igreja Presbiteriana Renovada, where a student named Silvio from our seminary in Cianorte was a member.

The pastor of Silvio's church invited teammate Sergio and me to go with him to visit a family from Guará. When we arrived, I saw a very sad picture of a family in ruins. A little eight-year-old girl was being held captive in a fortified room because she was wild and dangerous. She broke everything around her to pieces. She pulled and grabbed and tore at everything and everyone. She could break through walls, even the thick walls they constructed to confine her. Though they had boarded up the windows and cemented the cracks of her bedroom in the house, she had still broken her way out. In desperation, her family had placed the child behind iron bars in their garage. We had never heard or seen anything like this wild little girl, literally a prisoner at her house. When I sat there in that home, I felt the presence of something very strange and malevolent.

"Sergio, we have to do something," I pleaded. "Pastor, the girl is like an animal, a beast. What is going on here?" I found it impossible to just accept this situation and walk away. How many more years could she live like this with no one to love her and no one to love? I thought of the ten years of isolation and separation from my family I had chosen for myself in ignorance.

"She's been like this for a long time," reasoned the pastor. "They've already taken her to doctors, given her medicines, and they don't know what else to do but confine her."

"Couldn't we pray for her?" I begged, feeling so much heaviness in my heart for her.

"Sure, we could pray for her," agreed the pastor. "I'm just not sure how best to do it."

At first, we prayed for her through the closed garage doors. She couldn't be allowed out because of what she might do to her family, the neighborhood, and everything around her. We prayed fervently, compelled by the anxiety we felt and the hopeless brokenness we saw in her family. We prayed, asking God to take her over, overwhelm her strength, and heal her.

After a while, from our limited point of view, things began to change; we sensed things were different with her. At least she had quieted.

"Open the door. Let's go in," I said.

I felt so sure we needed to do this. We went into that jail of iron where no one had entered for years. Her mother had brought her meals in a pan which she passed through the bars as if to feed an animal. She was dirty, nude. She had no clothes. She was too violent, too dangerous, to be fed or dressed like a normal child. Everyone was terrified of her. Not one of her family offered to come into her cage with us.

But the little girl let us come in to pray for her! Jesus powerfully answered our prayers for her freedom. That day we encountered a phenomenon that is very hard to describe or even understand. What is important is that the power of Jesus Christ healed this little girl. Jesus Christ brings God's power and people together, giving us access to God and to His great restorative love.

The evil one had stolen this child's most basic needs—proper food, shelter, human contact. Her village was full of fear. Her family was devastated. *Deus libertou aquela menina!* God freed that little girl! The evil thing that had possessed her left her!

Now God had restored her life. She was free!

This was the first miracle, outside of my own restoration, that I witnessed in my life. I felt it was as much for my benefit as for this little girl and her family. I was deeply affected by her healing. I have always associated this miracle with the day God spoke to me. He rescued me, too, you see. I was learning that our God speaks and heals. He makes us better than we were before. He rescues us from evil.

Almost daily, little things were now happening to show me that the voice I heard was surely o Próprio Senhor, the Lord Himself. He was faithful to His word, even when I wasn't. He was near, and I belonged to Him when I didn't seem to belong anywhere. Things that God had placed in my mind, things that I had hardly known how to imagine, were now taking place right before my eyes. I was experiencing the love and power of God not only for myself but with others too. I was learning to share with others the riches of the kingdom of God.

CHAPTER 4

HUMBLE COUNTRY BOY

From our hometowns, and from school at Cianorte, all of the missionary groups would now travel to Brasília, the new capital and heart of Brazil, where we would be hosted by sponsoring churches. In Brasília we would make connections for the long journey north into the Amazonas. Some of our groups were coming from Belo Horizonte and São Paulo in the west to join us in Brasília. From Brasília we would all go to Anápolis where the whole team would come together before we branched out on buses, trains, and planes on our different journeys up to Belém and then finally over to Manaus and into the northwest territory of Amazonas.

Fortunately, my mentor, Pastor Arthur, had my back for the first legs of my travels. I was in need of his patience and guidance. We arrived in Brasília, and within two weeks my money was completely gone. I had another problem as well. It was a seminary rule that no one on the team could *namorar*, participate in romantic relationships. We were all single and were prohibited to mix even socially with the opposite sex. For the first time in my life, I was becoming attractive to the opposite sex. The *moças*, young ladies, in Brasília had begun to seek me out. My bogus indifference to them and innate chilly exterior made me an item of interest. The moças were sending little playful notes to me, which was against our team rules, and ignoring the young ladies just seemed to make things worse. Arthur said I was sending out mixed signals, but he knew I did not understand how not to do that.

I was very new at managing myself socially. People at the host churches even invited me to *viajar*, to travel, on holiday with their families. I learned to politely refuse invitations, explaining that we were not permitted to be alone with the opposite sex. Though I had no intentions to date any girls, a pastor at one of our hosting churches was not convinced I wasn't encouraging their flirting. Jealousies actually began to develop among some of our team members. Pastor Arthur stayed near me like a bodyguard, and I valued his protection. He said my inexperience and simplicity were somehow appealing, and my naïveté could be exploited to impede the plans of God for my life or others on my team. Unfortunately, being forbidden fruit had only made me more of an item.

One of the young ladies in the Brasília church youth group supposedly had a crush on me, and she pursued me relentlessly while we were there. One day her friend had her stand next to me while she took a prohibited snapshot of the two of us standing together. Then her friend delivered that photo to me to take to Amazonas. I accepted the photo, wrapped in paper, and put it into the pocket of my shirt. "Better to accept it than let it float around," I thought. When I later looked at the photo in private, I saw that the girl who had stood beside me did not appear in the picture! I was alone in the picture. I still have that mysterious photo today. I certainly cannot explain it. I should have recognized something odd about that girl. But most social situations were novel to me. Little by little I was discovering how unsophisticated I was. I was seriously untested in all avenues of life.

One day we went to the house of a man who was the local director of the Banco do Brasil, João Marcus. His wife was named Berenice. His house was magnificent with its balconies, stairways, hallways, and huge rooms full of elegant furniture. I had difficulty eating in the midst of such refinement. I had felt the same way at the house of the Canadian ambassador in Brasília where Arthur and I were invited. Arthur wanted me to go into other homes even when it was uncomfortable. I could no longer say I didn't go to the homes of others. Here at the house of João Marcus we were invited to dinner. It was distressing for me, a simple country boy, to sit down at a grand table with matching decorated plates, shiny glasses, and silverware.

"Arthur," I whispered. "I don't know how to eat in a place like this. It feels like a dream. I don't know what to do."

"You'll be fine, Justino. Just sit beside me and do what I do," Arthur assured me.

I discovered in this house of Dono João Marcus and Dona Berenice a huge bath in their outside garden! You see, my friend, I had never seen a swimming pool, and so I just assumed it was their bathtub. Arthur's steady signaling helped me as I was continually bombarded with new surroundings, novel cultural situations, and enigmatic people. He never acted surprised or teased or patronized me for my awkwardness or my anxiety. Arthur was a true gentleman.

The Empresa Braga, a travel agency, arranged for our travel to Belém using all the funds gathered by and provided for the missionary team. We were each to have contributed our share into the total sum. It was now determined which students had contributed enough funds to travel by plane. And it was decided that those without funds who were women would go by ônibus. It was time to go now, and I had contributed *absolutamente nada* to the travel fund! Not only was I embarrassed that I had no ticket and no money, I also worried that the mission might think it risky to allow me to travel in a coed group because of my reputation for flirting. I was still afraid I might be left behind. Arthur asked me if I was ever going to quit worrying. I didn't know how to answer that question.

I wasn't alone in having insufficient funding, either. Samuel didn't have any money. Bruno didn't have any money. Sergio, Talito, and others came up short. And I would, fortunately, soon be far away from girl problems. We country boys would all have to swallow our pride and find our way to Belém, some two thousand kilometers from Anápolis—apart from our team. But not apart from God. We were going with God and in His planning and timing. For the meantime, we would practice waiting for His plan for us in Anápolis.

Our team practiced ministry in the communities where we stayed in Anápolis until all the arrangements were made for the next phase of our travel. We all gathered together at a church to talk and pray about going to our different lodgings and future destinations. All of our plans were bathed in prayer. While we were at that church in Anápolis, a man who spoke with a heavy Arabic accent told me the story of how he had become a believer in Jesus.

"I was walking along the street when I heard someone speaking my own language," the church member said.

"Amazed to hear the Arabic language spoken here in Brazil, I stopped and listened and noticed the voice I heard was coming from a little house. I could hear someone speaking all about God's great love. Soon I heard him praying in the name of Isa, Jesus. This prayer was a powerful thing to hear, especially in my own language—this conversation with Allāh, God! To hear that God is merciful and compassionate and has provided the Good Shepherd, Isa al-Maseeh, to pay the penalty for us!"

The Árabe said he stepped closer to investigate and discovered there was a meeting of people in the basement of the house. He wondered if their voices were carried to the street with the help of a cable that came up through the basement window and out to the sidewalk. So, the man found the stairwell into the little house church, made his way into the gathering, and sat down with the worshipers, hoping for an opportunity to talk with them. The Árabe believed the message was personally for him, since it was in Arabic rather than Portuguese.

"Who has been speaking to me in Arabic about the sacrifice of God?" the Árabe asked the group.

"*Ninguém,*" they answered. "No one. None of us has been speaking in Arabic. We were just praying."

"But someone was speaking to me in Arabic. I heard him in my language, and I understood everything!"

"*Não, Senhor.* No one here speaks Arabic, *meu amigo,*" assured one of the fellows.

As they talked, the Árabe recognized the sound of the praying man's voice.

"It was you. It was your voice! You spoke in Arabic, and you said these things to me!"

The Árabe repeated the things he had heard from the street that had impressed him so deeply.

"You said that God is holy and just and He Himself provided forgiveness by coming to die for our sins."

The people agreed the things had been spoken, but not in Arabic—in Portuguese.

The Árabe told us that the prayers and the message he heard had converted him to faith. Because of what he heard in his own language, he personally experienced God's love for him and became a believer in Jesus. He believed they were miraculously placed in Arabic for him as he walked by. How could he reject this miracle of God?

Soon the man told us he was a seller of shoes. He was preparing to make deliveries to the many *sapatarias*, shoe stores, on his distribution route north. He was a local merchant who imported shoes from Spain, Italy,

Taiwan, and also São Paulo, Brazil, in order to bring them to buyers in the north. The shops of his clients were in the little villages from Anápolis to Belém. Isalino, Sergio, and I walked with him to his truck parked outside the church as he told his story. When we saw his truck, we lit up! It was big! I asked him about taking the three of us along with him to Belém as part of his cargo. Isalino and Sergio were nodding their support of the idea; Belem was just where we were going. But the Arabic man didn't seem to like the idea.

"*Não cabe mais tres pessoas no caminhão,*" the man declined in his heavy foreign accent. "Three more people won't fit. The truck isn't that big." His answer was settled by the shaking of his head, and his head remained bowed in finality.

The truck looked big enough to us. Our disappointment permeated the air, and the man offered to take just one of us. "I guess one person could sit in the *cabine* with me," he proposed.

"And the other two could ride in the back with the shoes!" I chimed in as convincingly as possible.

"You should know, amigo, there is a lot of open floor over the asphalt. The shoes would be bouncing all around you."

"That's okay, we can handle it," I interrupted with resolve. He had given me the opening. I didn't want him to change his mind. Here was our way to Belém! Our problem was solved.

The Árabe remained skeptical. He didn't know how desperate we were to commence our journey to the Amazonas! Most of our team members were already on their way.

"There is barely enough room for two *rapazes*, lads, in the back, one in each corner. The truck will be loaded up with *caixas de sapatos*, boxes of shoes."

We were happy with that.

"You will have to decide who will ride in the cabine with me and who will have to ride in the back and then rotate," said the Árabe in resignation.

"*Tudo bem, tudo bem, sem problema.* Okay, okay, no problem," we all agreed, the three of us nodding our heads eagerly. We felt so blessed to have this ride from heaven! We thought.

Two weeks later we helped the Árabe stack the boxed shoes in rows in the truck, and early the next morning we began our journey north. Within an hour we perceived our mistake. It was *duro*, rough, in the back of the truck, two of us seated on a ledge watching the asphalt speed away under us like a dirty river. We couldn't rest even a *minuto* or we might slip off the ledge and right through the floor.

At each sapataria we had to stop, scrutinize the order, unload the allotment of boxes from its compartment, haul the delivery in, and stock the boxes in the proper arrangement for the client. By fifty kilometers we were so caked with the dirt and dust that sifted up from the highway, you could no longer see our eyes. The roads were full of potholes, and the ride shook us until our bones ached.

Naturally, we had no money for food. The *irmãos*, brothers and sisters, of the church had given us a sack lunch, but it was ruined by the heat and dirt of the highway before the middle of the first day. For our daily sustenance, we had nothing to eat but the corn and watermelons that we found in the fields on the way. We boiled the corn in the rinds of the watermelons over little fires we made by the road. When our driver stopped for his meals at truck stops, we could only wander around outside hungry.

At the bridges, we descended to the streams and creeks to fill our bottles with water and wash the grime off our skin and clothing. We washed our faces gingerly, allowing a layer of muck to cover the blisters. After a few days of seeing us endure and weaken like this, the Árabe, who had very little money himself, began buying a little something for us to eat once a day. Willingly we suffered, and gratefully, for without his truck we were well aware we would have had to make our way by foot. Imagina!

As the days passed, we cleared room in the truck because we had delivered the shoes. But this only gave us more open space in which to be bounced around, and we had bruises and raw sores on our hips, legs, and backs. This was January, the summer season. The intense heat from the blazing sun above and the relentless highway below was baking us alive. We were approaching the *norte*, near the equator, and we were all from Paraná in the much cooler south. At each stop, one of us rotated to the cabin to help the Arabic merchant stay awake at the wheel. We could only nap when he stopped for a short rest. But we endured. We had that common goal and that call of God to reach Belém. We were resolute. Whether by foot, by horse, by truck, *fomos indo*, we were on our way!

After twelve grueling days, we arrived at a restaurant in a town called Piriá, just hours from Belém. Our battered bodies were dangerously dehydrated. Truly, we were all gravely ill from diarrhea, vomiting, hunger, thirst, and fatigue. There was a message at the restaurant for us. It was from a family who knew of our pending arrival because they were part of a northern church in Belém where many of our team had arrived before us. The family paid our way to stay the night in the very hotel next to the restaurant. The Árabe drove away, content to be rid of us.

We were overwhelmed with *tanta alegria*, so much joy! How thrilled we were to stop and lie down in a bed indoors! Though we had nearly reached Belém, we felt we couldn't endure another day on the road. We were very bad off, desperate for respite and care. *Mas eramos tão felizes*, but how happy we were! We were given food *tão delicioso*, it seemed out of this world. I remember the taste of the milk, yogurt, cheese—just what we had wished for! The family that liberated us owned another farm and business in Piriá, a dairy in Belém, and owned the restaurant and hotel where we stayed as well. The brand name of the food we ate was Piriá, the same name as the town. To us it was *paraíso!* Paradise!

We were given a stay at the lodge in Piriá for a few days to regain our strength before riding the last 150 kilometers by bus to Belém. In Belém we were received by more members of the same Piriá family and finally reunited with our team members—which, to us, was arriving in heaven! Our hearts were full.

CHAPTER 5

BOUND FOR BELÉM

We *pobres*, the penniless, still had not raised even a *centavo* to pay for the voyage to Manaus, so we were to stay in Belém until the *passagem* amount could be raised by funds that might be donated toward the mission. This time we could not hitchhike or walk. A road to Manaus didn't exist, you see. The only way to get there was by plane or ship. After twenty days in Belém, God secured our funds for passage on the ship *Augusto Montenegro* through the gift of two brothers. I still recall the house where we stayed with those kind boys those last weeks— in house number 1111—the place where we were first called *missionários voluntários*. It was good to be called missionaries now that we were getting closer to that identity, that destiny we had been summoned to. These two dear brothers had made a pledge to God to buy the boat passage for their guests, whoever they were and wherever God was taking them! These friends bought our tickets all the way to Manaus!

Estes caras, these guys, wanted to buy tickets for the most luxurious quarters for us on this ship. But we explained to them the practicality of buying the least expensive tickets so that we might have money left over for food. *Terceira*, third deck, was the area where the poorest voyagers sailed, where there were no beds, bunks, or cots. People brought their own *redes*, hammocks, but we did not yet have ours. So, the brothers took us to the *feira*, open market, in Belém and bought all of us our own hammocks for the voyage.

When we arrived at our area on the *navio*, ship, there were already myriads of redes hanging in their places in uncountable, flamboyantly colorful rows. We didn't know where the best places were at first as we gazed at the menagerie of ropes and people. We soon learned how to squeeze into some very small places. The hammocks were hung in vertical tiers, accessible by ladders, allowing for only a few inches between people above and below. This sandwiching was daunting for me, a person who was unaccustomed to being close to people. I had trouble even relating to people, and now this situation had become problematic. *Tanta gente!* So many people! Never had I seen a huge group of people so tightly packed together horizontally! I didn't want my hammock touching anyone else's, so I arranged it high up on the ladder and as straight and tight as possible from one cord to the other. I wouldn't be touching anyone above, below, or beside me.

Now because my hammock had brand new, stiff plastic ties rather than worn, fibrous fabric, my knots refused to stay taut. The first time I lay down in it and got myself comfortable, the knots spun right open, and I and my hammock fell about two and a half meters. I hit the iron ship deck below me dead-on my back, smack between my shoulders. I lay there stunned, seeing stars. I couldn't get any air in my lungs. Yeda, a girl on our team, saw me fall. She ran to me and began thumping me on the back to help me catch my breath. I'll never forget how much her pounding hurt! At least I had not broken my neck or head. This is when I learned how to tie safe knots for my hammock. It didn't occur to me what I really needed to learn. I had arranged my hammock tightrope-high and straight as an arrow in order to avoid any contact with humans. I was a *missionário voluntário* endeavoring to avoid people.

The journey on the ocean from Belém west to Manaus was absolutely amazing. I was seeing so many things for the first time that it was impossible to take it all in. Before walking along the beach in Belém I had had no previous concept in my mind of the Oceano Atlántico. The briny waves breaking on my trouser legs and the sand in my toes gave me joy. I had no words to describe the many birds offering their companionship; the salty, wet wind on my face; the splendor and grandeur all around me. I was very much humbled that God would allow me to enjoy such beauty close up, to feel His great power and glory in this prayerful way. I recognized how small and uninformed I was, that I had not even seen pictures or read books to teach me how to contemplate such loveliness all about me. I reached up into the pink, cloudy sky and said, *"Obrigado, Senhor!* Thank you, Lord!"

Back on our ship traveling from Belém west to Manaus, I heard the rushing waters of the Rio Amazonas moving strongly against the resisting ocean waters while the ship rested.

The *capitan* traveled at night in order to take advantage of the calmest water as he crossed over into the Amazon River. He navigated through these mysterious currents, sometimes pausing in the open water to make the best use of this exchange of river and ocean to maneuver and propel the navio on course. These nightly observations thrilled me and helped me to endure what were for me, the extreme sleeping conditions—suspended in air like a thousand bats!

In our hanging quarters, the ship's stewards served us *abóbora cozida*, boiled pumpkin, *mandioca cozida*, boiled yuca root, *arroz*, rice, and mysterious, leather-like *carne*, meat. After sailing with three thousand people, terrible food, an aching back, laborious starts and stops in open water, and monotonous pauses at various little ports, I was feverish to dive off the boat when we reached Manaus. Five days had miraculously passed, and we were once again on land!

We realized that we had actually arrived a few days early, even before our leader, Pastor Arthur. Though Arthur had left Anápolis with us, he had traveled back to Belo Horizonte and São Paulo before coming north again to join the team. Because he was delayed, we had no one to tell us what to do. We needed to find a place to stay in this foreign land. The members of the team traveling on our ship gathered their belongings and found one another at the praça de Manaus. Jaime, now our group leader, had an idea.

"Look, there should be a Pastor Ageu Bandeira at a little Baptist church in the Bairro Vitória-Régia. We could go there."

And so, we found our way to the church and knocked on the parish door. The pastor's wife, Rosali, looked a little intimidated by our group. Eleven people! But she bravely took us into the church and showed us where we could sleep on the *bancos*, pews. Then she rounded up food for all of us to eat. We all felt so happy. We were in Manaus! We had kept our pledge. Our goal was honored. Our conquest was taken. And now, together, we began to pray.

"*Senhor, O que vamos fazer agora?* Lord, now what do we do? Where do we go from here?"

We had begun to divide into certain clusters, each group having a certain character but unified in our hope and purpose for ministry to the indigenous tribes still north of us. The girls—Daisy, Irani, Carleide, and

Yeda—would stay together and go to a certain tribe. Helio, Mario, Bruno, and Somagio were to go to another tribe. Isalino, Sergio, and I were the least sophisticated of the whole assembly, and we three would go to another tribe. Each of our groups sought the direction of God in how and where we would travel. Now from Manaus, Brazil, we would journey across the Amazon basin to indigenous tribes as far away as Colombia and Peru. This is what we had been preparing for all these months. This was our basic plan in order to share the love of Jesus with the *povos indígenas do Amazonas*. Only God knew the details.

Mas nós não tinhamos nenhum centavo! But we still didn't have a single centavo! *Nada, nada, nada!* Nothing! What we had was God's provision, and we did find it lacking at times. We did not understand how little our financial status had to do with our success as missionaries. Isalino, Sergio, and I passed the night together kneeling in prayer for direction. Where did the Lord want us, and how were we to get there without money?

"God spoke a name to me—Benjamin Constant," said Isalino.

We asked around the larger group to see if anyone had heard of Benjamin Constant. No one had heard of him. Then someone remembered that Benjamin Constant is a *cidade*, city! In fact, it is the very last port in Brazil before the Rio Amazonas reaches outside of Brazil and into Peru and Colombia. Indeed, the mighty waters of the Amazon River stretch all the way from the Atlantic Ocean at Belém and Macapa, cut across Brazil to Manaus, and continue on to Benjamin Constant at Brazil's border and then west into Peru and Colombia. We couldn't appreciate this majestic terrestrial wonder at the time. We just wanted to get where we were going.

We soon learned from the local people in Manaus that we would be changing waterways on our way to Benjamin Constant. The Rio Solimões in the west meets the Rio Negro from the north, and these two gigantic rivers join to form the great Rio Amazonas. Isalino had received a name of a specific place in this vast territory in answer to our specific prayer—the city where we were to go. Benjamin Constant was unfathomably far away, we could only get there by navio, and of course, we did not have any money for passage. And so, we learned to never stop praying for God's direction.

A great tangled neighborhood of little houses, stores, and churches built on wooden planks and logs seemed to be floating all around this "jungle metropolis" called Manaus. This city would be a home base for most of us, so we needed to consider the matter of our lodging right away. On Sunday we attended a supporting church, and Pastor Bandeira asked his kind congregation if there were some who could take these young missionaries into their homes for a few days. Several responded right away.

A senhora raised up her hand saying, *"Eu posso levar um para minha casa.* I can take one of them to my house."

At the end of the service the senhora did just that. She took me to her house. Well, she didn't actually have a house. She had a little piece of land by a dirt road where there were two walls of wood constructed to form a kind of corner. The corner was crowned by a roof of brush and some pieces of wood.

"I wouldn't call myself *pobre* comparing myself to this family," I quietly observed.

In her little *casa*, there was pretty much *nada*. On the two corner walls hung four *redes* to sleep in out of the rain. These were for her and her three children, strung from one wall to the only other wall. Her oldest child was Joanna; next a boy, Danilo, of twelve or so; and a *garotinha*, little girl, of about ten.

"Pode por sua rede, irmão," said the senhora. "You can go ahead and hang your hammock, brother." The little lady, who was smaller than all three of her children, motioned to where the hammocks were hung.

I couldn't figure out where to hang my *rede* in that little corner of two walls where four hammocks were already hanging together. Since I obviously didn't know how to do it, she took my *rede* and hung it for me. I would be sleeping with the rest of the family in the corner. *Que coisa!* Oh boy!

"Você gostaria comer alguma coisa? Would you like to eat something?" she asked.

I glanced around and saw nothing to eat, no table, no dishes. She had offered me food, but I could see she had no cupboard, no icebox. She waved me outside the corner walls where a few dried fish hung near a little outdoor woodburning stove.

"You may choose one of these fish for your dinner," she said with cheerful hospitality. I thanked her and told her I had already eaten. I was dumbfounded by her generosity. She was so ready to share her home and food with me, and yet she really did not have either food or shelter. My sleep was troubled that night, though I now knew well not to toss and turn in my hammock.

When morning came, I asked Danilo, "*Onde eu poderia tomar banho? Where should I take my bath?*"

"*Sim, sim. Eu te levo. Podemos ir agora.* Sure, I'll take you. We can go now if you want."

I got my *saquinho*, bag, which contained my toothbrush, toothpaste, and soap and followed him with my towel in my hand. The boy Danilo was enchanted with my towel. After I explained its use, he said he had never dried off with a towel before. We walked for quite a distance through the forested area and came to a clearing where there was a spring with about seventy bathing people in and around it. These were people of all ages and sizes—women, men, children, everyone nude to my wonder. At first, I averted my eyes while I waited there for people to leave. But as soon as some left, more people came. I felt rather out of place stepping in with this naked crowd. With a closer look I spotted many washing clothes too. I surmised the crowd was apparently not going to thin out. I gave up and entered the water and timidly washed my legs, neck, and arms.

"Isn't there another place to wash?" I asked Danilo, softly.

"Sure," he answered. "Next time I will take you to another place."

The next day Danilo took me to another place along the river. Of course, it was exactly the same situation. I had gained the knowledge that if you want to take a bath in Manaus, you jump in with the rest of the city.

After spending a number of days at the senhora's casa, I began putting things in order in my little suitcase, knowing that I would be leaving soon. I remembered that not a long time before, I had refused to go to anyone's house. It was good to feel comfortable with this sweet family sharing their palace with no windows or doors with me. For everything they had, they had shared with me. I picked up my *colcha*, bedspread, that my mother had quilted for me, and watched the afternoon sunlight catch its sheen. It was very pretty, made of soft crushed velvet and trimmed with satin. I rearranged it in my *mala*, suitcase, smoothing it out nicely over the top of my belongings. I remembered my mother with *saudades*, quiet longing.

"Now, that's something I've wanted to have all my life," interrupted my hostess, who was standing right next to me since there were no chairs or private rooms in her house.

"*Sim*, how I would love to have something like that one day," she sighed, stroking the velvet as I had.

"But why would you want something like this, Senhora?" I asked, looking up at her. "This is something you put on a bed. It's a colcha, and you don't have a bed to put it on." *Where on earth would she put it?* was my juvenile thinking.

"I would like to have something like that so that when I die, I could be buried in it."

I was honestly surprised when she said this. I had always lived on a farm, in a house, and slept in a bed. I had thought that one was buried in a casket.

"But aren't you buried in a wooden box, like a *caixão*?"

"*Não, irmão*. Here we are wrapped in our hammocks to be buried when we die."

She gestured toward her hammock. It was old and faded and threadbare. It would barely cover anyone. She was tiny and very thin, and yet her hammock would not even wrap her little body properly. She really did make a good point.

"Here, Senhora. Take my *cobertor*, blanket, as a *presente* for you. You may keep it," I said, and I gave the blanket to her.

Her eyes shone as she held the velvet bedspread to her chest and hugged it, *tão feliz*, so happy! Then she called her children to her. The three heard her and came quickly.

"*Olha, eu tenho um cobertor! Eu tenho um cobertor!*" she said. "Look, I have a blanket! I have a blanket!"

Her children seemed very happy for her too. I was happy also, though I couldn't really grasp the measure of their joy. It was always very warm in Manaus and she had no bed and there was really no need of such things. She had her life ahead of her and nowhere at all to store a bedspread. But I was so very glad to have made her happy. Little had I ever given away in my eighteen years of life, and it felt good. We stayed in many other places, but I always remembered fondly the sweet little senhora who took me home when she had no house, who shared food and lodging with me when, by most considerations, she had none.

You may remember, when Isalino first heard a name as we kneeled in prayer for direction for where we were to go and how we were to get there without money, I had thought, "Who is Benjamin Constant, and what does he have to do with us?" If I had been better educated, I would have known Benjamin Constant was a city named after a French nobleman who had influenced Brazil's culture and government in the late 1700s. We soon discovered this city to be over a thousand kilometers away, and we could only go there by ship or plane. In *His* time, God provided the *passagens de navio*, boat tickets, to Benjamin Constant.

Through the generosity of another believer from the compassionate church of Pastor Ageu Bandeira, the three of us were now on our way to our next destination along the Amazon River. Our ship taxied the three of us from Manaus to Benjamin Constant. This was a seven-day boat trip, taking us very near to the countries of Peru and Colombia, since Benjamin Constant was the very last city along the Rio Solimões of the great Rio Amazonas do Brasil.

CHAPTER 6

BENJAMIN CONSTANT

Looking out, we could see the city from the ship, and we could feel and smell the humidity wafting up from the water. There were about five hundred people on our crowded *navio*, and it was a March evening in 1970. It had been a stifling sail, but our journey was almost over. Many of the passengers were standing triumphantly as our ship approached the docks of Benjamin Constant. But then our boat broke down in the harbor! We were stopped dead in the middle of the river and could move no further. Using a bullhorn, the *capitan* advised his sweltering passengers that everyone aboard would have to wait on the ship until a secure way was arranged for us to be ferried to the pier.

"Então, precisamos orar. Well then, we need to pray," Isalino, Sergio, and I agreed together. We had been learning together that conversation with God needed to be our first response.

There on that ship we had a very deep, unforgettable encounter with God. As he had in the previous days on the boat trip, Sergio played his guitar as we prayed and worshiped. Others listened and participated in the worship of the Creator of the glory surrounding us in the beautiful Amazonas.

Back in our home state, Paraná, Sergio had composed a hymn praising God for His creation: *"Olha a natureza, criada pela mão do Criador...* Look at the natural world, created by the hand of the Creator..." The melody still carries me back to the ship. We were assembled on the front deck of the boat, praying and singing, when God began to speak to us all through Sergio's song. That night, Sergio led us into a wonderful fellowship with God. He sang his hymn, which he had written about God's creation—*in the Spirit*. He explained that God had brought him to this very place in the world at the time when he had composed the hymn at home. And now that he was reliving it again, he realized that God had given him the song.

"It was about these very birds soaring above us, the *selva*, wild forest, the *mata*, jungle, the fish we hear jumping in the water. It was here, right here! He brought me here when I wrote the hymn," Sergio said with brimming emotion. "He gave the lyrics to me here long before I came here!"

We knew the validity of his testimony, because his lyrics, wholly divine to hear, described exactly the place where we looked out from the ship. This beauty which we saw with our eyes, the lyrics of Sergio's song, touched by heaven, brought about an *experiência profunda*, profound experience, for all of us. We shared together the knowledge that God is the Creator of a greater reality. And He invites us to join Him.

Passengers came from all over the ship and gathered in close communion around us, hundreds of them. Together we partook in this same blessing. Everyone on the ship was affected by Sergio's singing. The *som glorioso*, glorious sound, of his voice, the language that came from him was so extraordinary, so lovely, so moving—I have never heard its equal! And then he preached to everyone on the ship, and many, many people on the ship believed on Jesus as Lord and God of all. Sincerely, God was glorified for His majestic creation and awesome presence.

A friendship with the people came to us on that powerful night with God. They bonded with us. They did everything for us. They even brought us the best food on the ship and made sure we had every possible need supplied. When we finally came nearer to the port, the navio still had to come in and go out, letting off only a few passengers at a time. That took nearly three days. We enjoyed those muggy, hot days of fellowship with them, even while we were stopped between currents in the middle of the river just outside of Benjamin Constant. The capitan told us it was a question of timing with the tides and currents of the Amazon. He knew the river. He was destined for one more stop at a military base, and then he would be turning the boat around for the sail back to Manaus.

The capitan walked with us as we disembarked and made our way into the town. This gesture of honor boosted our spirits, though we knew the deference he was showing to us belonged to God. Ironically, as we were walking together, we saw a man being arrested near the entrance of the city. His hands and feet and mouth were being bound as he was taken prisoner.

"Não fala que vocês são missionários," cautioned the captain. "Do not say that you are missionaries. They will find any way to keep you out of the city if they find out that you are missionaries."

"Mas, por que? But why?"

"You just listen to me. Keep quiet about your work or they will not let you into Benjamin Constant. Just go about your business and enter the city without calling attention to yourselves."

It wasn't long before we discovered the identity of the man we had seen being bound and gagged. He was the town *padre*, priest, being expelled from the city. The capitan thought that the same thing could happen to us. Others later informed us that the padre had made a bad impression on the town by getting four young *moças* pregnant. We were shocked to hear this right at the beginning of our stay. We couldn't imagine being accused of the things this padre had done. We had just enjoyed three days of worship and friendship and kindness on the ship, which made such wrongdoings or even allegations seem impossible.

Quickly we discovered that people like us, who come from the "south of Brazil," are those who know everything and have everything. Though we arrived green and inexperienced, knowing little and having nothing, these people didn't see us that way at all. Their humble circumstances and isolation from the world gave them to believe we were like *deuses*, gods! We had stepped down to them from a lofty modern world. To them we were important and rich, though we knew ourselves to be small and insignificant.

Isalino was accepted into the home of a pastor of the Assembleia de Deus, Assembly of God. Sergio stayed at the house of another family from the church, a family with adolescents—two *moças* and one *rapaz*, two young ladies and one young man. I stayed at the home of a young man who was a leader of the same Assembleia de Deus. This is how we began our work by assisting the local Assembly of God congregation in worship, preaching, and the pastoral care of its members.

However new on the job we were, we had the exuberance and joy of our faith in the God who had brought us there! The reality had finally come when God would use us to reach out to people and bring them into His kingdom. We invited people to come to the church so that we could pray for them. Many came just to see us, having heard about us. In only a short time, the pastor's church was crowded with people from all over. People who had never attended before were now coming to his church. Even the mayor of the town, who had two teenage children, was now bringing his family to the church.

The pastor of the church, absurdly, became jealous because of the popularity of these "rich, educated young men from the *sul*, south." He understood that it was human nature that drew crowds to his church for lesser motives than the desire to know Jesus. But he still felt undermined by us. Sergio was a talented guitar player and singer and very sociable. He was about nineteen. I was actually very bad at relating to people, but I had unexpected passion and zeal when praying or teaching. I would soon be nineteen on my birthday that October of our journey. Isalino was older, about twenty-four, and a good preacher. And so, while we three began to preach a message of hope and peace in the city of Benjamin Constant, we were soon to see a thought-provoking reality of resentment and conflict awaiting us in the houses where we stayed.

Most houses were made of straw. In the house where I lived, my host worked in the sawmill, and so the house was made of brush and pieces of wood. The straw roof was reinforced with interwoven coconut palm leaves. We ate while bent over with head, shoulders, and chest protecting our food because the slightest breeze sent dust, dirt, bark, or bugs falling into our plates from the roof. The outdoor kitchen had a tarp for a cover. A board rested over sawhorses for a bench to sit upon during our meals— but no table. Next to the kitchen there was a bedroom with no door, windows, or furniture. Hammocks hung on the wall.

I hung my hammock in the "living room" where there was nothing but space. No chairs, no sofa, no sawhorse bench, nada. A rope crossed from one wall to another for hanging clothing not being worn. To wash clothes, we went down to the river and used a scrub board and homemade soap. *Todas as casas eram assim!* All the houses were like this! A very few casas had tile roofs or adobe walls, but not many. My brothers and I had helped our father build our house and tend his fields, so this kind of poverty was unfathomable to me. I wanted to help my host build a door, but there were no tools, and why would someone want a door?

We did find Benjamin Constant to have something striking that most of the towns did not: a movie theatre. A single *filme Americano de bang bang*, dubbed American Western movie, would show for a couple months at a time. I have a picture of the city of Benjamin Constant with Sergio, Isalino, and myself in a canoe in front of that theater. A canoe was handier than a car there, and cars were very rare. The rainy climate created waterways that functioned better for travel than muddy, unpaved roads. In 1969, Benjamin Constant was Venice in 969. Apart from the theater, we felt we had gone back in time a thousand years.

We tried not to judge the people we stayed with for some of their unorthodox behavior and justifiable ignorance. They were untaught, poor, and simple people, just like us. But they also lacked a standard of living, a stable community, and a work ethic to help them grow up. There was no privacy or security. The city was wild and free. It was seemingly free of morality: little girls of twelve and thirteen years were commonly seen pregnant or tending their own children. Prostitution was everywhere. People pursued us with promiscuous plans for us, too, with no shame at all. In the home where Sergio stayed, the host mother and a daughter both propositioned him. Where Isalino lived, the very wife of the pastor of the church tried to seduce him. This was a red alert. How could we continue working in this church with Isalino being pursued by the pastor's wife?

Our missionary work in the Amazonas had finally begun, and we were ready to leave after a month. Up until then, our journey had felt like an adventure. Now it was wearisome and frightening. We took needed time to pray together and comprehend that our struggles had only just begun. We were in training and too green to know how difficult the work of God could be. It was good to consider those days we spent stuck on the ship in the city's harbor singing with the crowded boat of worshipers. Many of those people lived right here in the city. God loves all the people, whether his servants do or not.

CHAPTER 7

TABATINGA BASE

After a few weeks in Benjamin Constant, our domestic complications persisted. Now the woman where I stayed was approaching me in over-friendly and inappropriate ways. The three of us tried to contact one another, whispering at common gatherings, "I need to have a talk with you." When we finally found a justifiable errand to get away and meet with each other, we comprehended that we were all in serious predicaments.

I was very much a boy and so was Sergio. Isalino was older and more experienced with dating and dealing with the opposite sex, but this state of affairs made all three of us nervous. We dreaded the consequences of rejecting what we interpreted to be blatant advances coming our way, and obviously we couldn't accept them. We discussed the ship captain's warning and the padre we had seen banished at the city entrance. We considered banishing ourselves before we got arrested like Joseph, the son of Jacob, in the Bible. We chuckled at the insanity, but frankly, we wanted to avoid all the awkwardness and get out of the city. To wait for a ship might take a month, and besides, we had no money for passage. We speculated about how we could earn money for the boat tickets.

There wasn't much money in the city to earn. The three of us had been working for the local church, but our pay was food and board in return for our labor. The church could not pay us. The people in the area seemed to have little use for money and little understanding of it. We found the way of life in this undeveloped place to be rather *triste*, sad.

51

From what we could see, the land was bountiful, but the people had little developing culture, little society, and little opportunity. We needed work to earn our passage out, but Benjamin Constant did not have organized work—no fields, no companies, no stores, no services. Money might have only complicated the simple trade that was sufficient for the way of life. A currency is based on something of value to everyone. The currency here was not money. To some outsiders this may have seemed like a paradise, but we all felt a kind of inner distress signal. We prayerfully awaited an escape.

Our lack of experience kept us from understanding upon our arrival that this settlement where we lived, close to Benjamin Constant, was still a trading village. The people pulled mandioca roots from the ground or fish from the river to eat. They killed wild animals from the forest to eat rather than domesticate them. Everywhere there were *chu chu*, a green pear-shaped squash variety, growing wild. There was not yet the need for large fields or gardens intended to feed many. Growing near every house was the staple mandioca, and the plentiful root was ground into flour that could be traded for portions of the meat of sloths, monkeys, turtles, tapir, and snakes. Trees grew wild, blossoming with every kind of fruit and berry. Some people had chickens for eggs.

Along the river there was a hardworking man who had a little boat that he used to transport people and goods to different areas. He gave a boat ride for a piece of meat, a bit of flour, eggs, a chicken, or whatever you had with you. He would take the lot of his daily collection of goods to larger towns to trade. There he would find more domesticated food such as pigs, ducks, chickens, a whole basketful of eggs, or almost anything people requested from the smaller villages.

Though Benjamin Constant did not have a school, this place was certainly an education for us! We felt our short month stay had been tremendously worthwhile, especially to teach us about our own anxiety. We needed to learn what God was doing in cultures different from our own. If we were to live with indigenous tribes, we would need to learn to live by another currency other than money. We imagined that some of the people might feel as helpless and frustrated as we did, but unlike us, they had no hope of leaving. We did not feel equipped to work there any longer, but we realized how blessed we were to have visited. It was a perfect place to learn important lessons to prepare us for the days ahead of us. Here we learned that though we were young and insignificant, the people thought we were attractive and important. How easily we could have taken advantage of others more vulnerable than we were and corrupted our calling.

We began to explore the surrounding area and soon became familiar with nearby Tabatinga, a military base for the Brazilian Army. We earned a little money there by working in the church on the base. We met some soldiers from the south like us—from Minas Gerais, Espírito Santos, and Brasília—and this made us feel more at peace.

From the base we made the first trip of our lives outside of Brazil—to Leticia, Colombia, just across the Amazon River from Benjamin Constant. We visited a little church in Leticia, spent the night there, and then came back the next day—a significant event for three Brazilian *caipiras*, country boys.

During our stay at the Tabatinga base, we visited our first tribe of *índios*, indigenous people, who lived nearby along the river. They were called the Ticunas. A man had lived with this Ticuna tribe for the past six years. He had come all the way from the southeastern state of Minas Gerais. When we met this man and he admitted he had a family in Minas Gerais, with children and even grandchildren, we wondered why the man was so far from home.

I asked his name, but he didn't give it and didn't divulge the name of his city or any other personal details of his life. He was very handsome with sun-bronzed skin and educated with a profession, having completed the Ginasial degree of study. The levels of study in Brazil are Primário, Ginasial, and Colegial, which can be compared to grade school, middle school, and high school. A Ginasial degree was pretty well educated in my book. I had not even officially completed Primário.

Isalino, Sergio, and I were suspicious. Maybe this man had left his family, his work, and his life in the modern state of Minas Gerais because he had committed some crime and was hiding from the police. But when the man invited us to his house in the jungle, we accepted the invitation. Hadn't we left our families too? We accepted the trip into the jungle out of sheer curiosity and swallowed our questions about his history and his motives for living there. We spent a whole day of canoeing through the forest to reach his dwelling by nightfall. When we prepared to bed down for the night, we were glad we had brought mosquito netting. As twilight turned to dusk, mosquitoes buzzed in thick clouds all about us, entering our ears, circling our faces and necks hungrily. The night air was thick with them. A bath in the river only kept the bugs in a hover, attacking whatever parts of us emerged from the water. We put mosquito netting close around us for protection wherever we shifted. We ate beneath the netting, or the insects entered our mouths with every bite. *Mosquitos, borrachudos, pernilongos, mutuca*—never in my life have I seen the air so concentrated with so many varieties of mosquitoes!

The man introduced us to his indigenous wife and child in his home, and soon we met a group of believers he had won to Jesus. He told us he assembled with this Amazonian church two times a week to encourage and teach them. We stayed with him a couple of days to pray and worship with the people he had been teaching to follow Christ.

I respected this man's ministry to the tribe, but I especially admired his endurance of the mosquitoes! We were on our first missionary journey, not even thinking how strange our own motives and adventures might sound to others one day. We had just been given a taste of the future, and it was the last thing on our minds. After canoeing all day again, we were just glad to finally get back to the base with the *caras*, guys, at Tabatinga.

CHAPTER 8

THE BIG FISH

Now that we had earned a little money at Tabatinga Base Militar, we believed we should return to Manaus. Our first boat traveled over 1100 kilometers along the Amazon River until we made our first stop at the port town of Fonte Boa, which means "good spring water." Our training instructions were to visit towns and take every opportunity to preach about the love of Jesus to people we met. We found a little Baptist church that had no pastor in Fonte Boa, and the people welcomed our help. The lifestyle and ministry tasks there were very like what we had seen in Benjamin Constant, but the social climate felt less threatening to us. We were more aware and more transparent with these folks about being in training, and they welcomed us with open warmth and friendliness. We were grateful for what appeared to be a healthier experience for all of us without the entanglements we encountered in Benjamin Constant. Or so we thought. We did not yet understand that we would find some kind of trouble wherever we went. But we knew that Jesus was our ever-present help in times of trouble.

Within the first week of our stay, we helped the local church members to gather visitors for a worship service, which would meet as a kind of house church. The meeting time came, and the little house was soon jam-packed with people from all around the area, *animado*, excited, to meet the three celebrities from the south. We were eager to bring a good message and pray for them too. Sergio, Isalino, and I stood at a corner where we could each be seen by all. Isalino and I introduced ourselves to many families we had not yet met, and Sergio strummed his guitar to a popular hymn that the Fonte Boa church knew by heart. The people had soon begun to join the singing, and all was going brilliantly when Sergio became very stiff and his guitar dropped to the ground.

Then Sergio fell down on the ground shaking and kicking in spasms. His face looked like he was in pain. Desperate to help our friend, we did nothing but stand there and helplessly watch him with no idea of what to do. Sergio continued this startling twitching and jerking for what seemed like a long time but probably was just a minute or two. The people assembled nearer to him, and in a little while he was better, conscious, and almost peaceful. We helped him up and found him a comfortable seat on the floor against the wall. Of course, there was no couch or bed. There was no doctor to send for. We prayed with the people for Sergio and for the needs of the people who had gathered together with us.

Fonte Boa was a town very proud of having electricity a couple of hours a day. They even had a single city light post with an electric light on the one street of the town. Our partner Sergio threw a stone and accidentally knocked out this legendary city light. That was pretty embarrassing for him, a guest in their village just recovering from the seizure. He was twice made famous now. Fortunately, the people were understanding about the loss of their light, which might not be repaired for many months. Sergio was very well liked. They enjoyed the way he would pick up his guitar and sing while people gathered out on the street in the twilight.

Isalino often joined him with his guitar too. After there was a good crowd, the three of us missionaries-in-training read the Bible to the townspeople and preached and prayed with them. Then we followed the townspeople as they walked from house to house, praying for all the families of the town to trust Jesus as Master and King of their lives. It was an amazing time for us. Many people of Fonte Boa believed and wanted to follow the living Jesus Cristo.

In the midst of our happy stay, we were with some families near the shore of the river. We watched as two teenaged brothers suddenly began thrashing in the water. They were wrestling with a huge fish near the riverbank, struggling with its weight, trying to tug it in with a fishnet. Then their little brother jumped into the water to help them. He was about nine years old and not much bigger than the fish. The fish twisted away from the older brothers and grabbed hold of the little boy, right at his neck. From the bank, we watched in horror while these boys tried to separate their little brother from the giant fish.

From our point of view, the only way to save the boy would be to pry open the jaws of the fish. But the brothers were too afraid to touch the mouth of the fish. The fish's jaws had locked around the boy's throat and neck. Maddened with what was happening before my eyes, I dove in to try to rip open the mouth of that fish. I pounded the fish in the eyes and mouth. The water was full of blood all around us. I was too late. The fish let go, but the damage was done. The little boy died in our arms just as we pulled him up to the embankment.

All of us took this very hard, especially Sergio. He was already confused and stricken with anxiety over his health. He was weighed down with the unknown reality and limitations of his epilepsy. He couldn't swim, and we were always on or near water. He had become afraid of the wild animals all around us. It was traumatic for him to see the tragic death of this little boy while in his state of mind; the sight of it was too much for him. He couldn't shake this growing self-doubt after the little boy's death. He would not have gone in the water to help. He questioned whether he had what it took to go on with us. He felt he had turned *medroso*, cowardly. Sergio became depressed and withdrawn.

Isalino and I did what we could to support the child's family, praying for them and explaining that the little boy was safe with Jesus. We were saddened even more when we saw the mother and father clearly hold the brothers responsible for the little brother's death. The older brothers felt great shame for not having fought the fish that took their brother's life. We learned that local legends and superstitions about the giant fish had put such fear in their hearts that the older sons were simply paralyzed when their little brother needed them. We tried to comfort them, knowing that they were in agony too. If only the little boy would not have joined his brothers in the water!

According to the village custom, the dead were buried wrapped up in their hammocks. But this little boy had shared a hammock with an older brother. The family had no choice but to bury this little boy without a wooden box, without a hammock, without even a blanket. I bowed my head in disbelief. This little boy was to be laid to rest in the dirt wearing only a pair of short pants with no shirt. Shattered, I took off my shirt and dressed his little body in it.

We wanted to help, so we asked around for a shovel so that we could dig the grave. A shovel? No one knew what we were talking about. They placed him into a shallow grave, the earth dug away by hand. Then they covered the place with a rock. Such profound poverty was very hard for us to accept. Compared to these people, we were not poor, no. *Éramos ricos*, we were rich, even though we were the poorest missionaries of our team.

The people of Fonte Boa told us about a family of *crentes*, believers, who had moved away from them. They didn't want this family to miss out on our missionary visit and assumed that we would want to meet them and encourage them too. They said we might face some challenges in finding them. We would have to hike a full day and then find our way across the river. There were many tributaries of the Rio Amazonas all around us. Some of these smaller waterways in the Amazonas region were not so small at all. They were a long way across, maybe a kilometer or more. We talked it over. This was our work—to meet with other believers, to worship with them and learn from them and try to help them if we could. Though we were from a different world in the sul, we shared the same God and Father, the same family. We would go and encourage our brothers and sisters across the river.

Sergio was relieved to stay behind and rest in Fonte Boa for a while. Isalino and I packed a bag of provisions and set off to find this Christian family who lived down the river. Just as we were instructed, we trekked much of the day on paths we discovered through the jungle until we came to a little village near the river. We felt strong and courageous, like bold explorers. The walk through the jungle was fascinating and invigorating. Monkeys and birds seemed to make themselves our companions, traveling near or just ahead of us. Like guides, they escorted us right up to a sudden clearing there at the waterfront.

The river was enormous; the shoreline looked like the ocean to us. Waves crested and swept toward us where we stood gaping at this vast body of brownish water so full of mysterious creatures. It was afternoon and we needed to get started. We asked around how best to get across. A small man with a kind face gave us a warning that the river was too wide for us to swim across. He provided us with a canoe to use.

Inexperienced with the paddling, Isalino and I awkwardly worked out a system that eventually got us out to the middle of the river. We were just getting the rhythm down and feeling confident when we suddenly flipped over the canoe. It was only a little boat, and I was amazed we had stayed afloat as long as we did. While Isalino and I struggled to right the canoe, he thought he saw and felt something in the water.

"It's the fish!" he called out in panic. "That big fish is swimming around down there!" He was absolutely sure he saw the fish that killed the boy in Fonte Boa, the very one. We tried harder to make it back into the canoe but were unable to do it. We steadied the boat for each other, but nothing worked. The struggle was taking all my reserves. I gave up.

"Isalino, we've got to swim across!" I called out.

I couldn't tread water any longer. I started swimming towards the other side since we were already halfway there. In my head, I remembered seeing him coming after me in the water, his stroke steady. I kept that picture in my mind and tried not to worry because it sapped my strength to think of being alone. I clawed my hands through the water, my arms aching. I believed he could make it. Isalino was well built, muscular. I was wiry and thin. If I could get across, couldn't he?

My legs felt as heavy as lead. When I turned to swim on my back, I lost momentum. Turning back over, I reached out farther and tried to kick harder to power through the wall of exhaustion incapacitating me. After a long while I treaded water and looked for Isalino. There he was, maybe a hundred meters behind. Then, heartened but feeling the pull of the current against me, I recommitted to swimming the rest of the way across. I believed I had to keep moving while I had the might and the will to do so.

After what seemed like hours, I finally reached the shore and climbed out onto the muddy bank. The forest grew right up to the edge. I could see a picture of the trees towering behind me in the reflection of the water. It was nearly sundown. I felt guilty for leaving Isalino behind. He had pleaded with me to wait for him, but I just couldn't. I had to keep swimming because I didn't think I would last treading water. I scrambled up higher onto the grasses of the shore to rest for a while, amazed at how far I had swum and sincerely wondering if Isalino could do it too.

Weary but worried, I shaded my eyes and began searching the glinting, ashen waters. I walked up and down the shoreline impatiently praying for a glimpse of Isalino. The sun dropped in the horizon. It had been more than an hour since I had seen my friend, maybe two. Mentally, I wrestled with myself. It appeared that I was a more experienced swimmer, but I was not confident that I could help Isalino. He was years older and bigger and stronger than I was.

"*Isalino, vamos lá, amigo!* Isalino, come on, man!" I cried, scanning the water impatiently. "Where are you, brother?"

Then I spotted him. He was still pretty far away, barely moving in the water. Maybe he was resting, I hoped. What seemed like hours passed as I sat on the shoreline, anxiously watching his form. I began to doubt that he would make it to shore. I became desperately afraid that he would drown and I would be there alone in the *mata*, jungle. The dense forest all around me was threatening. The current had surely taken us far from where we were meant to land, far from any remnant of civilization.

Hardly blinking, I watched Isalino's little body float as motionless as a piece of driftwood. I studied carefully to see if he was getting any bigger, closer. The last of the sunset turned to moonlight while I kept my eyes on him. The refracted light of the moon on the surface helped me distinguish his floating form from the smooth waters, even in the dark. Time crawled until Isalino got to a place where I thought I could swim out and bring him in. With that glimmer of hope, I dove in and gave it my all.

When I reached him, he was talking gibberish and moving erratically. I wondered how he had survived. I simply don't know how he didn't drown. He was shaking, trembling all over, and talking crazy. Part of the time I swam under him to avoid his flailing grasps and keep him from pulling me under. Miraculously, using the last of my strength, I dragged him across the remaining distance and out of the water, both of us nearly dead.

Isalino was so very bad off that he couldn't stand up, much less walk. He was sick and he had diarrhea. He cried out for his mother, calling out her name over and over. He insanely talked about the fish that had killed the boy. There was no stopping him. I couldn't convince him that he was okay, that he was not in the water anymore. My efforts to calm him had no effect at all.

"Yes, yes, we could have been grabbed by that fish, but now we are safe," I reassured him.

I didn't mention how lucky we were to be alive, fish or no fish. I didn't mention our good fortune to have spent that much time in the water without being attacked by the fish. Nor had we fought off any piranha, anaconda, or *crocodilo*! He was too cold and feverish to understand anything I said, anyway. He was very bad off, very bad!

I was depending on Isalino, you see, to get us through the night in the jungle. I looked up to him. He was older, wiser, stronger, more tested. I needed him. I was eighteen and he was twenty-four. I didn't know what to do. How could he be worse off than I was? Isalino lay there shaking, ranting, and raving. He had to snap out of it so we could deal with our latest grim reality together.

"The fish, the fish was there...I saw the fish! It was the very same fish... the fish!" he repeated with every trembling breath, yelling that, just like the little boy, we would die and have no proper burial. He was terrifying me. *Ele não dava conta de nada!* He was out of his mind!

Isalino refused to face our immediate reality. We were wet, cold, exhausted. It was dark, and we had no flashlight and nothing to make a fire to keep the wild animals away. Amazonian *jacarés*, alligators, *onças*, jaguars, and *cobras*, snakes, were probably all out hunting near us. The river had many undercurrents and so we didn't know where it had taken us. We weren't sure how far we had drifted or in what direction. Our boat, our clothes, our journals, and our Bibles were gone. We had come to the end of our rope. We were lost—in the middle of the Amazon jungle! What could be worse?

I needed to figure out what to do now—obviously without Isalino. "Our dreams and our zeal and our commitment to God have brought us to this point," I thought, my head in my hands. It couldn't be over now. Isalino and I were possibly suffering from hypothermia. If we stayed near the water, we would be even colder. If we moved away from the water a few meters, we might miss someone passing by who could help us. I could not see any lights from settlements up or downriver. Should we try to sleep, or were we in imminent danger? Near the water there could be jacarés. In the forest, the jaguars. Anacondas anywhere. I didn't have the strength to carry Isalino very far, a man much bigger than I was. I tried to comfort him, but he was *louco*, crazy. This surely was the most difficult moment of my life.

With Isalino in shock, feverish, and continuing with diarrhea, maybe it was better not to move him. He continued to call the name of his mother. I decided to stay where we were until he improved. Not far from us was a tree that we could climb for protection. I half dragged, half carried Isalino there and propped him up at the foot of the tree. I found a big stick to hold in my hand and sat there watching him drift in and out of consciousness the entire night.

At dawn, Isalino awakened feeling better. He asked me if it was true, what he thought had happened, or had he just had a terrible nightmare? I assured him it was true!

"Now that you are better, we have to get started walking. We have to get out of here, Isalino!"

Isalino agreed. I gambled that we were at least a half-day hike downriver from where we had planned to put the canoe. After a day's trek along the river and often through jungle, we still had not found the area where we had meant to land the canoe. At dark we slept at the foot of another tree. This time I slept too. We were both too worn out to keep watch or do anything to protect ourselves.

The next morning, we hiked about two hundred meters and quickly realized we had arrived at our actual destination. We had spent a second night at the foot of a tree with only a half an hour hike left! We chuckled at this. Hungry from two days without food, our feet bleeding, we were just happy we didn't have another long day of hiking. We were grateful to find the family we were looking for. These dear people prayed for us, fed us, encouraged us, and blessed us the way we had intended to bless them. They even solved our worst problem—the canoe.

We had borrowed the canoe in good faith and had lost it in the river. It was crudely made, unstable, and of little value to us, but it had gotten us at least halfway across the river. The Christian family arranged for a new boat to be made to replace the lost one. When the new little craft was ready, we crossed the river again, returned the new canoe to the nice man, and walked back to Fonte Boa to find Sergio. The three of us were greatly cheered to be together again.

Our original plan was to go from village to village along the Amazon all the way back to Manaus. But we were so shaken by all that had happened so far, we decided to return straight to Manaus without stopping along the way. Sergio, Isalino, and I had traveled along the Amazon River from Manaus to Benjamin Constant to Tabatinga to Fonte Boa to Cafezal, and now we were traveling by riverboat back to Manaus to enjoy a time of recovery and rest. We had a lot to think about. One thing stood out in my mind: if Sergio had gone with Isalino and me across the river to find the Christian family, he would not be going back with us now to Manaus. His fear of the water was a good and healthy thing. Our colleague would stay on in Manaus where he could get treatment for his seizures. He worked in a church there where he continued writing songs and eventually married and had a family. This is how God took care of our brother Sergio.

CHAPTER 9

DR. JOÃO

I looked forward to seeing the little senhora, the lady who had brought me to her house when we had first landed in Manaus a couple of months earlier. I had felt an affinity with that sweet family. "They feel like my mother and little brother and sisters in this strange, foreign land," I thought sentimentally. I recalled the cobertor, the pretty blanket that my own mother had made for me. When I had put it in the senhora's arms, she had shown such delight. She had called her children in to look at it, saying, "Look what I have now! I have a cobertor, and now I can die because I have something to be buried in!"

"No, you are strong. You will not need this cobertor for a long time," I had said.

When we reached Manaus, I went to the senhora's little house with two walls. When I arrived, only the children were there—the young moça, Joanna, the oldest; the boy of twelve or so; and the little girl. They welcomed me as their friend.

"And your mother, how is she?" I asked.

"*Ela morreu, Justino*. She died, Justino," Joanna told me.

"What? She died?"

"Yes, and she was buried in your cobertor," they said.

I could hardly believe my ears as they related this unhappy news with wide-eyed serenity. I hadn't realized what this woman clearly knew well about herself! She had a serious lung condition and only a little time to live. God had comforted her and her children through my mother's gift to me. The children were happy that their mother's one wish had been granted, that she could be wrapped in my beautiful quilt. I wept. As I tell this today, my friend, tears stream down my cheeks, again. This family showed me true hospitality and taught me that you can give even when you have nothing. A few years later, Joanna traveled all the way down to Belo Horizonte and married the brother of a pastor I knew.

~

The team had been living in the north for many months now. We had finally shifted from school and travel to settle into our new life in the Amazonas. In Manaus I began to get to know some special people who made a lasting impact on me. I attended a meeting of prayer and *adoracão*, praise, in a house where I first met Dona (Madam) Jacobede. She invited me to have *café da manhã*, breakfast, at her home in Manaus in order to meet her husband, Dr. João Chrisostomo, a Presbyterian minister. I marked the date to have café da manhã with her at her home, but when I arrived, she was leaving for the school where she was the Diretora do Instituto de Educação de Manaus. She was too busy to receive me that morning.

"Oh, Justino, there's a problem at the school and I can't have breakfast with you now. Would you mind going into the living room and waiting for Dr. João? The *empregada*, servant, will advise him that you are waiting and serve you both café da manhã."

And then she was off! I waited awkwardly in the *sala*, living room, for Dr. João until he finally came down the stairs, still in his dressing robe. He gazed down at me sitting alone in the sala.

"Who are you?"

"Justino."

"Justino. And who is Justino?" he asked again.

I said, "What do you mean, 'who is Justino?' Justino is me," pointing to myself a little defensively.

"I mean, what are you doing here? Where did you come from? Who invited you into my house?"

"Well, sir, I met your wife at a prayer vigil, and she invited me to have breakfast this morning. And then she had to leave and told me to stay and have café da manhã with you, sir."

"I certainly didn't invite you here. Don't you go telling people that you met my wife at an all-night revival service, or she could be thrown out of our church," said Dr. João. I gathered that Dr. João might not like Dona Jacobede attending other churches outside of his own church. He was the pastor of a traditional church like the one I grew up in.

"I'm sorry, sir. She just invited me here to have breakfast," I said, staying on subject.

Because I was backward and simple, I didn't know how to be anything but straight. I should have politely gone home when Dona Jacobede couldn't receive me, but I wasn't sure that was the appropriate thing to do. She had told me to wait for Dr. João. On the other hand, Pastor João wasn't making politeness easy for me, grilling me with questions.

"What do you do?" asked Dr. João.

"I'm a missionary."

"A missionary, how? You can't even speak well. How do you know you're a missionary?"

"Well, I know the Lord Jesus."

"Well, how do you know Jesus?"

And so, from the chair in the living room, I told him what I knew about Jesus, and the Presbyterian minister sat down to continue his interview. I told him my own father was Presbyterian and that I had been brought up in Paraná. At this, he began to show more interest. I told the story of my conversion and the vision I received and the call from God to go to the indigenous peoples in the Amazonas. I told him of our recent travel along the Amazon River from Manaus to Benjamin Constant to Tabatinga to Fonte Boa to Cafezal and back again. I told him about many of the things God had done on our journey from the south to the north of Brazil—how He had cured people, freed people from darkness, delivered us from dangers, and sustained us far away from home.

The empregada entered and said, *"Senhor João, café está na mesa.* Breakfast is on the table."

The pastor said, "Now, it is I, not my wife, Jacobede, inviting you to breakfast, Justino."

We both stood up and followed his servant into the breakfast room. Sitting down, he pressed me to tell more of my recent experiences in the Norte de Brasil. He asked me where I lived now.

"I'm staying in a room of the church at Batista Emanuel."

"While you finish your breakfast, I'm going upstairs to get dressed. I need to go into the city to work, and I'll drop you off on my way."

Dr. João explained that he was not just a minister but also the

Secretário de Governo da Cultura do Amazonas. "That is a long title for a government official," I thought. And it was not his only title. Soon the pastor descended the stairs dressed in a suit and tie with a white shirt, *muito chique*, very sharp. Here was an important, educated man, a government administrator, the pastor of his church, with a beautiful home and family, and he was spending all this time with me. Imagina!

"Let's go," he said, and I obediently followed him out of the house. His *motorista* opened the car doors for us to sit side by side in back. Dr. João gave directions to the church where I lived in the basement. He had some final words for me before we arrived.

"Justino, I want you to know I don't believe a single thing you've told me. But I believe in *you*." The car pulled up to Bastista Emanuel, and Dr. João said, "I'll see you another day," and he let me out.

I stood there wondering how this man could have any confidence in me if he thought I was lying to him. For the next few days, I repeated to myself, "Someone believes in me but doesn't believe what I say," and chuckled.

I went into the church and told my colleagues who were there that I had just had a pretty baffling experience.

"I had breakfast with the husband of Dona Jacobede, and he just drove me home and left me here at the door! Did you know he's the Secretário do Governo?"

I hoped that I had not said something that would get Dona Jacobede in hot water with her husband by talking about our church and our work, which she obviously supported. I didn't hear anything for a few days until I was told that someone was outside the church waiting for me. I went outside and recognized Dr. João's driver near the entranceway.

"Dr. João wants to speak with you," he said. "He's in the car."

My stomach lurched. I really didn't want to cause any trouble or be in the middle of anything. The man made me nervous. I followed the driver to the car and saw Dr. João in the back seat.

"I passed by here to invite you to *almoçar*, have lunch, with me, Justino."

He said this through the car window, and he seemed pleasant enough.

"Let me just check with my colleagues, sir," I answered.

The members of our team tried to keep each other informed so that we could keep in step with one another. This gave us community and accountability with each other for our time, our whereabouts, and our comportment when we were apart. Communication was limited in those days when few telephones were available. We were diligent to arrange time together to pray, worship, study, and to discuss God's leading. We shared all our food and supplies that we had among us like a family. Often there was nothing to eat except a little bread. We were glad if someone brought something home or if one of us had a little money to buy something. Here in our missionary life, we were all poor and yet had rich *comunhão*, fellowship. We tried to keep our needs simple and focus on harmony and rapport with others. This harmony was something I had gone without my entire life. Until now. The other things were easy for me. I ate little and weighed only *quarenta nove kilos*, a little over 100 pounds. I had few articles of clothing—a couple of pants and shirts. Maybe three pairs of underwear. A pair of shoes. We knew that these things didn't matter right now. And so, I went in to see what my *colegas* would think of my going out to lunch with this important man, Dr. João.

"Sure, go ahead!" they agreed.

I got into the car, and Dr. João took me to his house. As we sat at almoço, he tried to interview me.

"*Quero ouvir mais da sua historia*. I want to hear more of your story."

"Senhor, I really don't have any more to tell. I told you everything. But I would like to understand what you said to me when we parted. The Senhor says that he believes in me but not in what I said? What did you mean by that, sir?"

"Oh, Justino, the things you said were strange to me. I can see that you are a young man who is *sincero*, candid. I perceive that you are *honesto*, you are *verdadeiro*, authentic. But the things you say God did— that He spoke, that He cured, that He cast out demons, and that He blessed you the way you think He did—this I don't believe. I don't believe in this."

Now, I was saddened by what he said. This man of God didn't believe that God did these things? I was a new believer and so I didn't realize there were many different perceptions of God and many groups of followers all over the world. In the beginning, Dr. João had been short with me. But now he treated me with open *carinho*, affection. I had never been singled out by anyone so kind and encouraging before. Pastor Arthur was like Dr. João in this way, but he had dozens of young people to take care of.

Dr. João and I ate the noon meal together that day at his house, and then he went upstairs to where his office was. He hung a hammock there for me to lie down and rest after lunch. He went to his own bedroom to take a *soneca*, nap, on his bed. A *repouso*, rest, after the midday meal is a common custom in Brazil. In the north, a hammock is often more comfortable to sleep in than a bed because it is cooler.

After we rested, Dr. João said he wanted to talk with me some more. He showed me to the back porch where he had a rocking bench. This is where we first sat down looking out at his beautiful *jardim*, backyard garden. Every kind of tree was planted there, and the breeze rustled their leaves and blossoms. Sculpted bushes stood guard at the sides of the cobbled steps down to the lawn where there stood a painted bath on a pedestal, full of noisy, colorful, splashing birds. This is when he told me how he wanted to help me.

"I need to tell you something, son. You need to learn how to speak. You speak very badly. Would you let me be your teacher?"

I knew it was obvious that I needed help with speaking. I said yes, wholeheartedly! Dr. João began to pick me up regularly and bring me to his house for a meal and for individual lessons in Portuguese. When he brought me back to our team home, his parting words were always the same: "*Ore por mim*. Pray for me."

Dr. João studied with me at least three times a week. Sometimes it was quite late in the day when we finished, and he insisted that I sleep in the hammock in his office. Other times he and Jacobede would have me stay for a few days. Once, another traveling couple needed to stay at the pastor's house on a night when I was there.

"But where will we put Justino?" Dona Jacobede asked her husband.

"Hang a hammock in our bedroom for him," Dr. João said.

They treated me just like family. I was surprised when Jacobede actually told me Dr. João liked me better than he did her! The favor that Dr. João showed me by being my mentor, my teacher, and my guardian was inestimable to me. They had four children and yet I never saw him show more warmth toward any of them than he did to me. They all had good reason to be jealous of the time Dr. João spent with me during those four months of culture and language lessons. I suppose they endured me because they knew it was only for a season.

Dr. João began taking me to his downtown office so he could make use of his time there to work with me. He wanted me to practice speaking with the other educated men in his cabinet.

"This is Justino—*meu irmão*, my brother," he introduced me.

From then on, when I arrived at the office of the Secretário de

Governo da Cultura do Amazonas, I was given the respect of an important man.

"That's the brother of the Secretário," people would say, though I was *mal calçado, mal vestido, mal falado*, wearing worn shoes, shabbily dressed, and poorly spoken. This makes me smile whenever I think of it.

At the office when no one was near, Dr. João never missed an opportunity to coach my speech, continually having me repeat words and phrases after him. Dr. João made this his mission and recruited Dona Jacobede to work with me too. For countless hours during those months, they drilled me. He had me read aloud to him from the Bible. This really helped me to see how badly I needed to improve my pronunciation, my endings, my tenses, even change the very structure of my speech to answer God's call on my life. It was like learning a whole new language. Dr. João and Dona Jacobede taught me not only my mother tongue but gave me speech therapy as well. I accepted this amazing gift of their time and their skill as goodness from God's own hand.

"I want you to preach at my church for our anniversary celebration," Dr. João said one night as we sat outside on the bench in the jardim.

"*Eu?* Me?" He must have thought I was progressing!

"*Sim, você!* Yes, you!"

He liked my idea to enlist my team members to canvass the surrounding area and invite everyone to come to the church that celebration weekend. We did this and sure enough, the church was packed for all three of my sermons, Friday night, Saturday night, and Sunday. On Saturday night when I gave the invitation for the people to come for prayer, Dr. João's own son was one of those who came forward. This young man was studying medicine and was already the leader of the church youth program. Yet, he came forward that night asking to receive Jesus Christ as Lord of his life.

After the service, Dr. João and I talked this over. "My son is already a believer," said Dr. João. "He's the president of our youth. What happened here?"

"Dr. João, I preached what God put on my heart. Your son came forward to receive the power and love of Jesus Christ over his life. This is all I know that happened."

At this time in my life, I had no theology, no opinions. All I had was Jesus as my Lord and King. I was only a witness to what He was doing in my life and the lives of others. Dr. João and I agreed that we were both amazed at all that had gone on at his church that weekend. This generous and distinguished minister was still open to new ways to learn from God and was unafraid of repentance and change. At the end of the Sunday night service, his congregation thanked me for my preaching and gave me an *oferta*, offering, to bring home to my team. This gave me such a very glad feeling, I had to blink away tears. I was finally going to be able to share God's blessing with my brothers and sisters! I had so wanted to be able to give to someone else what I had received from Dr. João, who had helped me in so many ways, asking nothing in return. I marveled at how he loved to help people, to be connected to people. He modeled this for me.

CHAPTER 10

DAVID COOPER

Soon I met an American named David Cooper, who would greatly affect the course of my life. David had invited me to come for a visit to his house in a town named Maués, twelve hours by ferry from Manaus, where he had lived for the last eleven years. Being a less introverted and more emotionally adjusted person now, I didn't say no. I gladly accepted his invitation! I was comprehending how God was teaching me and preparing me through different people I encountered. In due course I became very close to David's whole família—his British wife, Gina, and their children Davina, Helena, Angela, Breen, and the littlest, Kevin, born years later. This family became precious to me, and I still have contact with them now, decades later.

David Cooper was an experienced missionary himself. He once visited with the Auca tribe, now called the Donane or Huaorani, who were infamous at the time for having killed five missionaries in Ecuador. David met Gina in Peru when he was a missionary there. Before Peru, David Cooper was a missionary in Mexico with his first wife and six children. In Mexico, there was a terrible traffic accident in which his wife and four of his children were killed. Other students from the children's school were also killed in the accident. David's two surviving children were Timothy and Alice. David then left Mexico and became a missionary to Peru, taking Timothy and Alice with him. In Peru he met Gina, and they later married and eventually had five children of their own. After they moved to Brazil and had been living there a few years, Gina went back to England with the children for an extended time for their child Breen's health care.

The first time I saw David, I was impressed with how elegantly dressed he was. He had on a white linen jacket and dress trousers and looked like a movie star. You would never know from looking on the outside the heartbreak and loss he had experienced. Later, maybe as a spiritual discipline, he decided that he would no longer use dress pants and shirts or even good shoes. He wore only overalls, without a shirt, and *sandálias de borracha*, flip-flops. He gave away his good clothes and kept just two overalls, two pairs of underwear, his sandálias, and his backpack.

David Cooper is the man who showed me how to pray. He taught me how to lie back in the warm waters of the Rio Amazonas and float, look up into the starry heavens, and pray all night long. Every Friday night we prayed until morning, praying for the nations, all the nations of the earth, praying for God's presence and power on earth. We prayed for the reign of the kingdom of heaven within us. David had many griefs within and helped me to know that I did too. His inner struggles went deep, so he had lots to pray about. His prayers for himself and for me taught me lessons about God's understanding and forgiveness, which I might not have learned without experiencing his heart-to-hearts with God.

There was a young indigenous woman who had lived with the Cooper family since she was a child in Peru. She had joined the family after leaving her tribe where David and his wife Gina had worked years earlier. The family named her Tina and had called her this name since she was a little girl. Now, as a young woman, Tina continued to live in David's home and kept house for him. Years later it was determined that Tina was a member of the Sateré nation of original indigenous peoples of the Americas. The story of her personal struggle and survival is one that would fill the pages of another book.

One day David and I were on the veranda of his house looking out on the river, and we began to pray. This was a time when we felt the *presença de Deus com muita força*, presence of God with great power. It was something unforgettable, tremendous, those prayers on that veranda. We were deeply moved. Tina was nearby where she could hear our prayers and came to us, interrupting with gentle but insistent *solicitações*, requests.

She was speaking directly to me, not David. But I didn't understand a word of what she was saying to me! So, she spoke in our common language, Portuguese.

"*Fale comigo agora!* Talk to me now! *Fale comigo!* Talk to me, Justino! You can speak my language!"

She explained that she had heard and understood everything I said while I was praying because I had been praying in the very tongue of her tribe. Actually, I didn't know what I had just prayed, only that the presence of God was marvelous to me during that prayer. I didn't even know that I was speaking in any tongue but my own. It was then that I realized I had spoken in a foreign tongue. Tina then interpreted the words of my prayers to me.

Tina said that I had been telling a story. She said the story was that I had fasted and prayed with young people in the woods and God spoke to me. Tina described the day when I had knelt down on the log, when I first received God's direction in my life. Tina described that day that had changed my life, that everyone doubted. She described it as if she had been there. She said that when I told of a revelation from God in her language, she thought I was speaking to her. She described my experience back to me in Portuguese, insisting that she had heard me tell it all in her own indigenous tongue. Wait a minute here. This was astonishing. I hardly knew what to say or how to react. I did not know any of Tina's language at all. Tina knew nothing of my experience with God. She could not know any of this without the Spirit of God telling her.

Surely God had prepared me to be there in that very place at that very time for Tina to hear her language and encourage me, I was thinking. And just as I was coming to this understanding, she said that I had said that. Tina believed that I was surely going to her very own people. She said they were a rare tribe of the Amazonas who had never had contact with modern man. This young woman knew more about what I was going to do than I did, and she was saying that I had just told her all this in her mother tongue, her first language. This was incredible.

"My tribe does not know any other language than what you spoke! The one *I speak!*" Tina claimed. I listened to her in awe. I did not know the strange tongue I had spoken. I could not explain what had just happened. I knew only that I had experienced a *louvor*, praise, of God Almighty within me that felt magnificent. David reaffirmed Tina's interpretation of the language I spoke. David had learned to speak a little of her language too.

"*Justino, você falou da lingua dela, mesmo.* You did speak in Tina's native tongue. I heard it too!"

Tina had much more to say. She said that I had said in my prayers that there was a group of her people who had never wanted any contact with the white man. In spite of this, she said, they would still receive me into their tribe because it was God who was sending me there. She said that I had told her that God had brought me to that very place today and was preparing me, and He Himself would take me to the place where the tribe lived in the rainforest. She said that I would be a *benção*, blessing, to her *povo nativo*, native people. She said I had told her all of this in her native tongue.

"Justino, you said this: 'God is calling me to this people because that is where He wants me. God will guard and protect me. *Deus está comigo.* God is with me.'"

I said all that? My mind raced as I began to ponder the profound meaning of what Tina said. I had received a specific calling and yet, thinking practically, how was I to find this place in the jungle? How would I find this unique tribe of natives? What kinds of supplies would I need? What about my colleagues, the missionary team waiting for me in Manaus? I had lots of questions! I had spent weeks away with David Cooper, and it was high time to rejoin the team. Now I would be seeing Arthur and my companions only to say goodbye. The importance of this time spent in prayer with David was illuminated by Tina's unexpected translation, input, and understanding. Her presence was not a coincidence but divine guidance for the next steps on my path, whatever they were.

David and I discussed the region where I might look for the tribe since he knew of the area and had actually lived in wilderness territory in Peru and in the Amazon Territory. David was a wealth of information, well equipped to inform me, but he wanted me to go to see his friend Victor. Victor, he said, would be the one to show me how I should make this uncommon journey deep into the Amazon basin, alone. I was sincerely grateful but surprised David was so concerned and guarded.

"Justino, the people of this tribe are very remote, very shy; they stay hidden, and even if you find them, they will not receive you. You are the white man. They don't relate to the white man at all. They don't want any contact with us. Many people have tried to contact them, but they will not receive anyone because the white man is bad blood to them. They bring disease, murder, smog, and devastation of the forests. The cattle ranchers and the miners and rubber kings are extracting resources and illegally taking their habitat. The *tribos* have to hide to save their families. If you go in there, and near them, you must know they are justified in killing you. I just don't want to be responsible for anything that might happen to you."

In earnest, Tina interrupted and repeated that I *must* go and talk to *her* people, that I should *not* be afraid of them because this was the will of God. He would lead and protect me. She had heard me, Justino, say so. Then she left our conversation with those encouraging words and didn't come back.

David was still conflicted. He knew the risks and felt he should inform me of them.

"The risks are for them too. You must realize the threat you are to their culture and way of life as well as the threat they are to you. I know this is your decision and that of Arthur and your team brothers and not mine."

"David, don't worry. God has spoken this to me and confirmed this over and over. You heard Tina today. This is another confirmation. God has even shown me the place. I am going with God there. He will not let me harm them. You are not responsible for me."

Still filled with reservations, he said, "If God is sending you, you must do what you believe is the will of God."

"Pray for me, David, that I do the will of God. He wants them to know He loves them."

And so, David Cooper took me back from his house into Manaus to talk to Victor, his friend from the Fundação Nacional do Índio. Victor was an authority on the well-being and location of the indigenous peoples living in the Amazon Territory. He agreed that there was a place down the river where some of Tina's tribe may have been seen passing by on rare occasions. He would take me to where I might watch for them. He would show me where I could stay and then leave me there. It was better, Victor said, to go alone because one person would be less threatening than two or more. Advising Victor of my intentions was following good protocol because he helped me to register with the Fundação Nacional do Índio, the Brazilian Bureau of Indian Affairs. I would go with federal permission and cross into protected lands. This registration process was as much for my security as it was for any of the uncontacted Amazonian tribes of the Brazilian rainforest. In the event that I did not come back out of the rainforest, an attempt would be made by the FUNAI to locate me.

CHAPTER 11

THE LONG WAIT

We were clad in good boots and both carrying heavy packs as we moved through the green forest, Victor ahead using his machete when needed. He was using a compass, and he showed me our progress on his map a couple of times a day. After a few days' hike trailing Victor through the *selva*, jungle, we arrived at the planned destination. We were in the middle of Amazônia and had finally come to what the government of Brazil called the Posto FUNAI, the FUNAI outpost. I don't know what I expected, but it turned out to be no more than a tiny shelter in the dense *floresta tropical*, rainforest, near the river. Here at the FUNAI outpost, we would try to find out more about the tribe of índios Tina called her own people. Victor had said this was the first place we should go to search for the tribe, because it was here in this area that members of the tribe had been spotted.

A conversation with a man stationed there at the Posto FUNAI reiterated David's doubts about finding the tribe I was looking for. Yes, many índios did come near along the river, but hardly ever did anyone see any members of the tribo I was seeking. That tribe wanted nothing to do with the white man, the man said. Victor shrugged and told me not to expect to make any actual contact because this tribe did not want it. I would still be permitted to stay at the Posto FUNAI as long as I wanted. Maybe I would at least see some of the tribe members if anyone showed up. But probably not. Victor left me there to wait for God's will. He would be back. He was a jungle dweller as much as a government employee from Manaus.

For four weeks, I camped at the outpost where Victor had left me. I had begun to memorize the area as my home. The tangled jungle seemed thickest at the river's edge. It must have taken men a long time to clear the area where I now camped—an open island in a sea of trees, bushes, and vines. This place was a hub of wildlife with sensational sounds and silence I would never have appreciated until now. I kept watch over the river all day as my respect grew for all the natives of this ancient, sacred world. Tina's assurance of God's protection quieted me like a mother's whisper.

Then one day two young male índios, who were surely of the rare tribe I was seeking, appeared in the clearing. I wouldn't have known them on my own, of course. But there just happened to be an indigenous woman passing nearby with five or six dozen bananas strapped onto her back. I thought she may have been bringing them to me. I approached her with a greeting in Português, and she responded with a *Bom dia* in turn. I asked her where the bananas were growing, and she handed me a bunch, not really understanding. We had been speaking in broken Português mixed with her Tupi Guarani language only a moment or so when the two shy natives appeared. They must have heard our conversation, which was ironically about them. She greeted them before they could pass by, in very quiet, almost subtle, sounds. This woman recognized these two young men as being from the tribe I had told her about. Assuming she was divinely appointed, I asked her to interpret for me. I hoped she could speak a little of their dialect, trusting it was related to hers.

I swiftly grasped this God-given opportunity to make my intentions known. They were not afraid of this woman! Through her, I asked these two young men if I could come with them and if they would receive me. I told them I wanted to come and stay with them for a little while and get to know them. The woman helped me understand their answer through her sketchy Portuguese. Their answer was that they would take this up with Tuxaua, their leader. If Tuxaua permits this, they said, then they would come back for me another day and take me. I was heartened.

For two more weeks I camped at the shelter, watching the river all day, every day, especially the place where I had first seen Tina's relatives. I began to wonder if I should go to another place. How long would it take to get the chief's consent? How far away was the tribe? I waited another ten days, trying to suppress my urge to ask unanswerable questions. And then, out of the blue, the men reappeared.

"Tuxaua says you can come with us" was what I hoped they said. It was a guess. This time, I had no interpreter.

Really? I grabbed my backpack wondering where I was really going. And, not just that, but with whom was I going? Of course, they didn't know whom they were taking with them, either.

We set off into the selva. I worked hard to keep up with them, walking all day, hardly sleeping in the night, walking again all day through unknown territory. Dense tropical forest entwined us like a mysterious dream. My pathway through I could not retrace. It was already unknown to me and maybe every other modern man. The path I made may have been the first ever made by boots. All around we were surrounded by selva, selva, selva, everywhere selva!

And then, suddenly before me, I saw another native. With his appearance our journey came to a standstill. This other tribesman made it understood by all, including myself, that they *não podia*, could not, take me with them any further. That was the end of that! They disappeared as if into thin air. I could no longer see or hear them. They were gone.

After walking nearly two days without proper rest or food, I had to turn back. Try to find my way back! Frustrated, exhausted, disgusted, I hiked back through the forest in the right general direction, I hoped. At night I attached my hammock as Victor had shown me.

A couple of days later I miraculously arrived back at the Posto FUNAI where I had stayed the last two months. I contemplated my status. It seemed I had not progressed very far. Two months ago, I did not know what I should do, and still I did not know much more than that. I hung my hammock again under the lonesome shelter made of bamboo and other jungle foliage. There I tried to be thankful for the little roof I used to keep the rains off while I waited to know more. I tried to be thankful for having found my way back. It didn't occur to me that everything was going according to God's plan and I should not be in a hurry.

I had a natural sense of determination and a temperament that adapted well to solitude. Here at the Posto FUNAI I could at least get flour and fish and even meat from the forest *bichos*, animals. Fruit grew everywhere on the trees. This was a place with everything—except people. The next tiny one-room dwelling along the river was many miles away. At least I was in an area where índios from different tribes might pass by on the river any day now. I watched and waited for the sight of that special tribe I believed I was meant to be with.

Sometimes I took a trip up or down the river with Victor, who also kept a hammock at the Posto FUNAI shelter for when he visited the area. It was getting to be about May or so. From Victor's *barco*, boat, we sometimes saw the boats of other índios passing by. With all of this waiting, I began to grow patient, rather than impatient. In my new patience, I gave up counting.

Just a few more days in my new state of mind, and they came back.

"You come with us," they ordered in their tongue.

I got my backpack and my hammock and started out with them again. From the beginning of our journey, it began to rain. *Chovia, chovia, chovia!* It rained and rained and rained. Four days we walked through this downpour of unstoppable *chuva, chuva* battering us all day! Hiking, slogging through it, sleeping in it, day and night, *completemente* soaked, I embraced this rain as a blissful greeting. This chuva was not something bad but something in cold contrast with the fire that burned within me. I was burning to get there, to finally come to the place of my call, my dream, the Lord's purpose for me. Wet and cold, I trailed the lithe nude bodies leading me through the *mata*, dense undergrowth.

Now, they were impatient with me, impervious to my inexperience, unsympathetic toward my wet clothing and my heavy backpack. I did my best to fall in line, between the one in front and the one behind. When I stumbled, they picked me up and shoved me ahead, sometimes dragging me along. After this eternal slog pressed on like this, I thought I had dreamed of an arrival. We had stopped. I assumed we were at the village of the tribe because they positioned me at the foot of a tree and promptly disappeared. I looked everywhere for a sign of them or their camp so I could follow them. Nada. Nothing. I sat there alone the rest of the day, wondering what in the world could have happened.

"Meu Deus!" I cried in dismay. A helpless prayer.

From where they left me, I could not see or hear any movement—no huts, fires, people, nothing—anywhere. So, I stayed there, under that tree, sopping wet and completely lost in the middle of the selva for days while it continued raining without letup.

When I awakened the third morning, the rain had stopped and the river nearby had sun on the water. *Que visão linda!* What a beautiful sight! I moved into the sun for a while to dry off and warm myself. I waited there all the day, wondering what I should do. At nightfall I returned to my tree.

The next day, late that afternoon, a group of índios gathered a little way from me and began to walk around me. I didn't know their intentions, didn't understand their gestures or anything about them. For hours, I watched them and they watched me until it was too dark to see.

In the early dawn of the fifth day, I heard a lot of noise along the river, some distance up from where I was. Something was happening, but what? I was *muito preocupado*, very worried. About mid-morning the two índios who had led me into the jungle appeared. They had brought me a present—a roasted monkey. This monkey had been blackened over a fire in its skin and had the putrid smell of burnt hair. I understood that this was something for me to eat, but I didn't know how. I was definitely feeling fear. I accepted the monkey and tried to take a bite of it.

I discovered that a roasted monkey is pure dense gristle and muscle, and I couldn't get my teeth through one morsel. I just sat chewing on the burnt monkey, watching the tribesmen as they gathered nearer. Here was my chance to really see these people. Young and old they assembled around me, some passing very close to the white man with the scorched monkey. When some children came right up to me, I held the monkey out to them. One grinned and took the *macaquinho*, little monkey, from me, skipping away *alegre*, joyful. The other children chased behind him, *feliz*, delighted. I was happy too! What relief it was to be liberated from that monkey!

After a while I stood up and began to look around. Without the hammering rain shower, I realized how close I had been to them all along. I let my eyes trace out their little lodges through the trees. Most had roofs and partial walls of *palha*, straw, and some had windows. The window openings were covered with the loose hanging stalks and leaves of *coqueiros*, coconut trees. The doorways also had these jungle-made vertical blinds from the coqueiros to be swung aside with your arms when passing through. All the casas were round, and there was a large circular lodge in the middle of the village. The big house was also made of straw with only one window and door of the hanging coqueiro leaves. With not a little trepidation, I began to make my way toward the huts, carrying my backpack in my hand. I hoped I was somewhat invited since they had spent the day with me and seemed interested and unafraid.

My backpack was full of things that Dr. João and Jacobede from Manaus and Victor, my friend from the Fundação Nacional do Índio, had given me for life in the rainforest. They had bought me the three different knives sheathed on my leg, the clothes on my back, and the boots on my feet. My pack contained a surgery of medical supplies. I had bandages, gauze, splints, tourniquets, compresses, dressings, and medicines including analgesics and *antibióticos*. I had syringes of *penicilina*; surgical supplies with scalpel, sutures, needles, and silk; bottles of antiseptics; and all kinds of medicinal *crèmes* and pills. I knew a little about how to use this medical kit from the first aid course I had taken with my team.

I had carried this heavy pack a long way and hoped to put it in a safe place. So, I just followed one of these young men into his brush shelter, his casa as I reckoned it to be, and put my bag there. I might have said "thank you for having me" if I had known his language, and he might have said "welcome" if he had known mine. But there was no attempt at communication at first, not even by gestures. If there had been visible emotions to read, I would have seen them. We must have mutually understood that language was neither needed nor possible.

I had arrived, found a place to stay, sat down, and there I was. That became my dwelling place.

CHAPTER 12

A VERY SICK MAN

I felt pretty uncomfortable in the beginning seeing that everyone was nude, completely nude, not a stitch on—man, woman, or child. I had on my white t-shirt and a pair of jeans which I had bought in Manaus. I was wearing the watch my brother gave to me at school. I still have that watch today. I had never felt so modern in what I was wearing!

A little while passed and someone brought me an antler with a piece of smoking carne on it. Like the monkey, the meat was as *preto*, black, as coal. *Preto, preto, preto!*

"*Ai meu Deus, o que vou fazer com isso?* Oh, my Lord, what am I going to do with this?" I thought to myself. I couldn't guess what animal this was from. I took out the smallest knife from the triple sheath at my right hip and carved off a piece. *Vermelhinha! Que coisa mais bonita!* Lovely rare red inside, it was the prettiest meat I had ever seen!

Every hut had a fire going just outside. I had a little frying pan and salt and oil in my pack, and so I sliced pieces of this beautiful, rare meat and fried it up for myself over the fire just outside the entrance to our place. It was the most wonderful taste I had ever had in my mouth. The meat was so tender that the pieces just disappeared on my tongue. A delicious venison!

Soon it got dark, so I tied up my rede onto the thatched wall of our *casinha*, little house, and went to sleep like the others. No one said or gestured anything to me, so I stayed put a few days while we were all getting accustomed to having me. During the day I wandered out near our hut and went about my own business of learning how to live in my new context, trying not to bother anyone.

Observing everything going on around me, I couldn't help noticing a tribesman acting strangely. He passed by and entered a hut nearby. Later he came out still looking very dark and troubled. He visited that hut often and always emerged looking upset. He stood out from all the other índios because of the adornments of feathers on his right wrist, his right thigh, his left ankle, and his head. My guess was that he must be the medicine man of the tribe, distressed about a sick person in that hut.

After becoming familiar with my new surroundings, I found I was free to move about wherever I wished, and no one seemed to take notice. I decided to peek into the hut where the feathered man kept visiting. There I saw a very sick man lying on the floor of the hut. Without even touching him it was clear he was burning up with fever. Moving nearer, I could feel the heat coming off his skin. This indigenous people were of a reddish-brown color, but this man was so deathly ill his skin was *amarelo esverdiado*, greenish yellow.

I was struck with my first real desire to talk. "How do you feel? What are you sick with?" I badly wanted to ask. As I stood over the poor man, two *jovens*, young men, came into the hut. Seeing me there seemed to put them in a panic. I watched the sick man writhing in pain and holding the right side of his abdomen.

"Appendicitis!" I surmised from his symptoms. He continued to moan and groan, suffering terribly from the deep pain. With his yellow-green coloring it was pretty clear to me his liver was losing its battle with peritonitis, the overwhelming infection of a ruptured appendix. I left to search my backpack and returned with a syringe and a bottle of penicillin.

Holding the medicine in plain view, I told the young lads that I had medicine that could cure their relative.

"*Tenho isso aqui para ele.* I have this here for him," I asserted in my softest urgent voice.

I pointed at the sick man and held out the syringe showing how I would use it, acting out a cure. This terrified them even more. I realized that they couldn't give me permission to take over the tribal doctor's job. They obviously knew that their loved one was dying. Should I let the man die? I filled the syringe and injected the penicillin into the man's hip.

Now, I suspected that I had put myself in danger with the medicine man or shaman. He was supposed to be in charge of this, and I had interfered. But I just couldn't let the man die knowing that penicillin could save him. I believed I had no choice but to do good. By the looks of the boys in the hut, the medicine man was someone to be feared more than death. I learned that this feathered *xamã*, shaman, was feared more than the death of a loved one too. At first sight, I figured that the man with the feathers was powerful and that the others respected and feared him. I was to learn soon enough that he was the revered *Pajé* and second in command of the tribe. And I had intruded into his healing ministry and jurisdiction. I knew what I did was risky but hoped it was not a terrible mistake. My first aid course had been brief, so I prayed I was doing the right thing.

I learned later that the sick man's *filho e sobrinho*, son and nephew, visiting him were also taking a risk. They were not supposed to be in the house, either. It was forbidden for anyone to be near a person approaching death. The escaping spirit of a dying person could enter those near them. Only Pajé had the knowledge and experience to manage the unpredictable spirits of the dead. Pajé's medicine and wishes were to be respected and obeyed. The three of us young men were out of line. None of us was supposed to be anywhere near this poor, tormented man. I left soon after giving the injection.

This man had not slept for many nights due to his pain and fever. He had already been sick for many days. But the night after the first injection of penicillin, he apparently slept through the night. This was an indication to me that I was on the right track. The next day I gave him another injection. When on the third day I entered his casa with another injection for him, the man was sitting up! He had regained strength. His pain had passed. His color had changed for the better. The son and nephew of the man were there with him, and this time they wanted to tell me something.

All that I could guess from their gestures, nods, and hand waves was that I was to guard myself. *They must mean the feathered Pajé.* They obviously couldn't openly point at Pajé, and they were forbidden to show me his house. But I was pretty sure they were referring to what I had done to provoke his ire. No doubt he was about to be in a very foul mood when he discovered he was no longer in charge of this man's spirit, his healing, or his burial. The emphatic gestures of the cousins could not tell me specifically, but I was certainly aware that I had overstepped in the treatment of the sick man.

I soon realized I was actually living in the casa of the brother of the sick man. The boys chose not to tell my host, the dying man's brother, what I had done. They kept the injections a secret to protect themselves and me from two dangers: If my medicine worked, there was the threat of the Pajé. If my medicine didn't work, there was the threat of the dying man's menacing spirit. Respecting their fears, I stayed on my guard and kept an eye out for Pajé. I returned to the casa every day continuing the injections of penicillin with the utmost of caution. The truth is, I could enter as I wished with no one stopping me, since nobody else dared to walk even near the dying man's house.

The sick man's son and his nephew knew that I had given the man five injections of medicine. They knew that I prayed for the man every day. Only they knew that this strange *homen branco*, white man, appeared to have a power greater than the Pajé. What intrigued these cousins was that the homen branco seemed oblivious to the threat of the Pajé, their spiritual leader and healer. To them I was both unafraid of a dying man's departing spirit and in possession of remarkable healing powers. They watched me curiously.

Kaúnã was the name of the nephew of the sick man. He seemed to understand that I was trying to do good to his uncle. He thought me brave and began to watch out for my welfare. Kaúnã chose to become my friend.

By the first moon of my arrival, the story of Kaúnã's uncle's recovery was no longer a secret. The way of life in this community was basically open and honest. Whatever the consequences of my actions, we were all to bear them together. After the fifth injection, the infection had essentially passed. The family returned to their house, and they were eating their meals together. They no longer feared the man's spirit and went back to their normal lives.

You might think the tribe would be happy with me for saving a man's life, but I had brought them into a new level of fear. A new state of trepidation came over the tribe after the recovery of the sick man. It gradually became known that I had something to do with it. I had jeopardized their way of life by ignoring their tribal code. All the people in the tribe were connected and all were affected. I had done something appallingly wrong in their eyes in undermining the power of the Pajé, their religious mediator. Kaúnã and his family assumed that Pajé would retaliate. His retaliation would be otherworldly, unpredictable, and could involve any one or all of us. The retaliation or punishment of Pajé would be meted out to rectify the offense, and in the view of every tribesman, it was completely justified.

As I lived with the tribe, I began to understand the order and beauty of their way of life and of their society and to deeply respect it. The tribe had three leaders. The political leader, or chief, was Tuxaua. The religious leader was Pajé. *Contador da historia*, the historian, Ais, was the beloved educator of the history, traditions, and culture of the tribe. With a *king*, *priest*, and *teacher*, this was not an uncivilized people, as some might presume. I soon learned this truth—that within the structure of their own society, they were highly civilized. There was no doubt that the most powerful of the three leaders was the honorable Tuxaua.

O Povo, the People, had their own culture, completely appropriate for them. I grew to admire their way of life and tried to live as a good citizen within it. It wasn't like my own culture, but it was just right for them.

CHAPTER 13

KAÚNÃ

My best bridge to understanding the ways and the language of the People was my friend, Kaúnã. He was my personal teacher. Our biggest communication barrier was what he thought I already understood. I would pick up some object and ask him what it was. Then Kaúnã would proceed to tell me its color or maybe its shape or its use or its danger or its history or just possibly its name. Only by constant repetition and association could I decipher what he meant. How I wished I could coach him on what information I wanted. I had no idea how to record the things I heard him say. I had no knowledge of phonetics. Every day was one of marvel and discovery. I marveled at what I did understand.

As time passed, I studied the language by copying the sounds, pronouncing the syllables—*e tu eh cah wah oo kah toh*—knowing these meant something but not knowing what. When I tried to make sense of these sounds, I couldn't write phonetically and so I couldn't record them properly. I couldn't read what I wrote down. Only like a baby did I begin understanding and growing my vocabulary, word by word. *Ooh wah hoo ka a daw—Eu estou bem.* I am well. *A toogh oogh eh—Eu te amo.* I love you.

One day, I had just had a swim with o Povo early in the morning before daybreak. When I got back to my hut there was a young girl lying in my hammock. This was a terrifying time for me. I was frozen with fear of the unknown. I didn't know the consequences of her presence. I didn't know the significance of her presence, except that it was great. I didn't know what would happen to her or to me if I sent her away. At first, I ignored her to see if she would become bored with me and leave. But she didn't go away. I began to point to her and the door. But then she ignored me.

How glad I was to be able to ask Kaúnã, who was always near, to explain the situation to me. I surmised from his few words, pointing and shrugging, that she was supposed to be there and I had no choice in the matter. Pajé, Tuxaua, and the Storyteller had brought her for me. There were no *solteiros*, unmarried men, in the tribe. A man without a wife would be alone and want a woman that belonged to someone else. *Não pode!* This can't happen! Each man must have his own wife. This is what I believed to be the gist of what Kaúnã was saying.

"Ai!" I thought. *"Um dia nunca passa que eu não aprender algo novo!* A day never passes that I don't learn something new here!"

I had observed that the old men of the tribe had little girls living with them and that the old women had little boys living with them. But I didn't realize that *no one* lived alone. I considered that when a man died here, his wife would belong to his brother. If a man's wife died, I supposed he was given another wife so that he would not want a wife that belonged to another man. Kaúnã confirmed this, saying that the way of the tribe was that there were no solteiros.

Especially after the initial trouble with Pajé, I didn't want to have another conflict. My sending mission had not allowed any fraternity with the opposite sex except in groups for worship. We were not even permitted to be alone together, and here this young girl had taken over my hammock as if she planned on living in my hut. I wanted to do things the tribe's way, but this was a time for some type of compromise.

"Who is this?" I asked Kaúnã.

"Your wife."

"No, I don't have a wife."

"Yes, you do. This is what a wife does. See how she has gathered wood and is now tending your fire."

"I don't want a wife; I don't need one."

"Yes, you do."

"No, I can't have a wife. You must bring back Tuxaua, Pajé, and the Storyteller and tell them for me."

"They won't come back here."

"They have to come back. You must call them here and talk to them for me. I can't keep her here."

Try as I might, I wouldn't be able to communicate my fear, my confusion, my beliefs, or my wishes to Tuxaua, Pajé, and Ais the Storyteller if they came back to talk to me about the young woman. I didn't know enough language to comprehend their response to me, either. I knew they would talk and talk, reasoning with me, insisting, but I wouldn't know what they were saying. Or, they could be very angry. How could I argue my position? I didn't have a leg to stand on. I had to depend on Kaúnã.

I understood that there was a complication to her being in my house. When three or four days had passed and she was still there, it appeared she was planning to stay. I had tried to send her away many times, and she wasn't leaving. I realized she could not disobey Tuxaua. And maybe no one else would take her for a wife now that she had been with me a few days.

Kaúnã decided that since the three would not come to my house again, he would take me to see them. First, we went to the house of Pajé, but he wouldn't receive me. Then we went to the house of the Storyteller, and he was open to talking to me. Kaúnã explained that I didn't want to have a wife, that I was different from the People. I didn't need a wife. Ais the Storyteller explained that o Povo would not accept my living alone. They would assume that I would want a wife and would covet one of their wives. There would be trouble.

I explained, with Kaúnã as my interpreter, that I would not take another man's wife. I would not be living with them for a lifetime. My stay with the People would not be a long enough time to take a wife. When I left, what would become of her? The Storyteller agreed that this was another problem that would come from having a wife given to me.

I asked Ais if I had done anything wrong. He said I had not done anything wrong but that I was in a difficult situation. There was a law that single men or women could not exist. Everyone had someone. Nobody lived alone. By being a single man, I was breaking the law, and this was not right for the People.

As my communicator, Kaúnã made my proposal to the Storyteller: "Allow me to stay with the tribe and continue unmarried. Watch me to see if there is anything about me that is suspect. If you do not trust me, I will leave the tribe. Or, allow me this choice, if I am not capable of gaining your trust as a single man, I will accept a wife."

This plea would have been impossible to communicate without

Kaúnã. He knew my feelings. He knew how to express my thoughts. He was a friend closer than a brother. He was my advocate before the Storyteller. I believe he had help from God. The Storyteller judged in our favor, and the three governors of the tribe went back to my dwelling and took the girl from my home. Only in this way could she have left. She would have never disobeyed her chief, Tuxaua. Whatever Tuxaua said was obeyed, however difficult. He carried authority over life and death. If Tuxaua told someone to jump off a cliff, without question the leap would be taken.

I had questioned the will of Tuxaua, Pajé, and the Storyteller. Never had I felt such fear and trembling. This was a humbling lesson for me in the complexities of human authority. I needed this lesson, considering the resistance I had shown my father. O Povo had demonstrated to me their commitment to obedience, and I admired their integrity.

The pretty young girl left with hurt feelings, I know, being essentially rejected by me. She might have had a position of some celebrity or novelty in being chosen for me. A husband who was already married was chosen for her because there was no other eligible male ready to take this young wife. She was only about thirteen or fourteen at the time. This was a very difficult time for her as well as for me. I felt very bad for her. Later, I took a picture of her with a comb of the *flor de taquara* flower in her hair.

This ancient forest life that I had been taken into was a marvel and a delight to me. Every day was a truly fascinating look into a world that made complete sense for where we lived. As I was able to understand the language more, I progressed from my babyhood. I began to learn as a child, appreciating the good insight of my teacher, Kaúnã.

There was a large, round house in the middle of the camp and smaller dwellings all around. The younger boys and girls all lived in the big house in the middle where they received their education. This is where Ais the Storyteller taught them the complete story of o Povo, their customs and their history. This included all the traditions, the way things had been done since creation. They learned how the Povo were meant to live their lives in the future and how their children were to live as well. This living arrangement continued even as they moved from time to time to other places in the forest. As babies became young children, they moved into the big house to be taught the story and way of their people. As the children came of age, they left the big house and were joined with spouses who were chosen for them.

I discovered something that deeply affected my life, which had been, until recently, a lonesome, single existence. Here with the Povo there was real community. This Amazonian culture was woven together with shared memory, not only as one people, but individually too. Each person had a living witness, a representative of his or her life. Each member of the tribe had someone who was being prepared to take his place in the event of his death. This way, no memory, knowledge, personal role, skill, or contribution would be lost. Every personal story would be known by someone. Each person was considered a part of someone else, prepared to take on the role of that someone else as well as that of his own life. If someone died, there would be someone to take his place in the tribe, to substitute for him or for her. This is how knowledge and remembrance were passed on without writing, through the ages, by a kind of one-on-one discipleship. No one was completely alone. Not even Pajé. And because of Kaúnã, I was not alone, either.

Within a few months, I had used up all my flour and oil. I thought I would either have to hike out and get more or try to eat the way the tribe ate. I was adapting to the ways of the People and they to mine. I went to take my bath in the river, and o Povo took my soap from me and played with it until they lost it in the river. They ate up my toothpaste. Whatever I had brought with me, if I didn't use it up myself, o Povo played with it until it was gone. They took it and lost it or ate it or ruined it not knowing its use or value. In this gradual way, the accouterments from my culture and my old life disappeared.

I eventually recognized that I didn't really need clothing. After several weeks, I had accepted nudity as normal and felt embarrassed wearing clothes when everyone else was completely naked. I packed my clothing away since it was so odd to them and cumbersome to me. You see, I felt silly dressing myself when everyone else was nude and the temperature ranged from hot to warm. I now had a more natural hammock to sleep in, woven from the jungle foliage. Sometimes I felt some discomfort from the straw on my bare back or the chill late in the night, but usually the relief of deep sleep overtook my need for covering.

I stopped shaving and destroyed my razor blades because I was afraid o Povo would hurt themselves on them. Emulating their way, I made all my things as available to them as their things were available to me. All that they had came from their selva and was liberally shared. There was actually no such thing as food belonging to someone. You couldn't steal food. No one owned it. You could enter a house and get all the food and take it to your own house and eat it without guilt. It was for everyone. My body quickly adapted to the new climate, diet, and vigorous exercise. Frequent walking, long hikes, and daily swimming for food were part of tribal life.

I passed every day learning the tribe's language and culture so that I could tell them about Jesus with what I learned. Most of what I gained in knowledge came from my friend Kaúnã. Anything I spoke I first practiced with Kaúnã, who was always near. He was my constant companion. *Eu caminhei com Kaúnã.* I walked with Kaúnã.

At the same time that Kaúnã was a *benção*, blessing, to me, he was a *problema* because he would not leave my side. I found his persistent closeness hard to adjust to. I was perturbed by this because I didn't understand how he had gotten so attached to me. Was this good? Night and day, he was with me absolutely wherever I went. Gradually I began to comprehend the reason.

It was Kaúnã's fear of the shaman, Pajé. He believed I could protect him. But in reality, Kaúnã was *my* protector! As time passed, it became clear that Pajé had violent intentions against me and his treachery and influence were great. Day by day, God used Kaúnã to guide my steps, to inform me, and to shield me from the perils of the jungle, from the foibles of my solitary nature, and from the constant threat of a strike from Pajé. He followed me like a disciple. But I was just as much his.

The *tribo* made everyday use of a type of tree in the forest. Underneath the thick bark of the trees grew layers of wood that were as thin as paper. The tribe used this paper to make wrappers for *cigarros*, cigarettes. They enclosed the meat and leaves from many varieties of foliage that grew everywhere. Many of the plants are related to varieties of tobacco but are much stronger than what is commercially grown. The constant smell of these many different burning cigarettes was quite dreadful. These cigarros, or *sahoot*, as they called them, were an addiction of the whole tribe, with most everyone smoking long, five- or six-inch cigarettes all the time, day and night.

During the *festas*, celebrations, the People smoked cigarros filled with the jungle tobacco and other more narcotic herbs all day and night. To enhance the experience, they added other substances of drink and inhalation, until most everyone had lost all presence of mind and body. These celebrations were religious customs as well as social. I wanted to talk to Kaúnã about the dangers of addiction or the use of harmful substances, but how could I guide him without language? I knew I must not lead him into deeper conflict with Pajé before I could talk to him about the help he could receive from Jesus. For now, I could only trust God to guide him the way God had guided me before I had known that I needed Him.

I began to pray intensely for Kaúnã, asking God to free him from those cigarros and the multiple harmful substances wrapped up in them. I couldn't yet clearly tell Kaúnã that Jesus was near us and would help him. Without more language, all I could do was pray for him.

One day I noticed he didn't have the sahoot in his hand all day. Without a single word from me, Kaúnã completely gave up smoking. Before my eyes, God began changing the life of Kaúnã. God must have revealed Himself to Kaúnã because he began to change in countless ways before I could ever begin to talk to him about life with Jesus. The transformation of Kaúnã's life was a daily inspiration and strength to me. The fact that he changed without a word from me was living proof of the supernatural power and presence of God right there in the wilderness where we lived.

The young man Kaúnã became God's gift to me, God's instrument, God's blessing to all of us in the tribe. And all this began because of, or in spite of, my first mistake. The healing of Kaúnã's dying uncle had broken the young man's trust in Pajé. It had put both Kaúnã and me in grave danger. But a life of fear is worse than a life of danger. Kaúnã chose to stay close to me rather than Pajé even though this choice placed him in constant danger. He didn't know that Jesus was the source of our peace, our security, and our very life!

Because Kaúnã chose to befriend me, at great risk to himself, he became a link to the other tribesmen for me. God used this life-giving friendship with Kaúnã to grow my own faith and teach me daily. I began to truly trust God for all that happened and take my life more completely as from His hand. I began to better understand that the Lord is all we have.

CHAPTER 14

NEW MOON FESTIVAL

After a few months, I realized the *lua nova*, new moon, was very important to the tribe. Every time the moon was new, there was an extravagant three- or four-day festa of celebration to observe. In preparation for this celebration, o Povo cut down the plentiful vines growing all around us in the *mata*, jungle vegetation. They beat the *videiras*, vines, with hard wood sticks to tenderize them. After the essence of the vines was processed in this way, the plants were immersed in wooden tubs of water to soak. A type of potent acidic *cipó*, wine, was rendered from the juice, which floated to the top of the liquid mixture like a foam topping. This mixture was traditionally their *bebida*, beverage, naturally distilled from religiously selected jungle vines for countless generations. I looked on as the partying tribe all drank from this tub full of the fruit of the vine, *cipó da videira*, and danced to their beating drums. It seemed this was their way of finding connection with the spiritual world, dancing with invisible ancestral souls.

As they danced, they called out in wails of what appeared to be agony. They stared wide-eyed into the forest or maybe at nothing at all. I was naive, uneducated, and knew nothing of "shamanic" journeys or mythical visions. Having lived with them a few months, I suspected that they sought protection, healing, help with hunting, knowledge of the future, or the will of their ancestors. I watched them stagger, eventually dropping, unconscious, one after another onto the ground. The drums beat incessantly—DOOM, do dom dom DOOM—DOOM, do dom

dom dom dom DOOM—DOOM, do dom dom dom dom DOOM—on and on, day and night for three days.

Their drums were made of large, cut, hollowed tree trunks with animal skins stretched over the ends. The drummers were sopping with sweat, as if they had just come out of the river. The dancers—men, women, and older children—were just as sweat-soaked, their hands making gleaming swirls with their glowing sahoot as they shook and spun and drank until they finally fainted. Naked, exposed, and sick, they lay where they had collapsed onto the ground until morning. Then the *celebração* started up again as soon as the People were able to rouse themselves. Every new moon I watched this three-day drama in quiet awe from *minha rede*, my hammock, in my corner of the camp.

Now, the *ayahuasca*, the fruit of the jungle vines, was continuously made a few times a week and then left to mature, fermenting in a large wooden basin. Sometimes the trimmings of the leaves of other selected plants were added by the Pajé, but I wasn't sure why. Another caldron of the concoction rested nearby on a little fire to simmer, the frothy top developing over the mixture maybe indicating where it was in the preparation process. A great amount had been brewed for the approaching new moon when all the people would drink and dance again. Each month I had become more curious, and so I walked over to sniff at it.

"*Porque fazer tudo isso?* What is the point of drinking this until you all faint from its effects?"

I murmured this to myself since Kaúnã would not be able to answer. He wouldn't know that I was curious as to why the whole tribe endured all of this for days with such conformity and compliance. Was the potion harmful, helpful, bitter, tasty, hypnotic, pleasant, life-changing? Was the whole tribe addicted—man, woman, and child? What was the allure of this new moon fascination?

I asked Kaúnã if I could test it myself. Kaúnã pointed to the stuff that had been bubbling for days and said no. Then he seemed to be explaining the dangers *por um tempo*, for a while.

"We are born to this and have grown up with this. You cannot drink this tea. This is very strong. You don't have experience with it. It will kill you."

I only understood the last couple words.

"What about the other, the newer?"

Kaúnã agreed that I might taste of the new basin that was being prepared at the moment but not the other mature cipó. But even my little experimentation came with a warning.

"*Muito pouco!* Only a little bit!"

I wondered what the exact difference was. Was the older preparation really stronger, or had it been *consagrado*, consecrated, by Pajé and set apart for the tribal ceremonies? Was it that I was "not permitted"? Forbidden fruit? Maybe because he forbade me, I actually preferred an authentic trial and wanted to experience the real thing, the fully prepared substance with all its properties. But I acquiesced and followed the strict instruction of my friend Kaúnã. I dipped my finger into the liquid that was in the earlier stages of preparation. After stirring my finger through the acidic foam, I put my wetted finger into my mouth.

Within a couple of seconds my vision turned dark. Quickly I dropped my head to keep from fainting dead away. My head began rushing and spinning, and my body seemed in motion inside and out though I was holding myself still to keep my balance. With careful determination, I stumbled to my rede and nearly fell past it. That is where I lay while the world spiraled around me for hours. I was too dizzy to sit up, much less get up.

That drop of ayahuasca, that indigenous hallucinogenic narcotic, was the extent of my 1960s experimentation with drugs. I suppose Kaúnã was right to insist that I NOT experience the effects of the forbidden consecrated batch. If I barely dipped the end of my finger in the potion and was completely incapacitated for hours, imagine if I had taken a sip of the *curtida*, more seasoned, distilled barrel. He was right! I may not have survived it.

How the Povo, boys and girls and their elders, drank the beverage day and night for three or four days a month for timeless generations remains a mystery to me. This was their tradition and very much a part of the life of the tribe. In my view, it certainly intoxicated everyone, but it didn't seem to poison them. For me it was not good medicine, and Kaúnã had advised me well.

When the Lua Nova celebration came after my first month with the tribe, my friend Kaúnã was out there dancing day and night as he must have since childhood. He smoked and danced and drank all night with all the others. The second new moon I saw him dance some, but not as much. The third celebration he came and sat down with me away from the festival. He had given it up. Why? Not for my approval, for I couldn't have given it. Not by any power of mine, for I had none.

Not only did he refuse to dance, but he had given up the *cipó da videira*, the potent ayahuasca, as well. And without a word from me, he had even given up the sahoot smoking. I was amazed that he had chosen to steel himself from the power of the sahoot and even the ayahuasca, for it seemed to have control over the whole tribe. The overwhelming influence of these substances and their value in this tribal setting cannot be calculated. So much went into this, and Kaúnã had given it up. There is no earthly reason for this. Only a heavenly one.

There is another important festival observed by o Povo. Every seven years the white jungle flower called *taquara branca* blooms, and a special celebration of the tribe marks that seven-year era for each person's life. " I've seen the taquara branca bloom three times," might be said by someone about twenty-five years old. What happens at the coming-of-age festival of Taquara Branca is always remembered, and it is celebrated as an anniversary of great importance. I was privileged to experience God's timing of this event during my few years with the tribe.

At this festival, the young men and boys are paired to do battle with one another to achieve the honor of becoming *older brother*. Being an older brother is a lifelong honor, achieved through victory at that seven-year festival when the flower is seen blooming. The young boys coming of age fight bare-handed, as gladiators without weapons, until one dominates the other and is pronounced the older brother. I was told this hand-to-hand combat actually led to death sometimes, though I did not see this happen. To lose and become the younger brother was to become the weaker brother, the servant of the older. The older brother became the leader, the more powerful, the more respected, the stronger voice, the more prominent of the two brothers. If one of the brothers were to die, the children and wife of the one would be given to the other brother, and the combined family all would become sisters and brothers, mothers and father. In this way, whether younger or older, serving or leading, these brothers took care of each other.

With this complex combination of families, it seemed everyone was a brother, sister, or cousin. I had never studied anthropology but knew the traditional way to diagram a family tree with branches from grandparents to parents and grandchildren, uncles, aunts, cousins, and so on. Being greatly confused about the tribe's relationships, I was enlightened after I witnessed the festival during my time with the tribe. Kaúnã explained how each person of the tribe was related in a familial, but not necessarily biological, way to someone else in the tribe.

When Kaúnã chose to befriend me rather than to practice the cultural rites of his people, I did not recognize the honor he had shown me. I could not know yet that he had chosen me as the older brother to him. He had chosen to become the weaker brother. In this way he forfeited to me his position and status and influence in the tribe. I didn't yet know his sacrifice when he preferred to stay by my side and abstain from these rituals that were so much a part of his life. Later I would better comprehend and appreciate the risks and cultural impact of the choice he made.

CHAPTER 15

WHEN THE SUN SETS

Here I was again, hiking through the *floresta*, forest, to somewhere unknown to me. As was the usual with these impromptu excursions, I knew not where I was nor where I was going. I had been with the tribe for about five months, but the tangled terrain was still incomprehensible, and keeping up with the tribesmen, quite impossible. *Destino desconhecido*, destination unknown, described my footpaths.

Besides those concerns, it had been raining heavily for some days, and the river beside our settlement was high and agitated. The índios showed me the place where we would cross over using a natural bridge, apparently familiar to them. They pointed to it, a skinny, tall tree without foliage that had fallen across the *barranco*, ravine. They promptly crossed over and then waited for me expectantly, unamused with my slowness.

I climbed onto the trunk and started across, trying to concentrate on my feet and yet not think about where I was really going. It was a precarious place, balancing on this wet, naked tree in a drenching rain shower, looking down at the rushing Amazon tributary below. The tree trunk was long but not wide at all. It didn't feel very solid under me. As I inched my way across, the trunk swayed and trembled under my boots. When I found some steadiness, I tried to move with its bending and had some success stepping and sliding up and out a few meters over the water.

My hiking buddies waited, wondering what the trouble was with me. I tried to ignore their clicking way of murmuring in the noise of the rain and the river. They were mocking my clothing, but I needed it when they took me away from the village.

My next step went wrong. I lost my balance and down I went, slipping backward off one side. I turned and reached out, grabbing the *madeira*, log, that had been under me. Hanging on for dear life, I hugged the mossy, slick tree bridge by my forearms, hoping to get my feet up to it. But quickly the weight of my backpack pulled my grip from my arms to my hands and then to just my fingers. My soaked frame and my heavy pack could not be sustained by my wet fingers. Leaving fingernails in the bark of the log, I went down, back first, tree trunk above me. Just as I touched the river with my pack down and my feet up, I felt myself raised back up! It was swift and sudden. Yes, my whole body with my backpack was raised up and set back down at the exact place where I had been inching along the tree bridge. *Um milagre!* A miracle!

I know this is an unexplainable phenomenon. It isn't believable. I hardly believed it. Awestruck, yet without pausing, I somehow slithered across to the other side of the ravine and joined my companions.

"Did you see?" I asked them, *espantado*, amazed, to be with them.

"You should have died," they said. I knew their meaning. It was only rational.

Returning to that place much later, I reconsidered that treacherous crossing. With certainty, encumbered by so much weight, I *should* have perished. By God's mercy I had been rescued. The *índios* would have survived had they fallen, being naked, carrying nothing, free-handed, and being skilled to swim hard and fast as they had since boyhood. But me, even if unencumbered by clothing, boots, and heavy pack, my stroke couldn't have managed the high current through the gorge that day. Neither could they nor would they have rescued me.

Wouldn't it have been just as easy for God to put me safely on the other side of the river beside my friends? He saves us but doesn't make things much easier. Getting that pack all those steps over a slippery, seesawing log to the other side seemed even harder after having once fallen! I hope it's not irreverent to wonder why God set me down at the very place I had fallen. Thinking through every step now brings home the reality that only God could have or would have rescued me. At the time, only He thought me worth saving. I thank Him!

The reason I carried such a heavy pack was that these men had already taken me to various places. At any time they fetched me, it was going to be a mystery—that is, where we were going and how long we would be gone. When we returned, I could not recall where in the selva we had been between our journeys. There was no map, no road, not even a path. So, I tried to be prepared for the unexpected.

One day I was with Kaúnã sitting near some of the other *jovens*, young men. They told me something intriguing.

"*Tem Povo nosso, Justino. No outro lugar.* There are more of our people. In another place," Kaúnã translated.

"*Como assim?* Really? How do you mean?" Kaúnã saw this piqued my curiosity and elaborated.

"The *caras*, guys, are saying we have relatives in another *aldeia*, village. This village is of our same tribe and can be found in the jungle not far from us. These are our *povo*, our brothers."

Kaúnã clarified that these people were of the very same tribal family. Kaúnã's tribe had split from their relations because his tribe did not want any contact with *homen branco*, modern man. Their relatives dwelled on another river and would accept a visit from us, explained Kaúnã.

This was an important and remarkable invitation to me. These were the same Povo and *do mesmo sangue*, of the same blood, and language of the tribe of Kaúnã. They were also an untouched Amazonian tribe as far as I knew. These young men were proposing a visit with their relatives and inviting me to go along with them. I surmised this meant we would *not* be in danger of a fight and we could even trade something with them. I suspected they wanted to show the odd human, Justino, to their cousins too.

"*Você quer ir lá?* Do you want to go there?" the guys asked me.

"Where do they live?" I asked Kaúnã.

"*No Andirá.* By the river Andirá." I had never heard of that place. I looked at Kaúnã. He was not familiar with the river.

"How far away?" I asked.

"When the sun sets, we are there," pronounced the hikers.

This was definitely something to consider. A day's hike to o Rio Andirá. I thought I could manage that.

"Okay, I want to go there," I agreed.

Kaúnã told them I wanted to go.

A couple of weeks later, the young men showed up looking for me and saying it was time to go. Kaúnã then told me that they were taking me to Andirá. I got my gear together and went off with them.

As I hiked along with my tribal brothers, I realized that many tribes could be known by their place of dwelling. O Povo could be known for the rivers close by. The Miriti was the name of the river nearest our dwelling place, which was also close by the Ibituí, the river on the other side of us. I had heard these names on occasion. These two waterways of the great Amazon, the Miriti and the Ibituí, were on nobody's map of South America, on nobody's map of Brazil or even of the Amazon Territory. They were indigenous names of rivers. And I was honored to walk on this ground, with these people, becoming possibly the first modern man who had ever had that privilege. This was an amazing reality to contemplate.

We were on our way to a village near the River Andirá, and it was a distance of "when the sun sets." After a few days' trek, at a relentless, punishing pace, I was very fatigued. I had run out of supplies, my body ached, my legs were cramping, and I began to doubt I had what it took for this expedition. Even my empty pack felt heavy. These boys did not pause to find food or duck out of the rain. The jungle was dense, and the path they made through the jungle was demanding. Without fruit, nuts, or drink, moving fast in the heat, rarely stopping, I had little energy now, and I was not able to keep hydrated to compensate for the prolonged, grueling advance. I was dripping with perspiration.

"*Onde está o Andirá?* Where is the Andirá?" I pleaded, every hour or so.

They didn't answer. I guessed speaking to me was Kaúnã's role, and he was not with us. They didn't know that almost any answer would have encouraged or quieted me.

"*O que está acontecendo?* What is going on here?" I pleaded.

They ignored me. I tried to remain focused on survival as a few more hot, humid days passed. Did it make them feel strong to see me so vulnerable and helpless? Did they plan all along to leave me in the forest as a test of my manhood? What would they say to my brother Kaúnã if I died? Did the Andirá cousins move their village?

By the fifth day I realized that I was an unexpected burden on them and that if I collapsed, it would put them at risk. They were hungry and tired too. They were not invincible. This trip was not one of recreation. It was a reconnaissance mission. If I had not been with them, they would have arrived by now, and they would have accomplished their assignment. I tried harder to keep up, but I was so bad off I now remember very little after five or six days of hiking with little rest or food.

Eventually we did find the river Andirá tribe of our people. The *rapazes,* guys, laid me down where I could recover in a sheltered place while they visited with their relatives. I slept solid for at least two days and nights. I imagine I was out of my head, but I know that o Povo Andirá fed me and were gracious to me. My own brothers took me home as soon as I gained enough strength to make the trip.

On that hike from our river Miriti to the relatives' river Andirá, I discovered that *when the sun sets* is an expression which could possibly mean "close to a week." When o Povo had said "let's go," I went with them because I thought they were talking about thirty or forty kilometers, not that distance times seven. I was as helpless to know *when* we were going as *where* we were going and *where* we had *been* when they finally brought me back. Not knowing the remoteness or the demands of these journeys, I tried to be prepared for any place they might take me, or leave me, for that matter. This is why I carried a heavy pack those first months with the tribe! Into that backpack I put my hammock and supplies for a couple of weeks, and I wore my boots and was fully dressed to protect myself from snakes, insects, and the elements.

The People knew of themselves, the surrounding rivers, and each other's villages, but to all others they were unknown. These two Indian villages in the forest along the Amazonian watercourses were brought into my mind, heart, and soul. I had seen them, eaten with them, received their protection and guidance. How easily o Povo could have killed me out of self-defense or by accident or by obedience to an order. But they didn't. I trusted them because they trusted me.

Many years later I learned that these two related indigenous nations would be called the Sateré. The two Sateré tribes that included Kaúnã's tribe and their relatives were the river Miriti tribe and the Andirá tribe named for the rivers of the dwelling places where they were discovered. Kaúnã's tribe lived by the river Miriti, part of a system of rivers coming off the waterway called Madeira, a large tributary of the Amazon River. The young men had asked me through Kaúnã if I wanted to meet their people living on the river called Andirá, which is part of the Amazon River, too, but runs out from a different tributary than the Madeira, at least 300 kilometers away—tough rainforest kilometers. I guess Kaúnã thought I was stronger than I was. At the time, I couldn't have survived the trip without these young men. I still had so much to learn from them.

Even though the rainforest all around contained countless dangers to me, I hadn't felt a heavy weight of fear or anxiety. The tribe and God's hand protected me from the jaguar, the anaconda, the black caiman. I had survived great *perigo*, danger, living with them. I felt safe in the water from piranha, poisonous frogs, and predatory fish for the same reason. I was essentially unaware of the numerous parasites and diseases and their carriers, assuming the indigenous people of the tribe were much more vulnerable than I. I was living in a place so remote that I was undiscoverable, yet I never really felt lost while with the People.

But just a few months later, I began to sense a different kind of enduring threat on my life. I could feel it, and I felt it daily. Kaúnã knew it too. For seven months now, I had been away from everything and everyone I had known in my nineteen years. Now, I recognized a growing menace of danger that persisted day and night. It was Pajé's discontent.

"I am actually fortunate to still be alive," I realized as I lay down to sleep in my hammock at night.

I reckoned with myself that along with the trust we enjoyed came more vulnerability and risk. It could be decided at the next meeting that I was a burden or an enemy to o Povo. This would give them reason to kill me. I wasn't ignorant, before, of this possibility. But now in my heart of hearts, I was convinced it was time to give the tribe a rest from me.

This was reinforced in my mind as I remembered that my friend David Cooper had told me stories about living near other tribes of the Amazon. Even my índio brother Kaúnã had made known to me some stories of o Povo having eaten their adversaries. Cannibalism is a common thread in the oral history of many indigenous tribes and may or may not be factual, I told myself. Either way, I didn't want to wear out my welcome. I decided my first term with o Povo had come to an appropriate end. I spoke to Kaúnã.

"*Eu quero voltar para meu povo.* I want to return to my people. But I'll come back to be with you and your people again."

Kaúnã looked at me, hearing me voice my decision in *his* language. His eyes told me that he didn't like what I said. But I was his older brother and so he wouldn't question it. I think Kaúnã may have agreed it was best because he notified Tuxaua of this news and helped me pack up my things that very day. Early the next morning, Kaúnã and two of the other hunters took me to a place where I could find my way to the Posto FUNAI, honoring my request with little fanfare. They accompanied me just as far as was needed and not a footstep further. We parted ways. Today o Povo would hunt for game like deer and musk hog. And I would hike out of the forest toward modern civilization.

CHAPTER 16

COMING HOME

Fortunately, I had gained a great deal of jungle survival expertise since my first walk into the Amazonas almost a year earlier. When I made it back to the towns and people of the modern world, friends and colleagues could hardly believe their eyes.

"*Rapaz, você está vivo!* Young man, you are alive!"

Apparently, few people believed that I would still be living! The worst possibilities had been assumed because I had not made contact with anyone at all. Not a word passed even to Victor at the Posto FUNAI. I might as well have come back from another planet. I had been completely unreachable and living a very different life, and the sight of me confirmed it.

My hair nearly reached my shoulders, and a long beard touched my chest. My skin was very dark from the sun. I was wiry and strong from the rugged life and eating the lean tribal diet. My teeth needed care, but I was in most ways strengthened rather than weakened by my experience in the remote territory of the Amazonas.

I first went to the house of David Cooper where he greeted me with unreserved emotion.

"*Me perdoe por não vir atrás de você!* Forgive me for not coming after you!"

He cried and hugged me, asking again and again for my forgiveness and confessing that he had believed I had died. I never once expected him to come after me. If he could have found me, which is unlikely, he probably could not have helped me. Two men may well have been more intimidating to the tribe than I was, alone. Tina, the young woman from Peru who worked for him, had told us both not to worry, that I was safe in God's care. Maybe David only half believed her. David had known so much loss in his life that he struggled with anxiety over dangers he couldn't predict or oversee. He said my life was inspiring and he hoped I would come back often. I told him I hoped so too.

After my visit with David, I went into the *cidade*, city, of Manaus, to the house of Dr. João Chrisostomo and his wife, Jacobede. It was the end of the year, already December 1970. When I greeted Dona Jacobede, I called her *Mãe*, Mom. Dr. João wept when he came down the stairs. Dona Jacobede said it was the first time she had ever seen him cry. This moved me greatly, as he had also become like a Papai to me.

Always planning for my further education, Dr. João told me that there was a new course in linguistics being offered in Belo Horizonte. He enrolled me in the course and wanted my promise to attend. I was glad to attend. I needed help. The language of Kaúnã was a tonal language with clicks of the tongue and guttural notes that matched no combinations of letters from Portuguese that I knew. I couldn't write down a single word of what I had learned. I needed intense study of what I had learned before I forgot it.

I loved my visit with Dr. João and Jacobede, but after only a few days, I was impatient to see my own family in southern Brazil. I had said goodbye to them on August 7, 1969, a year and a half ago. I missed them terribly, and I was anxious to know how they all were! Dr. João reassured me that I would see them again soon.

"*Não se preocupe*, don't worry, I'm going to take care of everything for you," said Dr. João. He smiled broadly and told me he knew I needed to see my family to feel myself again and was happy I came to see him first so he could help me do just that.

He then bought me an airplane ticket from Manaus to Brasília. That journey would have taken me weeks, and now it was going to be over in a day. This would be my first time on an airplane! I kept that ticket as a memory. He also gave me money to travel by bus from Brasília to the state of Paraná where my parents lived. In only a few days I would be home with them. I ardently imagined the joy of being together with my siblings and my parents on *Dia de Natal*, Christmas Day.

Dr. João was adamant that I go home with something for everyone in my family.

"*Você não estará de mãos vazias!* You will not be empty handed!" he insisted.

He took me to the luggage store and bought me a huge *mala,* suitcase. He took me shopping and filled the mala with new clothes. Then he wanted to know about all the members of my family. How good it was to talk about them! He bought *presentes* for Mamãe, Papai, and for every one of my ten brothers and sisters. I visualized myself having a presente for each of them at my homecoming and choked back my emotion. He wanted to know the name and age of each sibling so that we could choose just the right fine, imported material in Manaus at the *loja de tecidos,* fabric store, and then he labeled each gift carefully. He bought them all. *Foi muito bom!* It was tremendous!

I received another gift in Manaus from someone I knew through my friendship with Dr. João and Mãe Jacobede. An Italian Army captain, Iaco Astoriano de Sousa, gave me three polo shirts in white, yellow, and green. I will never forget getting those beautiful Italian shirts. After months of living nude in the rainforest, I was to be dressed in style.

Dr. João delivered me to the airport and escorted me through the line. The rules were unpredictable, and especially imports like those *elegante* shirts and fabrics could be a focus for a random high tax. He didn't want me to have to pay for anything. Dr. João escorted me to the baggage check carrying that heavy suitcase stuffed with all those presentes.

"*O Justino é gente minha.* Justino is my family. *Não precisa olhar para a dele, não.* You don't have to inspect his luggage, no."

The official passed me through just as if I were his son or Dr. João Chrisostomo himself. Government officials and their families were privileged to be exempt from these inconveniences of travel. Then Dr. João continued to escort me onto the airplane and to my seat. I had never been on an airplane. Never had a good leather suitcase to carry. Never had presents to bring to my big family. Never received this kind of preferential treatment. He hugged and kissed me goodbye. I had never known that kind of fatherly affection. It moves me to tears to this day.

"Will you come back?" he asked me.

"*Sim, eu vou voltar,*" I assured him.

"*Eu vou te esperar.* I will be waiting for you," he promised.

It was December 23, 1970, and I was on the ônibus from Brasília to the city of São Paulo! My dreams were coming true. It was *meu sonho,* my dream, to arrive by Christmas and be able to see all of my family together. It was my wish come true to surprise them with my arrival, bringing gifts in my arms for each of them. My heart ached with the joy of this vision of being reunited with my family.

I arrived at the *rodoviária*, bus station, in São Paulo finding my suitcase very heavy for my thin frame. It surely weighed as much as I did. Now São Paulo, an immense and populous city, had positively the largest bus terminal in all of Latin America—Rodoviária Tietê. There were dozens of travel companies operating scores of arrival and departure platforms serving hundreds of cities all over the twenty-six states of Brazil and several Latin American countries. The colorful Christmas crowds were in zigzagging mazes filing out of all the platforms, and I just needed to find a departure bus line to the state of Paraná so that I could be on my way. From line to line I lugged my mala, seeking any ticket south to any city in my state of Paraná.

I checked every bus to every city in the state of Paraná, dragging the suitcase, rambling from one ticket window to another. The earliest arrival I could find was January 1! This was a crushing blow. I looked around at thousands of people who were going home. I had only just enough money to get on a bus, no place to stay, and no money to pay for lodging. How could it be possible that there was no room for me on any bus at all? What a cruel disappointment this was—I couldn't believe it.

Through the deafness of my defeat, I heard the screech of a train. There was a train station a few blocks away from the bus station. I asked the porter if I could leave my suitcase at the rodoviária so that I could sprint to the train station and inquire about passage by train without my bag in tow. He agreed and I rushed to the Tietê train station.

A train was just leaving for Londrina, a city not far from my family! I went to the counter and waited in the line. No, they had no more seats available. I went to the railway, my envious eyes watching the people with their baggage. Everyone was boarding. The conductor shrugged and gave me a look of compassion.

"Do you really want to go so much? You really want to go that bad?"

"*Sim, eu quero ir!* Yes, I want to go!" I choked out, stifling tears.

"It's a long way," he sighed. "Would you be willing to take standing room only?"

"Yes, yes!" I was overcome with gratefulness.

Desperate for any way to get home, I hardly believed my good fortune. But the train was to leave in fifteen minutes, and I didn't have my bag. They wouldn't hold the train for me and so I couldn't buy the ticket and risk missing the train and losing the little money I had left. I couldn't go home without my bag! I ran like the wind to the rodoviária where I had left my suitcase.

I put the suitcase on my back and pressed through the thick crowds out to the street. The bus station was *lotada*, crammed tightly, with the holiday mobs. The noise and unfamiliar city lights from the shops and signs bolted out at me, charging me, threatening me. I ran like my life depended on it towards the train station, hardly noticing the weight of my bag now. I knew that train was my last chance out of São Paulo before Christmas! Or before the New Year!

Gasping, I stumbled up to the ticket counter at the train station, with no idea of whether the train had left me behind or not. After I insisted, the *agente*, officer, took my money, doubting I could make it.

"The train is leaving now! *Anda! Corre!* Run!" he said.

It was leaving indeed. I saw the stairs of steel moving towards me! I grabbed a rail as soon as it was near enough for me to reach. I jumped onto the first step, my other hand still holding my suitcase like it was light as a feather. The ground blurred away, and I stepped up through the door. Edging into the corridor, I found a niche to stand in. When I couldn't stand any longer, I sat down on my suitcase, still incredulous that I was a passenger. Through the night, I slept with my head in my hands or against the frame of the seats in the aisles, gratefully moving out of the way when people needed to pass. I was actually in their way because of the grace of God.

I was on my way to Londrina in Paraná, to the south of Brazil. I had traveled thousands of miles, and now I was a passenger on a train for the first time in my life. I flashed back to my first sighting of a train, when I was a little boy and first moving to Paraná. I had felt it make a mark on my life, and I believed now that it was God's gentle reminder of His presence on my journey wherever I would go. Unspeakable joy kept me strong for the many hours ahead.

When I arrived in the state of Paraná, still so far away from where my family had moved, I was losing hope of finding them by Christmas Day. They had let me know in a letter that the land we used to live on had been sold. They were now at a new farm in a town called Assis Chateaubriand. The little town of Assis Chateaubriand in my state of Paraná was not shown on any of the buses. Here I was in my home state of Paraná on Christmas Eve, watching lines of loaded, packed buses moving away, taking all these hundreds of people close to *my* family—to Maringá, to Rolândia, even to Londrina. But, not one seat for me!

As hard as I tried, I could not find one *ônibus* to take me even near the town of Assis Chateaubriand. Having come so far, I just couldn't bear the reality of it. I couldn't accept it. It was the death of my dream, the vision I had of embracing my brothers and sisters and parents at our Christmas gathering. Heartbroken, the tears streamed down my face.

"Meu Deus! Eu vou passar o Natal aqui? My God, I will spend Christmas here?" I cried openly. There was no holding back this waterfall of disappointment.

A repeating voice split through the bus station's commotion.

"Alguém quer ir para Maringá? Somebody want to go to Maringá? Somebody want to go to Maringá?"

It was a man calling out from his car for someone to ride with him and help him pay *gasolina* to his destination. Maringá was a step closer to home. I waved and quickly told him that I would go with him. He looked me over and grimaced, saying my suitcase was too big for his trunk. Then he sped away in his little Fusca, Volkswagen Bug.

"Não!" I watched his little Fusca meander around the lines of people in colorful summer clothing and the smelly buses of the busy rodoviária.

"Alguém quer ir para Maringá?" he sung out, circling the rodoviária and passing me by at least four more times. With all that effort, the man could not find another person willing to go with him. The morning was wasting away!

He came back to me. *"Eu vou te levar.* I will take you," he said. Complaining that my suitcase would not fit into his trunk, he wedged it into his back seat, and I took the front seat beside him. Soon we were at the bus station in Maringá.

It was there at Maringá that I finally accepted the probability that I would not see my family before Christmas Day. How could it be that no one would be taking me that little distance I had left to arrive home? Why couldn't I have arrived earlier yesterday! The closer I got to my home, the more it seemed I should have some choice in these matters. Yet, no matter how determined I was to make it happen and how many scenarios I imagined, it was there in Maringá that I had to give up all options. I would be spending the rest of Christmas Eve and much of the night right there at the rodoviária.

Maringá was the place where I finally figured out that God was already preparing the way home for me. As soon as I was still enough to sense God's gentle way in this, I let go of my disappointment. My wait in the Maringá bus station became a time of rest and of deep gratitude. I did not know that this interlude, this pause, was what I needed most.

I encountered several people I knew and some who knew of me or my family: Martin, Marlene, Paulo, César. César was a childhood friend with whom I had gone to school. How good it felt to be recognized, to be remembered. This pause in Maringá gave me the associations God used to make the last connections of my journey without my frantic worrying. These people brought me food and gave me satisfying company during the hours that passed. They made my stay quite bearable, even enjoyable. I was able to wash away forty-eight hours of travel with a shower at the rodoviária facilities.

César's family arranged for a friend to take me to Cianorte so that in the early morning I could catch all the right buses for my journey home. I arrived in Cianorte before midnight, in time to buy a ticket to Umuarama. I arrived in Umuarama *a madrugada*, before dawn. I was able to doze off a couple of hours before the next bus left about 4:00 a.m. to Assis Chateaubriand. The final bus to Assis Chateaubriand on Christmas Day and I was on it! A friend of my family actually delivered me from the rodoviária in Assis Chateaubriand right to my family's new home before noon on Christmas Day! I opened the door and walked in.

Ninguém estava! Nobody was home! *Ai! Fiquei muito triste!* I was shocked and crestfallen. This was something I had not even considered. Where were they? Did they go away for Christmas? They surely had been expecting me! I had written to tell them!

The house was nice, and for a change, was located in town. I found it *gostoso*, friendly and comfortable. I took a bath, changed my clothes, and decided to make the trip to the little town where two of my sisters lived, about thirty kilometers away. Maybe they were there, I thought, frustrated.

I walked back to the rodoviária of Assis Chateaubriand and bought the ticket. Sometime later I asked to be let off on the highway. I still had about five or six kilometers to walk before I would be on the *sítio*, the small farm that my sister lived on. I found some of my cousins and other relatives and friends at this sister's house, but they said my parents and brothers and sisters were at Celia's house, my other sister. Finally, I knew where my family was!

Perfeito! They would be there all together, and soon I was indeed going to be with them. My step was light. I had left my suitcase in my parents' home, but I didn't miss carrying it as I almost skipped for that last kilometer. *Era tão bom vêr-los!* Oh, it was good to see them! They were not expecting me, you see, since I had not arrived before Christmas as I had promised.

"*Coitado!* Poor thing, Tininho!" they said using my nickname as they embraced me. I was much thinner than they had ever seen me.

They enjoyed watching me eat so much Christmas dinner, and it was delicious. That night we all returned to my parents' home where I had left my suitcase. I could hardly wait to give each sister and brother the presents I had brought them. Dona Jacobede, in Manaus, had written a little card to each member of my family with words of fondness from me and a blessing from the Bíblia. They seemed surprised and happy to get the presents and received them one by one almost timidly. I looked over at my parents and noticed they had the same shy look, as if I were an important guest in their home.

"I am finally at home with myself, but they don't know me this way," I thought.

After most of the family had gone to bed, my father asked if he could talk to me. We walked outside together, quietly appreciating the breeze as it moved the clouds past the moon just above us like a floating heaven. It would soon rain on us, but it would be the warm summer blanket of December. We weren't far from the house when my father stopped and told me he wanted to ask me for my forgiveness.

His eyes teared up, and he choked out how he regretted not believing me when I had said that God had spoken to me. While wiping his face with the handkerchief he had pulled from his pocket, he said he knew that my words were always straight and honest and that he should have reinforced me in every way in the calling God had given to me. Sobbing now, he said that he would always support me and that he was proud of me. He said that since I had left, he had talked about me to others saying I was a missionário to Amazonas. He laid his hand on my shoulder and again asked if I would forgive him, his wet face blushing with sincerity. Dazed by his emotion and earnestness, I did my best to answer him plainly.

"*Claro que aceito seu pedido de desculpas, Pai.* Of course I accept your apology, Pai. I know I was so unfriendly and indifferent to you and to Mamãe and to my brothers and sisters, too, that I prejudiced you against me. I did not generate trust, and so you could not believe me. No one could for a long time, Pai, until Pastor Arthur. I did not hold this against you. I never did."

I took this rare privacy with Pai to share one more thing, though I hated disappointing him. When I attended the seminary at Cianorte, I discovered I must finish my theology studies in a college which allowed the belief that God communicates and acts today in miraculous ways by the Holy Spirit.

"Pai, I am not really a good Presbiteriano anymore. I cannot deny that I have seen amazing acts of God and have been led by His voice within me. Our church has taught me and given me so much, but it is difficult for them to accept what has become my experience with God."

My father looked at me with his moist eyes and nodded his head in alliance. He even smiled. It wasn't exactly agreement.

"I know you must be true to your convictions to be a servant of God, Justino."

After that I was convinced that the main division between us now was not so great and had come about by experiences we had not shared or even talked about. There was so much we didn't know about each other, but there was a new peace between us.

I stayed with my family for a month or so. After this time of rest, of visiting and reflection, I was ready to leave. This was not my home now and I didn't really fit in, even though we loved each other. I never had really known how to relate to any of my family, and now every day became more awkward. I had shared many stories of my life in the North, far away from them, which seemed to make the distance greater between us. My openness was met with astonishment, not understanding. They asked me questions, but their eyes glazed over before my answers could be heard. They didn't know what to make of me. The more I shared of myself, the more I distanced *them* from myself. This seemed to hurt my mother, and I very much hated making life harder for her. What was different about me or about them couldn't be resolved. We were not connected by strong family ties. Confused and disappointed that I couldn't fix the problem, I decided I couldn't stay there any longer. I just didn't belong.

I returned to Maringá to study and be with friends and people with whom I had more affinity. I stayed there for a couple of months to readjust to Brazilian culture. Maringá was a better debriefing place for me. Friends asked questions but didn't judge or worry like family. In those few months I had a hunger for food that was unquenchable. In the Amazonas I had no such appetite. But down here in Paraná I needed to get up in the middle of the night to eat. My thirst was incredible too. The hunger might have been from living on so little food for well over a year. The thirst might have been from moving from the rainforest down to the dry, cool climate of the *Sul*, South. In a few months I gained weight so that the pants Dr. João had bought me no longer fit me. Even my Italian polo shirts from the capitan were getting tight for me. I was eating myself out of my clothes.

CHAPTER 17

KARATE KIM

When it was time to start the Wycliffe linguistics courses in Belo Horizonte that Dr. João had arranged for me, I was refreshed and ready to work hard. These two-month courses from Wycliffe Bible Translators would enable me to develop a system to record what I heard and understood from my índio brother Kaúnã. I was honored and grateful to be part of Wycliffe's first linguistics courses in Brazil.

One of the later officials of the Posto FUNAI took the *second* Wycliffe course offered in Brazil, and I did too. I enjoyed working through the course a second time with him. Together we acknowledged the value of learning new skills for our work with Amazonian indigenous tribes. Every minute in class increased my ability to grasp and use the language of Kaúnã so that in the future I could better tell him about Jesus. I had read my Bible to Kaúnã even though it was in Portuguese. He listened and seemed to enjoy the music of the words. How much more he would enjoy hearing and understanding those words in his own language! I could hardly wait to share some of the things I had learned to write down in the very language of my brother!

Certainly, the Portuguese study I did under Dr. João was what enabled me to comprehend the Wycliffe linguistics course. Without Dr. João's honing of my Portuguese, I would have been too illiterate to handle the material. God had put me under his tutelage at just the right time so that I could learn to speak and read my own language first. He had been incredibly patient with me while I practiced on his porch in the swing. I am greatly stirred when I think of how I was given such privileges, such care, by the hand of God to prepare me for life with the tribe. God gave me Dr. João for his help in not only Portuguese but also in acquiring the language of "the People," o Povo.

The Wycliffe curso de linguística was given by five or six Wycliffe missionaries. I wasn't a very capable student, but I impressed these missionaries because I understood so much without ever having studied grammar or phonetics. You see, I had not studied any written language before, not even my native tongue. They were ironically trying to teach linguistics to an illiterate student. But, my experience with the índios of the Amazonas had given me knowledge of my own needs, which Wycliffe knew just how to meet. I asked questions and worked hard to use the tools they were giving me and, in the end, they passed me. Twice!

My older brother Gerci came to visit me at the school in Belo Horizonte all the way from Paraná. I was very emotional seeing my own brother at the Wycliffe Seminary, so far from his own home. He had traveled more than twenty hours by ônibus and still had the trip home before him. I had not known how to make a connection between us. But he did. Before he left, he took off his watch and put it in my hand.

"*Fica pra você. É seu.* Keep it. This is for you, now. It's yours."

I was speechless. This was an even greater sacrifice than forty long, sticky hours of travel by ônibus. I wore that watch from my big brother Gerci, always, even in the *selva*, jungle. One day after I had gone back to the tribe, I was out chopping tree branches with full force. My machete slipped from my hand and hit my arm. The blade hit the watch first, hard enough to break the bone in my arm under it. It cut the watch band in half. The band deflected the blow, and the machete only grazed my arm, leaving just a superficial cut. My arm swelled and turned black and blue, but with time it healed. Without my brother Gerci's watch, my arm would certainly have been severed and I would have quickly bled to death, being several days walk from any kind of medical help. I always remember that my brother's gift saved my life!

One of my fellow Wycliffe students, San Wan Kim, was a Koreano do Sul, South Korean, who had come as a missionary to Brazil. He was excellent at karate but spoke very little Portuguese. On the weekends, he and I went to the city parks of Belo Horizonte. While San Wan Kim demonstrated *caratê*, karate, I gave a message of God's love to the audiences that gathered to watch him. This was very enjoyable for both of us and for the people we met too. The people of Brazil have loved capoeira for centuries. This is a Brazilian/African art form that combines elements of martial arts, dance, acrobatics, and spirituality. When they watched San Wan Kim do the ancient Korean dance of karate with many similar moves, they were fascinated with his skill and finesse while they listened to the Word of God. Many asked us for prayer, and San Wan and I were delighted to pray for them.

As the Wycliffe linguistics classes eventually came to a finish and it was time to go back to o Povo, I found myself in that familiar predicament of NOT having even one centavo. At the school, my room and board had been paid by Dr. João. Now I couldn't pay for the bus to the next town!

"*O que vou fazer, agora, Senhor?* What do I do now, Lord? Where do I go?" I prayed pessimistically and with little faith.

I sensed I couldn't ever ask anyone for money. I picked up my suitcase, ready to leave the school, hoping nobody would see me leaving by foot. I waited near the stairs until I believed everyone had left before I began my exit. Descending the stairs, I felt angry and forsaken by God, and I told Him so.

"I am yours, Lord. I belong to you. But you have allowed me to be in this humiliated state again, ashamed to be seen, without a single centavo and no place to go!"

San Wan Kim the Koreano saw me going down the stairs and called out to me in his broken Portuguese. He called for me to wait.

"Justino—God say me help! What you need San Wan give Justino. *O que precisa?* What you need?" I could hardly understand his simple but clear words. He was offering me help, but I felt too lost to accept.

"*O, San, eu não tenho dinheiro nem para sair daqui.* Oh, San, I don't even have money to leave. From here, my plan is to return to Amazonas. I don't know if I should take a bus to Amazonas because I don't know how to get there from here!"

"God me say do for you. *O que você precisa?* What you need?"

My needs were more than I wanted to tell him. I couldn't admit needing so much. So, San Wan decided what it was that I needed.

"I give you for you return to Amazonas! *Quanto custa?* How much cost?" he asked.

"*Eu não sei.* I don't know. I don't have any idea," I answered. I needed so much I was paralyzed, body and mind.

Then San Wan proceeded to call a taxi to take me to the rodoviária in Belo Horizonte. While we waited for the taxi to arrive at the school, San

Wan made more calls. He booked a bus ticket from Belo Horizonte to Brasília, another from Brasília to Belém, and then the ticket for the journey by ship from Belém to Manaus. Then he gave me money for everything he thought I might need including the taxi he sent me away in. I don't know how San Wan Kim, a missionary sent to Brazil from South Korea, came to have this kind of money to share with me. I know only that he said God had instructed him to meet my need. San Wan Kim the Koreano put me on a journey of more than 2,500 *kilometres* all the way back to Amazonas!

After that, San Wan Kim went to Mato Grosso, a state in the interior of Brazil, to become a missionary to the indigenous people God called him to there. I will never forget San Wan Kim.

CHAPTER 18

THE WOODEN BOARD AND
THE DRAWING STICK

I had more confidence as I embarked on my second journey to the Amazon rainforest. I was better educated, more mature, and more chastened in my life with God. When I had been uncertain and doubting, God was always near. And so my faith and confidence increased. Wycliffe had awarded me a certificate of recommendation based on my personal experience and new training in linguistics. This certificate officially made me an *estajiário*, certified government intern, on assignment. I was now authorized to live with an Amazonian people group in order to study their culture and language. Before this, I had no financial backing, no education, and no support outside my amazing helpers along the way.

So, when I arrived back in Manaus, I presented myself with this document from Wycliffe as a certified *missionário* to the churches and to the Government of the Interior, seeking their sponsorship. The first response to my mission was astonishment that I had already spent time with an Amazonian tribe. People showed genuine interest, asking questions about things that my family and friends back home never mentioned.

"You were really there? For how long? How did you get there? Wasn't it dangerous? Were you afraid? Why did you go?"

It seemed everyone was amazed that I had survived, and they were astounded that I would want to go back to this work. After hearing the story of the journey there, of God's mercies and leading, of living with the tribe for seven months, they were anxious to help me get back in.

The churches helped me with my documentation and my travel, and they supported my endeavors as God's will. I would return trained by Wycliffe, sent by churches, with the governmental authority of the FUNAI, Fundação Nacional do Índio, which had officially recognized me as the first foreign contact of this indigenous people group in Amazonas. In the language of the 1960s, I was the *Primeira Emissario Branco*, first white contact, with the tribe. But I knew that I was not first. The Lord had gone before me. He had already chosen Kaúnã to be my friend and bodyguard. I could hardly wait to see him.

The FUNAI outpost was still in the same place by the river in the middle of the jungle, where I had originally spent about two months watching for Tina's people a year ago. It was not a simple thing to get back in contact with such a remote and isolated tribe. I could only follow the same routine as before. I stayed in the preferred place in the jungle watching the clearings, the banks, and the canoes that might have natives in them I knew. I was unable to find the dwelling place of o Povo on my own, and I was the only outsider who had been with them. I knew better than to enter the forest alone looking for them.

After some weeks I was finally recognized and picked up by a tribesman. When he delivered me with pack and boots, most of the tribe hardly knew me. Even Kaúnã was unsettled by my appearance. The shaggy, thin man they knew was now clean shaven, had short hair, and was quite a bit heavier. For weeks I was eyed with distrust.

O Povo did not have hair on their bodies, and my beard must have been an important characteristic that identified me. Since they didn't know other white men, they lacked that frame of reference. But as my beard grew and my skin tanned, most were reassured. Yet, some had real difficulty in believing I was really Justino because I was not acting as I did the year before. Even Kaúnã seemed annoyed with me and told me what people had been saying.

"Why must the pale man always have the wooden board, the white leaf, and the drawing stick with him? What does Justino's wrinkled face mean when he marks the wooden board with the drawing stick?"

I understood my new job made me different now, but I couldn't yet explain this to my friend. I had come into the village with a specific assignment. I was now equipped with the invaluable knowledge of phonetics. I was listening to their tonal language with the intention of writing down all the sounds I heard. It might be a rudimentary way, but hopefully it was a way that would be understood by me and others later.

There was first the matter of developing a kind of alphabet to match the sounds I heard. With diligence, I practiced using the tools I had learned from the Wycliffe courses, trying to make written sense of my daily experience with the language of the tribe. If I were faithful to the Wycliffe techniques, supposedly my records could actually be of value to others later. This method made what had been inconceivable for me possible.

I tried to be subtle in my efforts to record in detail what I was learning, noticing right away that my clipboard, my pencil, and my paper were helpful only to me. I was there with them to tell them of Jesus and His love and presence with them there in the forest, not to drive them crazy. My new training would not make a bit of sense to them, and I didn't want to distance them with the very thing that was supposed to bring us closer.

I did my best to come back into a friendly relationship with o Povo, and I understood I must try to be at peace with each member of the tribe. This was never going to be easy, as my presence stirred and reverberated troubled waters in the community. Taking care of this peace was an essential part of my assignment. I tried to follow the Holy Spirit's leading in this matter, praying for protection and guidance for myself as well as for the tribe.

After about four months back with the tribe, the adjustment and harmony seemed to be going really well and yet I felt it could be already time to leave again. After having been with the tribe more than a year now, Pajé, the spiritual leader, still saw me as a danger to the tribe's existence. From the first days, I felt that Tuxaua, the chief and political leader, and Ais, the storyteller and teacher, had tried to influence me to remain with the tribe. They trusted me, saw me as good for them, and had even tried to give me a wife. But Pajé had feared me and hated me and probably always would. I sensed that Pajé was becoming agitated and threatening and I needed to take a leave of absence. Even Kaúnã approved, knowing now I could make my way back.

I knew I might always be a bone of contention for the tribal leaders, especially Pajé. Change and different events caused tension in the leadership that had nothing to do with me. But when I was with them, and they had any annoyance, I became part of their larger problems. Their stress might be over decisions and laws of the tribe or even over the strong influence the Storyteller had over the people. But when I was present with the tribe, their disagreements became about me. My presence there had political, historical, and spiritual impact. My coming was an event and had effects that could not be avoided. So I decided I should give them a regular break from me every six months or less. I prayed that God would protect them and me in this matter of my coming and going.

I would hike out to Manaus for a time in order to pacify Pajé as well as guard my own safety and peace of mind. There was a Wycliffe base in Manaus, and this was a place I could visit for continued study of the language while I was away from the tribe. The more I could speak the language, the more I could put aside my clipboard and pencil and listen to them with understanding. In Manaus I would learn more about how to better hear their sounds and write them down. I longed to comprehend the ways and complex culture of this people I lived with.

CHAPTER 19

A HIDDEN PEOPLE

It was a singular experience to know this people, this undiscovered tribe, later to be called the Sateré! How to describe them justly? What things held my attention? It was extraordinary to look at them as a people, the first impression being that they were *muito idêntico* —almost impossible to tell apart! Like all of the tribes, these people had their characteristics—eyes, hair, height—peculiar to their people. They were not tall, with the tallest adults being not much more than a meter and a half, or five feet. They were strong, muscular, not fat, with dark eyes and thick, straight, black hair.

Women and girls grew their straight hair long, and men cut theirs in a short bowl cut with fringe across the forehead. The women were less muscular than the men, but fit, since they essentially did the work of the tribe, carrying water, gathering firewood, making the fires, grinding roots for baking bread, and totally caring for children. In the three years I lived with them, I do not remember any occasion when I saw a man with a child on his lap or a man looking after a child.

The women were mostly very pretty, and beauty and vanity were valued by the tribe. I noticed this because there were a few homely women in the tribe who were considered less desirable to look upon. It was common to see women untangling their long tresses using the dried, polished shell of a fruit, which became a brush. Combs were fashioned from the spinal part of the fish called the *cue*. Also, many fish have a bony structure with teeth called the *basihyal* on the floor of the mouth, which resembles a tongue. O Povo dried, polished, and decorated these parts of fish and fruit of the Amazon into a beautiful collection of combs, brushes, and tools for grooming, cleaning, and gardening. Many a young heart was won by a pretty, painted comb that once swam in the river.

Their *pintura*, makeup, they wore was well done and very individualized. Their body paint greatly helped me distinguish one from another since even the women looked alike to me. Red paint was made from a plant that had a red nut fruit. Blue paint was made from a mixture of a tree flower combined with white powder. Black dye was also made from plants, especially the *jenipapo*. Inside of the soft, unripe fruit of the *jenipapo* tree is a liquid that is used as a dye for tattoos, skin painting, and possibly insect repellent. When ripe, the harder-skinned fruit from this white-flowered tropical tree can be picked and eaten or squeezed into a sweet, fragrant drink.

The women mixed the dyes into diverse and lovely shades, and with finesse they expressed their style by their combinations of black, blue, and red. Their identities really came through in the body paint they used on their faces and across the neckline from shoulder to shoulder, and some women and girls painted creative artworks on their legs as well. Now these were not permanent tattoos but temporary illustrations used to commemorate the days of festivals and celebrations such as the new moon, good hunting, marriage, and war. Each event was marked by a different type of design or symbol to indicate the occasion, like a form of writing that was never learned by me but was taught by Ais, the teacher.

The young men could be very artistic too. Black hunting paint and black war paint were also used by the men. Those who did this sometimes elaborately painted themselves in a jungle camouflage. The paint never lasted long, being washed away naturally by their many dips in the river. What endured with permanence was their individual style, never failing to reappear in their new painted images.

O Povo are *muito limpo*, very clean, people! Before daybreak a loud yell always rang out into the camp. Everyone got up from their redes and went down to the river to take the morning bath and watch the first rays of light appear in the sky. Everyone answered this call. No one stayed in their warm hammock like I did. Often, I went with them, encouraged by the steamy clouds drifting above the water attesting to the cozy warmth below. Children, babies, and all the people in the village were in the river talking, laughing, and playing every morning. This community bath was really very pleasant, and it was difficult to sleep through it, especially when they shouted for me or when the boys came back to coerce me.

"*Justino morreu!* Justino is dead!" they teased, shaking and swinging my hammock. "*Justino morreu! Justino morreu!*"

I came with them, covered from head to toe with my blanket, something none of them owned. I always gave in to their pestering, unless, on rare occasions, I was not feeling well. Sometimes I caught a very bad fever, and they could not get me up for anything. I did not see any of o Povo sick with a cold or flu or malaria or any of the modern man's common diseases. Being their first contact, I was grateful that they never seemed to catch a fever from me.

The *cascadores*, hunters, used a type of repellent, an oil, on their skin to keep the insects from biting. I used this the few times they let me hunt with them. They insisted I put the oil all over me. I had noticed that they never really wanted me to go hunting with them. I asked them why.

"*Você cheira mal.* You smell bad. *Você espanta as animais.* You scare the animals."

So, my smell was so bad I scared the animals. I had never noticed this about myself. It must be something they had to endure about me. Later it was further clarified that my bad scent could be smelled from a long way off. The truth was, the animals quickly detected unfamiliar scents and I could be a factor, a liability. I continued to ask anyway.

There was a good reason the Povo took at least two baths a day. This was a way to clean the bugs off of their bodies, refresh and cool themselves, and enjoy together the warmth and beauty of the river. Maybe because of the dryness of my skin and my physical distance, I never had lice. But I often watched those tiny parasites hop from one body to another when two sat together. Then, in awe, I watched them eat the lice from one another. I learned to accept this as part of their nutrition and survival. I may have missed out on some of the properties of their immunities by keeping a physical distance from o Povo, but I didn't think of this at the time. It was my way to keep my distance, and it may have kept them from being exposed to the infirmities of my culture.

O Povo weren't a demonstrative tribe. You did not see them embracing. You didn't see them touch one other affectionately, and they didn't try to touch me to feel my skin or hair. They showed their curiosity about me by pointing at my characteristics and indicating my oddness with a high sound, "Peeeeeeeeeh!" My first thoughts when they did this to me were how right they were to sound off like they did. I was an odd-looking human next to their breathtaking natural beauty.

The most striking quality of these people was how they shared a consistent mindset to advance the serenity and survival of their community. They were submissive to their leaders; hardworking in order to meet the physical and social needs of the tribe; creative in dance, art, and self-expression; sacrificial in helping each other and me; inquisitive about me; and kind to me. I had lived most of my life without understanding my own need for community and without noticing the qualities and attributes of others. My life with the tribe was a time of passionate learning about how to get along with others. I gradually recognized this as a prized survival skill for the tribe that was extremely valuable to me personally. Because of my simple, solitary existence and growing up with few possessions, it actually wasn't so hard for me to transition into this tribal culture. I did not have much to give up. I arrived without a particular social structure confining me, and this made it possible to welcome the friendship o Povo offered me. As a person who struggled with his own identity formation as a child, I treasured the sense of belonging and acceptance I felt when Kaúnã called me brother.

CHAPTER 20

THE DECEIVER

From time to time, I left the tribe for a few weeks. I didn't stay away long because I couldn't let the present-day life spoil me, and I really missed o Povo, you see. I sensed that this break was for the tribe's protection as well as for my own, from Pajé. I felt I was a danger to the tribe because Pajé was a danger to me. But Pajé was an important leader who must be, at the very least, respected. Instability in the government of the tribe could be threatening to the survival of the tribe. So, I learned to come stay with them a few months and go away for a few weeks, hiking out of the selva and usually boating to the city of Manaus. The hike out of the forest was very difficult and lasted eight to fifteen days depending on the rains or what I encountered on my route. Every time I did this I wondered if I would survive, and then I wondered that I did survive.

After I trudged through approximately 200 kilometers of jungle, I took a boat a couple of days to Manaus for supplies, for perspective, and for the emotional support of friends living in the modern world. After a few days in Manaus staying with friends or with Pastor João, I traveled by riverboat to Maués, where David Cooper lived close to the jungle where I would later hike back to the tribe.

On this occasion I skipped the stay in Manaus and took the boat the 200 kilometers right to David's house. The tributary to David's cabin flowed east and then turned southwest down to his little river town. He was always glad to see me when I got there. David dreamed of starting a seedling church near his house. He wanted me to come and help him reach out to the diverse community there. He wanted us to work side-by-side to bring different groups of people together to follow Jesus. His efforts alone in Maués had not yet been successful.

David had made a meeting place ready and it was very simple, being a shelter of wooden posts with a canopy of branches. On this visit with him, I went out every day to the shelter about midday and again at night to pray for the people there. At first I was alone, but then Isalino came down from Manaus to stay with me at David's house for fifteen days or so. He joined me to pray, and sometimes people from the area unexpectedly gathered to join us for prayer in the evening. This gave us hope and encouragement that a seedling church could be started.

During Isalino's visit, the two of us went for a walk and we passed by a *sítio*, rural property, which belonged to a man named Raimundo. He had come to pray with us and had been inviting Isalino and me to spend a few days with him at his sítio. He had a river that flowed through his land, and it was unbelievably beautiful there. Seeing Raimundo's place, we promptly took him up on his invitation and had a great time of rest and recreation there.

On about the fifth day of our visit, Isalino and I hiked out to the river to bathe in the morning, and we decided to stay out there to swim and enjoy the day. We discovered long vines growing from the tall trees lining the riverbank, and we had a great time together swinging out over the water like monkeys and plunging ourselves into the river. Like boys, we laughed and played there all afternoon, forgetting all our missionary work.

In the early evening, we went back to Raimundo's house at the sítio, and there was David Cooper waiting for us. He had a serious, almost disapproving look on his face.

"*Justino, eu preciso que você va lá em casa.* Justino, I need you to come back to my place."

I told him I would really rather not, as I had just gotten back from a day at the river and was taking some time off with Isalino. But David was insistent.

"No, I have a man who is really messed up at my house. I really want you to see this man. *Ele está muito mal.* He's very bad off!"

David explained that he suspected the man was *demoniado*, demon possessed, and he wanted me to come and help him pray for him. David knew from personal experience that this was not something to deal with alone. I looked at Isalino.

"Let's go." I was persuaded.

Isalino refused to come with us. "Today I haven't prayed, I haven't read my Bible, I haven't fasted. I'm not prepared, no. I've spent the day just playing around. I can't go with you."

I was surprised and disappointed. David's call for help was not very inspiring to me, either, but I knew I needed to go. I fetched my Bible and walked back with David the three kilometers to his house.

When we arrived, the man was standing at the gate of David's house. He turned toward me, put his hands together as if in prayer, and bowed down very low, nearly squatting on the ground in this pretense of prayer. Then he jumped high, very high up off the ground, shouting.

"*Justino! Louva se Jesus Cristo!* Justino! Praise Jesus Christ!"

Then he crouched down again with his hands together and jumped high with his arms upward, shouting the same things again.

"*Justino! Louva se Jesus Cristo!*"

Three times he did this in a pretense of praise. This made my blood feel cold. I had a visceral feeling of icy dread under my ribs. I asked David if he had told him my name, and David shook his head no.

"How do you know my name?" I asked the man.

"*Sabia que ele foi te buscar.* I knew he went to get you."

From his odd words and gestures and excited jumping, I supposed it was a demon speaking. I felt my anxiety building and began to pray fervently from my heart. My thoughts were that this was an *espirito enganador*, spirit of deception. Meaning, I could be easily deceived. I must listen for God's voice over and beyond the forceful words uttered by this man.

"*Eu posso falar com você?* Can I talk to you?" asked the spirit, continuing to use the man's voice.

"*Tudo bem, pode.* Okay, go ahead," I agreed.

"*Eu ando sobre as aguas, Eu ando sobre as matas, Eu domino tudo neste região.* I walk over the waterways, I move over the forests, I have dominion over everything in this region. *Somente falta você.* Except for you." After that boasting and flattery, he continued to try to manipulate me with a deal.

"If you submit to me, the two of us together can do whatever you want to do."

"*Eu não tenho parte de você. Eu não quero nada seu.* I have no part of you. I want nothing that is yours," I said to this spirit, my heart pounding in my chest and in my head and ears.

He bowed again, saying my name, and rose up with the shout, "Cristo!"

Then this man's already intimidating countenance changed. It became very ugly and unnatural. Unnerving. Chilling, even. We waited, and as soon as he appeared more normal again, David and I brought him inside the house.

I began to pray aloud for this man in trouble. David joined in, and soon his wife, Gina, now home with his family from England, prayed with us too. Then Davina and Helena, their oldest daughters, came in and joined us in prayer for this *homem acorrentado*, man in chains, in spiritual prison. During the hours that passed, he showed many manifestations of demon possession. At times, he became very strange, grotesque, and disturbing. Soon the evil spirit dominating the possessed man began to make reference to Isalino.

"*O covarde está se preocupando por vocês. Ele vem.* The coward is worrying about you. He will come."

When it was close to midnight, I thought Isalino might become concerned about us because he expected me to return to Raimundo's place for the night.

"*O covarde está vindo pra ca.* The coward is on his way here."

When Isalino reached David's front gate, even before we had heard him, the man said, "*Ai, o covarde está chegando.* There he is. The coward has arrived."

When Isalino entered the room and joined us, the demon began to taunt him. "*Oi, Covarde! Está chegando agora?* Hello, Coward. So, now you show up?"

The unrelenting spirit continued to mock Isalino.

"You haven't prayed today, you haven't fasted, you haven't read the Bible. What are you doing here, *covarde*?"

Even so, I was heartened that Isalino had joined us in praying. Now we were all together, strengthened to participate in this *obra de Deus*, work of God. Yet after many hours, I was exhausted. I didn't know how much longer I could go on. I had spent the day outside playing in the river and had prayed for the man from about five o'clock in the afternoon to after one in the morning. All of us had our Bibles open, and each of us read a verse and prayed with the others. When it was Isalino's time to read, the demoniac continued his verbal abuse.

"*Covarde, você não precisa ler, não.* Coward, you don't need to read, no."

This meanness, this constant attack on my friend Isalino kept me awake. My senses were heightened for my friend's sake. When morning dawned, *o homen começou a ficar livre!* The man began to have freedom! The periods of peace between his outbursts were getting longer and more certain. This was a huge relief to all of us, but we were cautious. I knew the man in invisible chains was depleted, helpless, and vulnerable.

"*Não deixa ele ficar sozinho.* Don't leave him alone at all," I reminded David, as he well knew already.

It was my turn to get some rest. I would sleep until noon and come back and relieve David so he could sleep. Then Isalino would sleep and later rejoin us after he had rested. We took shifts in this way, with the help of the others in David's family, for seven days and nights until we were confident this man was finally free of the enemy. When it was over, and the man had received the *cura de libertação*, complete freedom and healing, he told us his story in his own voice.

This man explained that he had been kidnapped, his hands tied, and taken away in a boat upriver to Manaus. He spent his days on the boat mashed into a three-by-three-foot cargo container and locked in the bathroom. The container had only a tiny square opening, hardly enough to breathe through. When the captors got to Manaus, they unlocked the bathroom and pried open the cargo container to get their victim out, but they found no one there. How did the man get out? The *demonio das trevas*, demon of darkness, had won him over with the promise to help the man to escape. It seemed to be the same *espírito de engano*, spirit of deception, who had addressed me by name in front of David's house.

How happy we were to have that long week behind us! David hoped I would come back to help him, reminding me how difficult the work was in Maués. A palpable darkness still existed in that town. But now it was time for me to get back to my forest brothers.

CHAPTER 21

A TRIBAL TRINITY

As much as I might have liked to, I could never personally know the reserved Tuxaua, the chief of the tribe. Like all the members of the tribe, I looked up to him as a benevolent leader, admiring his position and importance. I esteemed him from a distance and respected his way of paying attention to all of his people in great detail without showing partiality. I supposed he was too busy governing the lives of his people to develop close relationships with any of us. Maybe it was improper for the chief to show any special alliances or friendship with any of the men or women of the tribe. He was conscientious, authentic, fair, and generous to all. He was at peace with the other two leaders. Tuxaua seemed neither to fear nor be under Pajé's influence the way the people were. He seemed capable and content in his role as honored judge and guardian over the tribe.

Tuxaua could usually be found in his house, where he received those who had needs or requests, unless he was called outside his home on business. I was fortunate to be able visit him at his house on rare occasions. The first time, he sent for me through Kaúnã, and the two of us arrived promptly without a whisper of apprehension. Tuxaua came out as we approached and opened his arms in a friendly gesture saying, "Nana karuka." I wanted to bow in some way, but when Kaúnã didn't, neither did I.

"Nana karuka," said Kaúnã, and so I said it too, not knowing it was the afternoon greeting. The chief smiled warmly and we smiled back.

No one went to Tuxaua's house as a frequent guest. I felt honored to follow him into his grass-thatched dwelling, and I believed Kaúnã did too. The chief's hut was not larger than mine. His home was just like any other in the village—a simple shelter of two walls, open on two sides to allow unwelcome spirits an easy passage out if they happened to fly in. In a more elaborate home built to shelter a large group, there would still be two open doorways for the spirits to pass through. Day or night, even the chief's house would not be closed up. Just like in all the shelters, Tuxaua had a warm cooking fire being tended by his wife near the end of one opening, and that was kept burning day and night to frighten wild animals and ward off insects with its smoke. We sat down on the floor, and Tuxaua must have asked Kaúnã how his odd friend was getting along. Within a few minutes we were on our way out.

Tuxaua, though he was chief, recognized the balance of power between himself, Ais the Storyteller, and Pajé, the medicine man. The governmental authority was Tuxaua, but his leadership was complemented by the wisdom and knowledge of the Storyteller and the cultic powers for finessing the spirits attributed to Pajé. In the tribe's recent history, there had been a shift in this governmental structure some fifty years earlier. When Tuxaua was a young man of about thirteen years, he was given the noble position of storyteller. As storyteller of the tribe, he had the duty to choose the next chief from another family and later sanction the family as the next in the royal lineage.

The ruling family must have been wiped out and possibly the storyteller position as well for a time. According to my understanding of Kaúnã's history lessons, this had not ever happened before in their past. Many environmental or political events could have devastated the workings of this ancient tribal government. It could have been a time of internal fighting, geographic movement, tribal wars, injury, illness, or deaths by natural causes. I never knew why or when he was moved from storyteller to chief, but maybe this experience in both roles educated him to be more receptive to change and new ideas.

I heard with my own ears at a public meeting led by our own Storyteller that Chief Tuxaua had served many years as an excellent chief before my arrival. I knew God's hand was at work in ways I could not fathom at nineteen years old, but I often wondered what made Tuxaua open the door to my presence there. I knew I would not be with the tribe unless Tuxaua had given his consent. The fact that I could come into his community and leave when I wished was certainly an honor and a privilege given by his ultimate authority.

Everything that happened in the tribe was Tuxaua's business. Any situation that arose in the tribe was taken to Tuxaua for a hearing. If anything happened that was not brought before him, those involved would run the risk of some kind of penalty. It was simply illegal to keep news or secrets from Tuxaua. Everything mattered to him. The first thing to do when returning to the village after a hunting expedition was to report to the chief all that had happened. If a hunter got hurt, this would be a matter to take before Tuxaua without delay. Tuxaua was chief administrator of all and needed to know everything for the sake of the welfare of the People.

Ais the Storyteller was the teacher of tribal history. He kept a very old wooden bar which was the *story stick*. On this ancient wooden bar were special cuts and grooves in the wood to indicate every one of the stories of the whole history of the tribe, passed down for countless generations. It was sacred and closely guarded. The many stories were taught carefully to the youth. These boys and girls as young as eight or nine years old lived in the large center hut and memorized the stories together as they were taught by Ais until they came of age.

The teacher's big house for the training of children was built to have the doors closed. His dwelling place was the exception to the tribe's open-door policy for the spirits. I could only guess that this was allowed because of the almost constant presence of their teacher with them. This was the schoolhouse and dormitory where children would come of age, where young boys would learn to be hunters and fishermen, and young girls would learn to take care of the village chores. You didn't see young children around the village very much. They were all in school with the Storyteller, who brought them all into adulthood.

Almost always, the lifelong career of a storyteller was passed down from father to son, usually to the oldest son. All these stories were known and were to be passed on by one storyteller until he died and then by the storyteller's son who inherited the position. A few members of the tribe knew *all* of the stories, but still none could ever become the storyteller, or teacher, of the tribe. This was with an exception, of course, in the case that both the storyteller and his son died. In that case, a new storyteller would be declared. The identity of the successor was already known and kept secret by the three current leaders—Tuxaua, Ais, and Pajé.

The customs and ceremonies which I was privileged to observe and learn were intriguing and fascinating for me as I lived with the tribe. After the Wycliffe courses, intense study, and practice, I found myself acquiring the language. I was gaining understanding and much more facility to speak. I was able to listen carefully to Ais the Storyteller as an industrious student, like the other adolescents did. As a student and an honorary member of the community, I could now understand, use, and record the words of this Stone Age language I was learning. I could listen with comprehension to Ais as he raised the story stick and gestured in his lively way to thrill all the People with their laws and stories.

I came to see the Storyteller as the most important person in the tribe —more feared than Pajé, more honored than Tuxaua. He was the wise counselor and the master of ceremonies. If any knowledge was sought, one asked the teacher. If a decision had to be made, his counsel was sought out, even by Tuxaua. The person who most influenced my continued stay was probably Ais the Storyteller. The person who gave permission for me to come in the beginning was Tuxaua, but the one who gave the sustained approval for me to stay and live with the tribe was the Storyteller.

He called and conducted the village meetings and honored the people for life's successes. The Storyteller chose the *premios*, prizes, judged the contenders, and gave recognition for best hunter or warrior. The prize would often be the best piece of meat and yet, what caught my attention was that the honored one always gave his piece of meat to the Storyteller. Ais would then sit down and enjoy this portion. Whatever the prize, it was given to the teacher. The winner received the premio, but he gave it up to that one who had raised and taught him. If a tribesman was given a seat of honor, he gave this seat up to the Storyteller. The Storyteller also called and conducted the village meeting for life's failures. If a serious crime was committed within the tribe, he was the magistrate who performed the duties of arranging for the execution. This included choosing the *fleixeiros*, archers, who must shoot the guilty.

No one knew the hearts, the stories, and the histories of the people like the Storyteller. He seemed to be a happy man, open, animated, often smiling. When he told the stories at the village meetings, he spoke with authority and confidence, as if he were part of the generation of which he spoke. It was a blessing that the Storyteller did not set himself against me like Pajé and did not monitor me or interfere with my life. His sustained approval was of great benefit to me. I could never have a close friendship with him though I learned a great deal from him about the tribe. He was deeply immersed in his vocation as village manager, teacher, and historian of the People.

Ais' own son, the descendant storyteller-in-training, was more approachable and available to be my friend. Though he was destined for authority, he was much more a fellow partaker of communal life with the people than his father, Pajé, and Tuxaua could ever be. He was closer to my generation, being maybe ten years older than I was, and he was always friendly toward me. It was hard to guess the age of the people. I estimated the Storyteller, Pajé, and Tuxaua all to be more than sixty years old when I was there, with Tuxaua likely the oldest of the three.

After the adolescent children lived in the center house for a few years, learning all the stories and culture from Ais, the teacher, they were ready to have a mate chosen for them. The coming of age for the boys was about twelve or thirteen years old and the girls as young as ten or eleven. First the Storyteller chose a girl to become the bride. Then the boys a couple of years older made a gift offering to please her. This might have been a kind of food, an artistic creation, or anything that might have won her affection. She was then allowed to make a choice of a mate. And yet, she was not obligated to accept any offering. The boy whose present was accepted by the girl became her bridegroom, and the two were promised to one another only. They were then betrothed.

From the day of betrothal on, of everything the boy gave to the girl, one half was given to her father. If the boy hunted, half the meat was given to her father. If he caught four fish, two were given to her father. If he made something for her, he made another for her father. This was a challenge, yet one readily accepted.

One day in the future, there would be a processional marriage ceremony in which all members of the tribe participated. The girl and boy would walk to the house of the boy's parents, who would take their place in front of the groom. Then they would all walk to the house of the parents of the bride, who would then take their place in front of the bride. As the parents of the bride and the parents of the groom walked to the center of the gathering, all would witness as the new bride and bridegroom took their places in front of their parents. Then the parents of the new couple were positioned to walk behind them in a procession, joined by others again and again as they passed in front of all the houses of the village. This procession continued from house to house until all the people of the village were walking behind the new bride and bridegroom.

The wedded children chose whether to live with the parents of the bride or the parents of the groom. The marriage ceremony ended at the house where they chose to live. The last part of the ritual was the cutting of a hammock. A hammock was placed for the boy and another was placed for the girl, the girl's above the boy's. When the cord was cut from the girl's hammock, her hammock would fall onto the boy's hammock, and the two were married. From that day forward, the young bride changed the decorative tie she wore at the top of her arm to her other arm.

The way of life for the people was not to walk around the village being seen by everyone. They each had their own roles and responsibilities, and life wasn't about socializing and getting around to see everyone in the tribe. Social meeting places didn't really exist except when the whole tribe was together at the river or for a celebration. Society was lived out between relatives and during traditional and religious festivals and in the special place of growing up, where boys and girls became men and women.

Pajé was the tribe's spiritual leader, and he saw me as a spiritual leader, too, in conflict with him. Everything about me, he was against. He would appear out of nowhere like magic, look right through me, and then turn his head in contempt. His stalking felt like a mental slap. I could feel my heart skip in response to his dark glare. And before I could think, he disappeared like smoke. A mysterious potency exuded from his fit, feathered form. Everything I did made him angry and vengeful simply because I existed and thrived in his territory. I was a menace to his stability, his dominion and influence, his very way of life. I knew he wanted to harm me and probably kill me, and I daily depended on God to protect me.

He could not really intimidate me. This was yet another frustration for Pajé. So, he used passive aggression to harass and punish me for living with the tribe. He distanced himself from all who became friendly with me. Anyone who wanted to befriend me or was influenced by me had to make a costly choice between Pajé and me. Friendship with me brought about the loss of Pajé's favor and any religious clout Pajé might wield on their behalf. A father would forfeit his creed and his family's trust if he made any connection with me. If his wife had a sick baby, she would resent enormously her husband who befriended me.

I felt concern for those who had the kind of courage or need that they could desert Pajé for me. I prayed God would take care of them! Pajé's potions, spells, and divinations were greatly desired and trusted by the members of the tribe to deal with the real and present dangers all around them. I also felt pity for Pajé because, though he looked at me with hostility, he carried a heavy burden being a shaman and dealing with the spiritual and physical world of o Povo. Every day his flock faced serious threats of deadly wildlife, criminal trespassers, torrential downpours, disease, tribal wars, and even starvation. As a teenager, I had no education or awareness of what this tribe had already survived for centuries or their vulnerability to what the future might hold. I only knew I was placed there to tell them Jesus would come to them and take care of their needs.

When there was a death, Pajé was called first, even before Tuxaua, because this was a spiritual matter. Pajé must manage the spirits. When someone died, in the law of the Povo, no one was allowed to touch the body, not mother, not child, no one. Everyone must leave the house immediately and Pajé must be called. He was quickly called for any severe infirmity or injury that could possibly result in death. If someone was killed on the hunt, Pajé would be taken out to the location of the body, because no one must touch or be near the dead. Pajé then performed his rituals and took the body away for burial.

Only twice did Pajé come personally to my house. The first time was with Tuxaua and the Storyteller to give me a wife. Pajé would appear among the people of the village more than Tuxaua. When he suddenly appeared near me, I usually remembered something that I had done to disturb him, such as praying with a couple of tribesmen when they asked me to. I wanted to tell people not to say they had seen me. But this seemed manipulative. I disliked the anxiety I felt when Pajé would come unexpectedly around a hut, glower at me, and walk away with an ominous, brooding gait as if he intended to put a snake in my hammock. From time to time, Pajé could be seen going from house to house holding the branch of a tree he had foreordained to expulse the spirits. He came to my house a second time but did no ritual for me. He must have decided to leave me with my spirits.

He didn't want me to have a clean house! I can say that some nights were very strange, indeed. The hammocks would swing without any wind to move them, and there were many voices and whisperings, which I assumed were the spirits he dealt with or sent my way. This kept me praying.

CHAPTER 22

HUNTING WITH JUSTINO

With much begging, I finally convinced o Povo to take me hunting with them. They painted my face in an animal camouflage. Black stripes were painted on my forehead, then tracks were made across my cheeks and around my eyes, and my beard already decorated my chin. Then *eles morreram de rir*, they died laughing. O Povo had nearly hairless bodies and so my beard was always a thing of amusement. They admired the way my beard enhanced my wild animal appearance.

We set off on the hunt, expecting to be away from the tribe for at least two or three days in the *mata*, jungle. The men let me know from the beginning that we would not find any game. They said I kept the animals away with my scent and with the noise I made. They couldn't know how I needed my clothing for protection from the sun, the biting insects, the inevitable scrapes and lashes of the brush, and the allergens or poisons of the plants. Despite the scolding of my naked companions, I kept my clothes on and my boots too.

I lightly protested their attitude because I wanted them to stop treating my hunting trip like a festa. I seriously wanted to join them in the kill of some big game, and I told them so. They laughed at me and said it wasn't going to happen. The hunt with Justino was a joke. For one thing, my hiking boots were not noiseless like their bare feet. I tried to be quiet, but the standard was absolute silence. When they walked beside me and I listened with every nerve, I could not hear a single sound coming from them. There was no rustle, no whisper, no step, not a breath could be heard.

"*Você cheira mal. Branco cheira forte,*" the men explained in their tongue. "You smell bad. White man stinks. *Animal percebe e corre.* Animals perceive and run."

On the first day I tried very hard to be quiet and not to smell bad, but just as they predicted, we found nothing. We climbed trees to pass the first night. Like the others, I chose a tree about four *metres* high and climbed high up and onto a branch that was capable of holding me securely against the trunk for the night. They all fell asleep balanced on their branches with their backs to the trunk. This was not a possibility for me. At my first slumber, I would have fallen from that very high place. I had planned to tie myself to the tree so I could doze off for at least a part of the night. But I had a powerful fear of *serpentes*. I was just discovering that snakes nested in the trees at night, and plenty of them were either venomous or were just big pythons. It wasn't possible to see these *cobras*, snakes, on the ground or hear them in the trees, unequipped with the heightened senses that these brave hunters had. I had to spend the entire first night eyes open, acutely alert, listening. I was soon grateful that our hunting trip was not to be long. I was a zombie going without rest into the second day.

We trekked away from all civilization to an area where we thought we might see *veado*, deer, *bicho de preguisa*, sloth, *tatu*, anteater, and plenty of *aves*, birds. One of the young hunters killed an anteater the second day, and that was just what they expected. I guess the gigantic sixty-kilo tatu, which live in little bands, are not fighters and don't run from my company. Big and slow, he was not the animal to proudly bring home to the table. The anteaters cleaned the forest floor by eating worms, insects, larvae, spiders, scorpions, snakes, lizards, termites, and mostly ants. So, in the forest the big anteaters are the bottom feeders, and this makes their carne distinct. The young men quietly celebrated with their eye roll—a drone of hissing while pointing at me. I was used to their teasing. It didn't offend me.

I have often been asked what the worst-tasting animal in the Amazon forest is. While the sloth carne is bitter, the stench of this anteater was *nojenta*, nauseating. No wonder the tatu was not shy of me or my body odor. This beast renders absolutely putrid meat. After choking some of it down, I could later smell it drifting up from my own pores. And it wasn't just me. All who ate of this *bicho*, animal, began to radiate the odor of this *carne horroroso*, horrible meat! I also cringe when remembering the *carne de bicho de preguica*, meat of the lazy beast, the sloth. This was a sour *amarga*, bitter taste! A nastier and longer-lasting aftertaste no one can imagine! I don't know which could be worse, to eat the bitter meat of the sloth or the smelly meat of the anteater!

When we got deeper into the mata, my eyes scanned through the tall trees longingly for veado. This was the marvelous game meat that I was eager to see hiding near us. And to be able to participate in killing deer with these brave hunters was something I could be proud of! I hoped the next kill would not be a sloth!

In the rainforest the *coqueiros*, coconut trees, stretch very tall to catch the sun on their leaves. I liked to look up and see the light shine through their star-shaped canopies. Their root systems are not deep and deteriorate under the damp forest floor. The coqueiros will eventually grow old and topple from age or be blown over during a storm. So, the rainforest floor is full of these long, fallen coconut trees, their soft trunks causing a man's footsteps to give in slightly. Like stepping on sand, even through my boots I could feel the inside of the coqueiro trunk shrink and crumble into pulp with my step.

As I was hiking, yearning for the sight of deer, I passingly noticed that the ground shifted under my feet like a moving staircase. Was I on quicksand? Suddenly the tree trunk under me rose straight up from the ground! As I spun away, I realized I had been standing on a *sucuri*, anaconda! My boots could feel no difference between the huge snake or the trunk of a tree. This giant anaconda I had stepped on was also looking for deer, ready to embrace it in an instant and crush its bones. I barely had time to gasp before the bold índio at my side had put an arrow in his bow and shot the snake. In the blink of an eye, the giant sucuri had changed her mind about me and slithered away into the underbrush.

"Aren't you going to kill it?" I asked, trembling. The snake was six meters long.

"No, we don't eat them."

"But, aren't they dangerous?"

"Dangerous to you, but not to us," explained my friend.

The tribesmen hunted only to eat. And the skilled hunter's trophy was in being a good provider to the tribe. I pondered the meaning of this simple ethic, sensing its importance to the survival of all of us there in the wild. I thought about the speed and accuracy of my friend's arrow for me. He had hit the snake in the head. All the hunters had this kind of skill with their carefully crafted handmade arrows. They were unbelievably accurate at short and long distances. Even the boys were born naturalists and brave archers.

"We aren't going to see any game at all. You make too much noise. And you smell bad. Take off these things on your feet."

The men were gesturing at my boots and complaining about me in clicks and low tones. They were right. We had found absolutely nothing worth eating for days. Nada, nada. I conceded. I was much more than a hindrance to their hunt. I frightened the animals away with my noise and my scent. They needed to do their job. We were now on our third day and I was exhausted.

I smiled as I imagined taking them on a trip to Manaus, expecting to get my work done with the distraction they would cause. I could see how reasonable they were in dealing with me. How well they knew this wilderness they lived in, and how well they cared for it and knew how to survive in it. I gained a great respect for them as the hours passed and my presence kept them from finding meat to feed their families.

"*Não vai matar nada?* You aren't going to kill anything, are you?"

"No, you don't let the animals come."

I gave my last challenge. "Well, I came to see you kill something. I came to see the hunt, and I still haven't seen anything."

So, the men took me to a place where we found some *cutia*, large rodents, armadillo, and some birds. It was not much for them to display their bravery and their prowess with their lightning bows and arrows. It was the third day in the afternoon when we got back to the village. We had not brought carne to be proud of back for the tribo. We slept that night at the village, and the next day the hunters headed out again.

"*Posso ir com vocês?* Can I go with you?" I asked, already knowing their answer.

They laughed at me.

"*Agora, vamos casar!* Now we are going to hunt!" they said.

Now that I wasn't with them, they could get the job done. That same afternoon they came back with wild pig, deer, birds, and plenty to eat. I was never completely sure if they just didn't want to hunt in front of me or that it was truly impossible to have any success with me along.

O Povo knew how to be undetectable by hiding in plain sight. My friend David had warned me how an untouched tribe blended so perfectly into the wildlife around them that they could be close by, watching me, and I would never know it. If there was a modern house near the edge of the jungle, they could enter it and hide, and nobody would ever know. They have the discipline to travel unnoticed to their hiding places, and they leave no evidence of their visits. For eons, o Povo have made and shared their life in the jungle as a dynamic part of it. They know how to do this. This beautiful forest garden is their shelter and oxygen. The wild game is their friend, not enemy. The river system is their domain, and they know it well.

I believed there was another reason why they couldn't have me with them on the hunt. It could have been that they didn't necessarily have Tuxaua's permission to take me along. There were places we may have passed that Tuxaua might not have wanted a modern man to see. When they brought me back to the village, I noticed that we made very good time. If I had come by myself, it would have taken me three days to travel what took us the afternoon to hike. I had to work hard just to keep up during those few hours. I would have quickly been lost on our hunting trip if they had moved about the forest in their normal way.

When I learned to travel back and forth to the tribe, I followed the Miriti, the river of the tribe as my guide, and I used my compass diligently. If I had cut across the rivers like the hunters did and not kept close to the Miriti River running near our dwelling place, I would have encountered other rivers and would have completely lost my way. I remembered how the tribesmen had practically dragged me through the forest when I first came to the tribe. They were more patient with me now. But they didn't have the patience it took to hunt with me.

CHAPTER 23

THE CHRONICLES OF BIDÚ AND AURÁ

The men in the tribe frequently gathered together to hear the Storyteller's oracles. The women were not invited. The men seated themselves on the ground in a circle around their historian ready to hear a legend or a word of wisdom. The Storyteller was dressed in his usual adornment of paint and feathers and stood on a platform near the fire where he could be seen and heard by all. It was a familiar ritual seeing him on his feet, gently dancing, turning to the left and to the right, and then spinning around in the firelight. Sometimes he moved all around the circle in front of each man, his voice and body producing the cherished rhythmic revelation. This was a spectacular time for me. First of all, being a man and living with the tribe meant I was invited. As my knowledge grew of the language, my understanding grew of these stories and their significance for all the men of the tribe in their roles as leaders and as providers from generation to generation. I felt I belonged with these men even though it was for a short time. They had let me in.

Usually, the session began with a mythology lesson about Bidú and Aurá, the very first ancestors and deities of the tribe. Bidú was the older brother and Aurá was the younger. Being the older brother, everything that Bidú did was perfect. He was handsome. He made close friendships. He told interesting stories. He could make a warm fire, swim, craft beautiful arrows, find the best meat, shoot the farthest, win any fight, catch the biggest fish. He was loved and respected by all. According to the

Storyteller, the older brothers were the best hunters, the best fishermen, the bravest, the strongest of the men. The younger brother, Aurá, didn't have this kind of good life to share with the people. He brought hardship and unhappiness to the people. He brought bad luck. All of his works were *malfeito*, badly done. He was unloved and unsuccessful. The stories we heard followed the theme of Bidú *o conquistador*, the conqueror, and Aurá the loser. They were about the successes of Bidú and the failures of Aurá. They were about the good fortune brought to being by Bidú and the regret, disappointment, and shame brought by Aurá.

One day Bidú was at the riverbank spearing one fish after another. Aurá wasn't having any luck at all. They each had a spear made of wood from the forest to stab the fish. Whenever Bidú stabbed a fish, he pulled his spear out of the water and there was the fish stuck on the spear. When Aurá stabbed down, the fish eluded him. His arm was too slow for them. This is why the men now have to work so hard to catch the fish they need.

The tribe presently hunted with arrows more frequently than with these spears spoken of by the Storyteller. For fishing, they usually caught the fish by hand. When hunting in the forest, a bow and arrow was a faster and more powerful weapon than a spear. But in the tales of the Storyteller, the *lança*, spear, was very prevalent and symbolic of bravery in the hunt, in war, and for survival in this ancient forest.

For the celebration of every seventh year's coming-of-age festival, Taquara Branca, all the young hunters prepared for their trials by carving a spear for themselves. On this occasion, they all went into the jungle, each with his own wooden spear. This was a genuine challenge because, whether to stalk and kill a deer, a wild pig, or a jaguar, this special hunt of the seven-year festival required a personal wooden spear. It was a risky and untrustworthy weapon to use since the young hunter was more highly skilled with his bow and arrow.

The Storyteller always gave Bidú honor for being a great fisherman or a great hunter. Bidú's spear struck the *veado*, deer, and then his spear left the veado and returned to him. Yes, it came all the way back to him as if it could fly. Then, when he saw the *onça-pintada*, jaguar, his spear was already in his hand, and Bidú was able to kill the jaguar too. With one swift cast, he could strike down that onça-pintada, and still his spear came back to his hand again and again. But Aurá was the worst hunter. If he did catch sight of game, he threw his spear and missed. Then he didn't have his spear when the game came near again. This happened to Aurá when fishing in the river as well.

The Storyteller said that one day Bidú was away from the tribe for a time. The tribe ran out of meat and the people were hungry. It was up to Aurá to hunt for o Povo since Bidú was not there to do it. This time Aurá had to hunt alone rather than help Bidú bring in the meat. Aurá set out into the forest and saw the game. He threw the spear, and it narrowly missed and came back to him. When the spear returned to Aurá, he tried to grab it from the air, but the spear flew past him and landed on the ground far away from Aurá. After that the spear became frustrated and wouldn't come back to Aurá anymore. Aurá's failure with the spear brought this hardship into the life of the tribe. Aurá was not a good hunter. I learned when the tribe goes hungry, this is because of Aurá's bad aim, his lack of affinity with the spear, and his historic failure to kill meat for the tribe.

Further, it was a comfort and a relief to have Bidú near when someone died. He was not afraid of the dead person's spirit. He carried the body to the river, said the appropriate words, and put the body in the river. Then the body sank down and was carried into the depths, never to be seen again. One day Bidú was away from the tribe for a time while someone died and needed burial. Aurá's heart was soft and he was full of fear. He took the corpse to the river for the burial. The people were gathered there, trusting him to take care of things. When he placed the body in the river, the body stayed on top of the waters. He tried to push it down, but no matter what he did, it floated. It didn't even float away but stayed near, frightening the people while the spirits poisoned the air.

"From that day on," explained the Storyteller, "all dead people float on the water, and Aurá is to blame for this."

From these stories, I learned Aurá brought suffering and hard times to the people. It is his fault that the hunter's spear doesn't come back to him. It is Aurá's fault that the hunter has fear and a soft heart and a poor aim. Aurá is to blame for the shortage of meat and for hunger. And Aurá brought hard work to the people because they have to use sticks to dig holes to bury people when they die. No longer do the dead sink down into the river like they did in the days when they were placed there by Bidú, the older brother.

When I, Justino, sat in the circle of men and heard the many stories of Bidú and Aurá, I listened with intense interest. Watching the Storyteller dance and hearing his poetry became a rich time of learning that I had never had in grade school or seminary. In the beginning, I understood very little and depended on Kaúnã to retell and explain everything to me.

But now the language was like music I could sing along to. I remembered what I heard. I could repeat it back. I was appreciating the customs, and I greatly valued taking part in the ceremonies of the tribesmen.

Unfamiliar with their ways and ignorant of the language, I always felt honored to be with o Povo. As time passed, I only felt more and more privileged and incredibly blessed to be living out the reality of the vision God had given to me a few years earlier when my life had first begun its transformation. I knew that God had spoken to me and had brought me to that place where He showed me this people. I was only an illiterate, inexperienced, ignorant farm boy, and so I could never make sense of it all. I had to leave making sense of this reality up to God.

CHAPTER 24

MY OLDER BROTHER

I had first arrived to the tribe more than two years earlier and had attended to the dying relative of two young men, giving the sick man injections of penicillin until he was well. The young men looking in on the dying man while I was looking after him were Kaúnã and his cousin, the sick man's son. I realized later that, because of the complex relationships of the Povo, this cousin of Kaúnã also had become his brother, by tribal ceremony. When they were younger, the two were chosen to do battle with each other, and Kaúnã was victorious. Kaúnã was now the older brother of his cousin since he was the victor in the duel.

This ceremonial day of reckoning between brothers was a very important day in each young man's life. It was a day of testing, a day of victory or loss, a day of identity and destiny for the people. Being a brother, whether older or younger, became the most important relationship in a man's life in the tribe. The older brother was leader and provider for this rainforest tribe in ways that were consistently complemented and supported by the servant younger brother. The social roles of leader and servant between men in the tribe might even have been more crucial than those between parents and children or man and wife. It seemed the actual survival of the tribe in the mata depended on men following the proper roles of brother to brother in service to the tribe.

When I understood how significant this concept of brotherhood was in the life of Kaúnã and his people, I was inspired to begin to tell him about my own Older Brother. Using the context of Kaúnã's own experience and culture, I hoped to make known to him the value of the daily presence of Jesus in my life, my own Older Brother.

"My Older Brother is very good to me," I told Kaúnã. "He is precious to me, *muito especial*, very special."

I told personal stories of how my Older Brother looked after me, gave me many presents, and loved me very much. I chose stories which were a testimony of my Brother's goodness and mercy. When Kaúnã wanted to know His name, I told him His name was Jesus. I explained that though Kaúnã couldn't see my Older Brother, He was with me always, living within me, doing everything for me, taking care of me.

"*Ele me da força, me cuida sempre, e jamais me deixará*. He gives me strength, takes care of me always, and He will never leave me."

Kaúnã wanted to know all about Jesus. Every description, every story I could tell, Kaúnã longed to hear over and over. It was an immense joy to be able to tell Kaúnã all about Jesus, especially speaking in his native tongue. The sounds and clicks of his language came to me as a gift from heaven. But the truths I wanted to share transcended human language. I say this because Kaúnã understood things I really couldn't say. God was his interpreter.

"What does your older brother look like?"

At first, I told Kaúnã that my Older Brother had big hair and a beautiful white robe, hinting at the image of God that I thought Kaúnã might envision. I tried to describe Jesus the way I pictured Jesus—as God here on earth, in Kaúnã's physical world. I didn't want to put any restrictions on Kaúnã's questions or limit his understanding in any way. I tried not to. I had not yet studied Revelation or Daniel to give me visual descriptions of the King of my heart and life. But I had a small paperback Gospel of John that I read often. I shared all that I had learned from John's story of Jesus as Creator of the world and the Light of the World.

"To me, Jesus is very fine to see. Very good, very beautiful."

I cautiously sought a way to frame Jesus in divine terms, since He is simply beyond our understanding and yet has made Himself comprehensible. He has come near to us, giving us understanding. And He is still here with us. I told him that Jesus is the life of God coming to be with us as the light and life of all mankind. Jesus is not abstract. He is real and present. I tried to tell this to Kaúnã.

Something that really attracted the attention of the tribe was the way rays of sunlight shone outward and penetrated the treetops in the forest at twilight. I was with some of the men once when the sunlight shone through the trees over the river causing marvelous colors to spill down over the water. Crystal streamers of light reached down from the sky and stretched out over us. We were awestruck by the brilliance of this show of dazzling light. I had no word for this kind of magnificence. Yet I reminded Kaúnã of that day and explained that Jesus looked like that.

"My Brother Jesus is light, like this, Kaúnã. *Meu Irmão Mais Velho*, My Older Brother, is amazing. He is as splendid and as beautiful as that light."

One day Kaúnã stayed out fishing until early evening. Using a long animal bone that he had sharpened to a point, he thrust his spear into the gathering schools of fish and threw his catch into his *barquinho*, little boat. The fish were plentiful that day and kept him busy until dusk.

While Kaúnã was fishing, he must have seen something incredibly overpowering, something that compelled him to run two or three kilometers to find me. He arrived so overcome and out of breath that, at first, I could not comprehend what he wanted.

"*Eazu, é Eazu! Eazu, é Eazu!*" he kept repeating. "*Seu Irmão é luz! Seu Irmão é luz!* Your Brother is light! Just like you told me! Your Brother is light!"

In his language, *eazu*, the word for "light," was very like *azul*, blue. I was struck by this. He then shook me by my shoulders to help me understand. He gestured and insisted that I pay attention. He pulled me to come with him, and so I began to run back with him. As we sprinted through the forest, I realized he was taking me to the place where he had just seen Jesus, my Older Brother, Eazu. At the place where Kaúnã had been fishing, we searched the trees by the water.

"Justino! Eazu was here! Here by the trees was your Brother! He is very beautiful! Your Brother is Eazu!" Though I looked to where he pointed over the water and saw nothing, I easily imagined what he must have seen—an appearance of incomparable beauty and light, so uncommon and powerful that he believed it had to be Jesus, my Older Brother. I wondered if an angel had come to him.

"Justino, it was here, right here. I talked with Him here!"

Kaúnã looked down. He felt so sorry that I had missed seeing my Brother.

"I talked to *Seu Irmão*, your Older Brother. I said to your Brother Eazu, 'I will go get Justino!'"

I waited with Kaúnã by the river, feeling the ache of his deferred joy turn to grief. He still hoped my Brother would reappear, but we could see nothing now.

"Justino, I told Eazu to wait for you so that I could bring you! I wanted Him to wait for you! Isn't He your Older Brother?"

"Yes, He is my Older Brother," I answered.

I felt so bad for Kaúnã's disappointment but was also discovering that Kaúnã had grasped that my Older Brother was much more than my brother: He was more than can be grasped or seen.

"Justino, why didn't Eazu wait here for you?" Kaúnã protested. "I spoke to Him! I told Him I was going to find you and bring you to Him," he cried out with emotion. Then he wept.

This was the first time I had seen such emotion in any member of the tribe, having lived with them for over two years. I was trying to take it in —Kaúnã's excitement, his shouting and jumping and waving his arms, his shaking me by the shoulders, begging me to come with him, running with such zeal. And now this heartbreak. His tears. These expressions of feeling were not part of his world, his life. All of this caused me to believe that Kaúnã had truly experienced Jesus, my Older Brother and his Older Brother too. I told Kaúnã this time Eazu had come to see *him*, not me. This gave me a thrill of happiness to say.

"*Seu Irmão é Eazu!* Your Brother is light!" Kaúnã said again and again on our way home.

"Yes. He is light. Your Brother is light." I said back to Kaúnã again and again.

This emotional exchange between us moved me deeply. Again, I tell you emotion was not something I had seen in this stoic people. Excitement was muted, like a vague curiosity, a quiet smile. Fear was silent, still. Even anger was manifested as a visceral, dry, stiffness of the body: a closed, controlled look. Arguments between men that I had heard had the benign, dull sound of harmless grumbling. Brooding bitterness that could lead to murder was barely detectable in the Povo's seeming cold indifference. With few exceptions, to give expression to emotion was appropriate only in a ritual or a celebration.

But Kaúnã was different now. Kaúnã was new, changed. His eyes were brimming with expectation even in his bewilderment. He had surely seen a glimpse of heaven. I think Jesus, my Older Brother, had come to him. From then on, Kaúnã kept even closer, often reminding me in his rich yet undiscovered language that *Eazu é kao kao toh!* Jesus is very, very good.

CHAPTER 25

DARKNESS IN MAUÉS

After living life another five months with the tribe, I noticed Pajé making fleeting appearances near me. I tried to avoid his lethal stare by getting myself busy doing something benign. I would write or draw with my paper and pencil or plant seeds or put mud on myself as mosquito repellent or talk with another young man near me. Still, anything could work against me. Before long I prepared to hike out of the forest. This trip, I would spend more time in ministry with my friend David Cooper in Maués. I left the tribe about twice a year, sometimes more often. This way o Povo could enjoy a reprieve from the inevitable tensions my presence caused them. When Pajé wasn't happy, no one was happy.

Maués was a good three hundred kilometers from our River Miriti, a long hike through pure natural jungle. It could take me more than two weeks to reach the River Maués-Açu trekking daily from sunrise into the night. I was daily drenched in rain, and it was hard to hike soaked. I felt cold and my legs felt leaden. So, I took cover under the umbrella of short, bushy trees or the fort-like walking palms to open my pack full of dried meat and nuts. Hanging fruit was not hard to find. A deluge forced a time-out that I usually needed and a time of less risk. In a heavy downpour, the land animals also retreated to their holes and dens.

All day I tried to move carefully, knowing how easy it was to fall into a ravine, enter a cave, trip over the roots of the big trees, or be unexpectedly walled in by the branches of entwined, close trees. The forest was so dense in places that I hiked into mazes of trees I couldn't get through and had to climb my way out. When climbing high up into a coconut or pineapple palm, I could get a better sense of my whereabouts. But climbing steals the energy needed for advancing thirty to thirty-five kilometers a day, finding food and a safe resting place, swinging the machete, swimming across moving water, and picking myself up after an abrupt slip in a patch of dry leaves covering solid rock.

In water, I kept my compass and torch in a bag in my hat or in my teeth. If my machete made a good trail for me, a few weeks later all signs of my path would disappear. I could never retrace it on my way back to the tribe. It was easier to avoid gators and piranhas swimming across rivers than broader lakes, which had to be slogged around, increasing my days of *perigo*, danger. I did not relax about poisonous reptiles, carnivorous fish, electric eels, and iguanas near or in the water. At twilight I always moved faster, rushing before the vast tree canopy blocked my last rays of daylight.

The fear that began at nightfall was terrible. I could never be calm about a jaguar, a leopard, or a pack of angry pigs, bats, or vultures. I had covered my clothing with insect repellent, but because the daily showers washed it off, with every step I prayed for safety from mosquitos, spiders, centipedes in the brush, and anthills, which could suddenly give way under my feet.

Whether big cats, snakes, sloths, monkeys, or birds, I could not distinguish foe from friend seeing their red and yellow glowing eyes. In the moonlight I first checked for vicious bullet ants around the base of my chosen tree, and then I climbed and strapped myself high up into the canopy. The Povo had spoiled me with their twenty-four-hour fires, which frightened away the *animais* and insects. I always shined my torch to check for a python or scorpions and hoped Káunã was right that I was the scariest beast in the jungle.

Each night I thanked God for another day of life unscathed before I collapsed into oblivion out of exhaustion. At least I was far from Pajé's malevolent glare and a sudden order to eliminate me. These breathtaking journeys through the forest taught me the critical need to choose faith over fear, continuously. In this way, my natural terror turned to awe and wonder and gratitude. Each morning I awakened refreshed, heartened that God had fortified me for the thrill and adventure of another day in His vast, wild forest.

Finally leaving the wilderness and stepping into the clearing, I again admired the pristine sand and thatch-roofed houses appearing off the banks of the River Maués-Açu, which ran out of the jungle and throughout the developing town. The little port of Maués was still a sparsely populated open territory of about a million acres, just becoming a growing municipality. The town was mostly indigenous communities and European settlers.

David welcomed my arrival, and I was soon cleaned up and resting on his little veranda. He had recently taken the two-day trip up the Amazon River to Manaus and had brought back equipment for us to use to gather the people in the area around the river for worship. He showed me a nice knapsack he had bought to carry food, Bible tracts, and a microphone for our outreach venture. After my grueling trek through the jungle, I thought walking along the beach and dirt roads of Maués would be *muito facil*, very easy.

The next day David secured the backpack with the microphone onto me, and I went walking through the village, teaching from the Bible, projecting my voice with the microphone. I walked about the roads and paths near the river and wherever I saw dwellings. I walked all day on the sandy, muddy roads until I saw a spectacular sunset of many red, orange, and peach tones spread across the sky and waters. The people did not emerge from their houses, even out of curiosity, hearing my Portuguese. Maués was the first stop out of the Amazon jungle, and so I suspected the residents could include shy, indigenous Mawé among other tribes not open to strangers.

My second day out, still no one gathered around. No one wanted to listen to me. I couldn't even find Christians anywhere who wanted to meet me or talk with me. Even David agreed that Maués appeared to be a resistant place. In my experience with Isalino and Sergio, the people in the settlements along the waterways and rivulets of the Amazon on the other side of Manaus were open to receiving prayer or medicine for their sick and were receptive to teaching about Jesus by visiting ministers. Even if they couldn't read, they sometimes liked having the tracts with pictures or Scripture so that they could learn their letters. But not in Maués.

And I was completely taken aback when the local padre and three nuns showed up, grabbed me, pushed me down, and took my microphone. They slammed the microphone on the road, breaking it. They sure did want to shut me up and give me a good scare. This distressed me. I wasn't really hurt by these local clergy people, just shaken. I walked back to David's house wondering what God planned for the area, sending us out when there was such resistance. In my walk with God over the last few years, I had learned that He was way ahead of me. He knew what the story was about in this place. I should be sensitive and see how He would lead the way.

I did continue going from door to door leaving leaflets with Bible stories while I still had them. But there was no interest shown, I was not able to gather any people for worship, and they didn't even want me to pray for them. I had come to Maués six months before, and a few men had come to pray with Isalino and me at the shelter David had built, but now even they had vanished. There was no sign of them.

Next I received an intimidating letter from the mayor telling me to leave his town. In only a few days they had already had enough of me. I didn't go out again. That very night even the padre, who had roughed me up a little, received an awful beating. David paid the padre a visit and discovered he was badly bruised all over his body and so traumatized he could not even identify who had done this to him. It seemed that anyone representing the Lord Jesus in this area was considered a nuisance. We certainly didn't want to be a part of stirring up antagonism or violence. This was a beautiful place where David believed God wanted him to plant a church. We were messengers of peace.

Then I received an official notice from the City of Maués giving me fifteen days to leave the town. I had every intention of leaving, but David convinced me to visit the mayor first. He said he had gone to see the mayor, who had sent me the mandate to leave town, and he now had a *new* request—a request for me to stay. I raised my eyebrows at first, but David insisted that the mayor had pleaded with him to ask me to come to his house. The mayor had asked David for help with a problem, and David had told him that Justino was the only one to talk to. He took David's advice and sent for me. The mayor was apparently in a rather dire situation and had decided to swallow his pride. We didn't know what was going on, and we didn't want to make things worse. I would visit the mayor.

There are many other Amazon tributaries around Maués, and so it was much easier to navigate the way to the mayor's house with the little boat David offered. It saved me hours. After I docked the boat, it was still a couple kilometers inland to the house. Propelled by the mysterious nature of this visit, I hurried the distance. When I finally arrived at his home, I immediately understood why he had become so desperate.

The mayor was completely distraught over the militias of ants that had taken over his nice cottage. Armies were crawling on the walls, in the bedrooms, and in the beds. They were in every room from *cozinha*, kitchen, to *sala*, living room. I suppose there were many hundreds of thousands of ants in his house. He raised his arms with disgust and alleged that nothing like this had ever happened before. Perplexed, he pointed to the colonies of ants, deliberately insinuating that I was involved. His look and tone were angry and accusatory.

I told the mayor that his ant problem had no connection to me. I had nothing to do with it. I had not brought this dilemma upon him. I was steadily thinking that this was a spiritual problem, and I told the mayor so. It had a bizarre feel to it. I was not unfeeling about this poor man's difficulty, but he had evicted me from his town because he thought I was a troublemaker, and now he wanted me to take care of the trouble he thought I had brought. I wanted to make it clear that God was the rescuer, and I was neither the mediator nor the perpetrator of his troubles.

"This is something between you and God, and there is nothing I can do about it," I said.

Then the mayor talked about the beating of the padre in a reproachful way. I again told him that I knew about it but I was not present and had nothing to do with that situation, either.

"I don't think you should make *me* responsible for your problems," I told him. So, the mayor took another approach and said that I could ignore the town eviction notice he had sent to me.

"Why do you now want to stop my eviction?" I asked.

"You can stay here as long as you like. I just want to get these ants out of my home. We can't relax, can't talk, can't eat, can't sleep without ants crawling all over us. It's a plague, day and night. No one wants to visit me. No one in my family even wants to live here now in these conditions. This is serious!"

I agreed with the gentleman that his problem was serious. I told him he was blaming the wrong person. I told him that he needed to make peace with God. God would shed His light on the source of these conditions in his home. He needed to invite the Lord into his home.

"Senhor, I am not the answer. You need to get down on your knees and ask the pardon of Almighty God and change your attitude before Him. If this is something that has to do with God, this will all stop."

I spoke to his wife and all of his children about their need for forgiveness and change and God's love and mercy, and they all agreed. They all knelt in prayer, every one of them, and accepted the forgiveness of Jesus. They invited God to dwell in their hearts and their home. As soon as this occurred, the ants disappeared, as simple as that. This was very strange and humanly inexplicable, but it happened, indeed. It was very exciting to understand that if we put ourselves in God's care, He will show His mercy and power. The world is full of conflict and grievous things we don't understand. We need God with us.

It was a difficult but rich and rewarding time working in Maués with David. It was there that he began to introduce me as *Príncipe de Jesus*, Prince of Jesus, and even called me by this name to local people. When someone needed help or prayer, he would say that they needed to talk to Príncipe de Jesus. This splendid name deeply touched my heart and humbled me every time I heard it. My life was marked profoundly by the work God gave me to do in that, at one time, God-forsaken place. It became a place that God shone in so that it was no longer forsaken or dominated by Satanás. A church was planted there that year, and the numbers of believers increased.

In the town there was one house that had a wall around it. This is not something you see often in the interior of Brazil, where most neighborhoods are open. I had been told there was a woman who lived there who had a son who threw rocks at people in the streets. The neighbors had built the wall around her house to protect people from her boy because they could not get him to stop. While I was meeting people in the neighborhood, I knocked on the door of the mother of the boy.

She was very friendly and told me that she wanted to come to my church and that she knew the Bible. But, though she wanted to come, she wasn't able to because her son Getúlio was sick in his mind and might injure people. She couldn't bring him anywhere where other people were. I asked if I could pray with her son and she said yes, but she doubted he would let me near him to pray for him.

When I saw the boy, I was surprised to see that he was probably close to my age. He was filthy, naked, with long, tangled hair, and seemingly not in his right mind. I believed at the time that he was developmentally disabled. When he walked the dirt roads, everyone was afraid of him because of his scary appearance. He was quiet when I prayed for him. As soon as I finished praying for him, Getúlio asked to take a bath. With joy, his mother and I took him down to the river, and together we washed him. She helped him dress, and that night she came to church with her Getúlio.

It was the first time in nearly twenty years she had been able to walk down the town road with her son. The people at the church were amazed and very emotional about what had happened in the life of Getúlio and his mother. Their faith in God was strengthened by the remarkable change in the life of this ill-famed young man.

Getúlio never missed a worship service after that. When his mother didn't bring him, he came alone. He had a favorite *corinho*, hymn, that the church played for him every service because it was so moving to hear him sing it. His voice could be heard stammering above all the others, making the people all smile with love for Getúlio and love for God. It was *muito bom*, very good, to be reminded of the transformation of his life and the power of God available to us on earth.

David Cooper continued to give me Bible story tracts, which I took to all the houses of the town each time I returned to Maués. Gradually the people of the town became more receptive. Most didn't have Bibles, and the tracts had Scripture to comfort them and help them know the God of love and power. Getúlio often insisted on coming along with me out of his love for Jesus and the joy of his new life with Him. He was always ready to participate in the *obra de Deus*, work of God. In fact, Getúlio knew that he himself was an obra de Deus.

CHAPTER 26
KAÚNÃ'S DILEMMA

We had lived in the same area in the jungle for nearly three years, and I assumed that life for o Povo was going well. But there came a period of time when we seemed to have less food than usual. The *cascadores e pescadores*, hunters and fishermen, were coming back with less and less. I supposed this was the sort of shortage that could necessitate a nomadic move to fresh rainforest.

The tribal government would not allow the people to become unhealthy or unhappy because of scarcity of such an essential as the game that sustained them. I surely didn't want them to move in my absence because then it might be impossible to find o Povo again. If I moved with them deeper into the rainforest, we could end up in a different country. Brazil, Peru, Bolivia, and Ecuador were all part of their rainforest, and this ancient people were not part of any nation but their own.

For the time being, the tribe was eating all sorts of things for which only real hunger could compel them. They were not starving, but they needed their favorite meat. With a sinking feeling inside, I wondered when I also would have to join their eating of these beasts and insects they found—roaches, rats, leeches, grubs, bats, larvae—things that they surely didn't like to eat at all. *Nem eu!* Nor I! They weren't complaining, but as they ate bugs, they were not celebrating feasts with the fervor I was used to seeing.

We would always have fish and birds. We were river and forest dwellers, I told myself. But, with the vague whisper of a move in the future, I wondered if the leaders could have a growing concern for the well-being and security of the tribe. So far nothing had happened. Maybe I was projecting my own discomfort to be more alarming than the present reality warranted. I wondered if game, like birds, moved as seasons changed and so would come back. The tribe did have a law forbidding a hunter to come back to the tribe empty-handed. I had heard the law recited with my own ears:

"He is permitted to stay in the forest until he finds food or dies, but he must not return from the hunt unless he has found food. To return without is a great dishonor. If the tribe dies of hunger, the hunters are responsible."

I was neither a hunter nor a fisherman. I was daily amazed at the skill of children grabbing fish with their quick little hands and stabbing fish with the spears they made. And yet I never did succeed at doing this for myself even once. The tribe never requested me to do anything, *nunca*, ever. Neither was it my place to assume the high position of a hunter. Kaúnã was a very fine hunter, and there was only one other young man more valuable than he was. Regardless of his reputation and notoriety in the past, a hunter must not, could not, return home without food for the tribe.

One day Kaúnã didn't come back. In fact, none of the hunters came back. Another day passed and then yet another day. Still, no one came back from the hunt. The tribe was eating all sorts of things that I couldn't stomach—beetles, ants, praying mantises, katydids, spiders, crickets, scorpions, caterpillars—while they clung to hope for meat. They also ate their forest *pão podre*, daily staple bread, which was roots dug up from the ground. I disliked the smell and taste of those roots, and so I lived off the *coqueiros*.

The *coqueiros* were plentiful, and I had resolutely learned to climb them. I knew how to grab the trunk with the arches of my feet, both knees bent outward in a squat. Then, keeping my back straight and grasping the trunk high up and away from me, I straightened my legs and moved up the tree like a frog, one length, bringing my legs up into a squat again. I sat on my heels to rest and leaped again. It took only a few body lengths to reach the fronds that held the coconuts. Resting on my heels at the top and hugging the tree with one arm, I freed each smooth green coconut by twisting it until the stem broke.

The brown ones let go more easily, and I dropped five or six to the ground some five meters below me. The sensational sight overlooking the treetops gave me a thrill from head to toe. I always brought some fresh fronds with me on the descent. The coconut tree fronds have stalks in the center that are good to eat. With my knife I cut and peeled these stalks into frond sticks and toasted them over the fire. With a hammer I had brought with me from Manaus I cracked open the hardest, toughest coconuts and shared the fruit with whoever was near.

During those days that the hunters didn't return, I mostly ate those roasted stalks. I had found my limit to how much fish boiled in water I could get down. Boiled fish had become *nojento*, nauseating, to me now. I wasn't the only one tired of fish. The whole tribe was accustomed to forest meat about twice a week. Any kind of meat that could be caught or killed with the hunter's knife or arrows would do—birds, small animals, or big game. Deer, anaconda, crocodile, parrots, toucans, turkey, wild pig, wildcat, monkey—anything would be delicious after a week without meat. Anteater and sloth would not be delicious but would still be more edible than fish.

On the fifth day that the hunters did not come back, I was lying down in my hammock asleep. It was late at night. In the darkness, I heard something under my hammock. I sat up with a shudder and looked around to see what had awakened me. Crouched down, motioning desperately with his hands for quiet, was Kaúnã. His signal was clear. He must not be heard by anyone.

"Justino, ask your Brother," he whispered. "You said that He is very good. I have not found any animals. You said that He is able to do anything. Please, Justino, ask your Brother! There is no food. Can your Brother help me? Is He able to do this?"

"He is able," I answered.

I prayed in a whisper with Kaúnã and asked my Lord and Older Brother Jesus to help him in the hunt, to bless him with animals, and to take care of him. Then Kaúnã left quickly and silently. No one could know that Kaúnã had come back home without food.

This was deadly serious. There were three crimes that carried a harsh penalty for those who committed them: One was to take another man's wife. The second was for the warrior of the tribe to run away from battle. The third was for the hunter to return home without meat. These three laws carried a penalty of death.

In the center of the village was a high platform built for public events. The adulterer, the coward in battle, or the dishonorable hunter would suffer the penalty of death on this platform. He would stand on the high landing while three men took their positions surrounding him. The three executioners would each take a bow and shoot three arrows at him, nine arrows in all. The criminal's only shield would be two animal skins, one for each hand, to deflect the arrows. If he survived, he would be pardoned and go free. In the history of Kaúnã's tribe, no one had ever come through this punishment alive. For this reason, a hunter preferred to die in the jungle rather than return home with nothing to feed his people. Famished, exhausted, desperate, Kaúnã had taken a great risk in coming home. He took this risk out of faith.

The following day, Kaúnã was seen returning from the hunt with the hunter's swaying victory walk and holding his banner. From side to side he stepped, demonstrating his triumph, and many in the village ran out to sing the song of the hunter's accomplishment and the tribe's good fortune and to dance with him. Young men ran out to meet him and find out where the slain game lay. The hunter did not carry the animals back to the village. There were others that had this happy assignment. Kaúnã was taken to a special house of honor to rest, to be brought refreshment, to be served, and to be fed the first portion of the meat as soon as it was ready.

Kaúnã was the first hunter to return home. The others came back happy that day, too, all with game for the people. They would have been allowed to return because of Kaúnã's kill. One hunter's success is counted for all of them. But each one had found abundant food to kill.

After Kaúnã returned, he didn't stay at the designated house of honor to rest with the other hunters. He came to see me.

"Justino, your Brother is very good," he said. "It is true, just as you said. He can do anything!"

Kaúnã had killed an elk, the largest beast to be found in the forest where we lived. He also killed a wild pig and a *cutia*, rodent, the size of a small deer. This was a fine kill for one hunter.

"*Eazu é kao kao toh,*" said Kaúnã in his tongue. "Jesus is very, very good."

Kaúnã went to the house of rest to receive his portion, but he didn't eat it. He brought it to me at my house.

"It's from your Brother," he said. "It wasn't my portion. The animals came to me. I didn't hunt them. They were gifts from your Brother. Eazu sent the animals to me."

Usually, whatever was killed in the hunt would be eaten on the same day. But that day there was more than the tribe could eat. It was a wonderful day not just because of the hunt, but also because Kaúnã began to tell the others about Jesus. Kaúnã had experienced going with Jesus from scarcity to abundance. What a great blessing this was for me, his brother. Together we shared this kingdom of God in the heavens experience.

After that, other men came to hear about Jesus from me and to ask me to pray with them. In time, they also brought others with them. Almost every day, the men came to meet with me in my house for prayer and to hear stories of Jesus. When I left the tribe, there were nineteen men who met with me nearly every day to learn about the Lord Jesus.

This time with Kaúnã and his people has echoed throughout my life as a reminder of God's destiny for me and for all who seek Him.

CHAPTER 27

DANIEL'S EDUCATION

On my last journey out of the jungle for supplies and rest, I knew that I would come back only one more time. I was conflicted as I envisioned the impact my leaving for good would have on the tribe, Kaúnã, and on me. I imagined the things I would say to the nineteen men who had come to faith in Jesus. Now there might be a cultural and social and spiritual shift within the tribe—a struggle between the leaders that would be best worked out without me. I practiced the words in their tongue of how I would say goodbye. I had been staying with o Povo for about three years now. Every five months or so I left for three or four weeks, and they seemed to like this rhythm.

From Stone Age to information age, from ancient to modern, I needed to shift many things in my outer life and maybe my inner life too. Giving up my concerns to God, for them and for myself, wasn't easy. Now they would have to understand a permanent goodbye. I needed to reset my own bearings and temperament to a more modern Brazilian life. My pace in life would need to pick up. I needed to be as patient and open with modern people as I had been with my indigenous friends. I suppose I knew to do this because of God's leading, not having had any training in mental or spiritual health issues.

I visited churches in the North of Brazil to report my experiences and to worship with other Christians. When I told of my encounter with an untouched tribe in the Amazon forest to a church in Manaus, a young man named Daniel became fascinated with my story of the índios. He was from Divinopolis in the state of Minas Gerais, far south of us. His interest led to a heartfelt request that when I returned to the tribe I might take him with me. He maintained this sustained desire to go with me and stay for the time I would be there. I thought this over. Since I only planned to stay a few months more, I agreed it could be a good experience for him and made plans to take him along.

Daniel must have had second thoughts long before we arrived anywhere near the settlement of o Povo. Within the first hours of our trek, I saw that Daniel didn't know anything about how to hike through the jungle and had not prepared for the challenge. He didn't seem to know how to motivate himself for the contest as he faced each trial. It had not occurred to me that he would be unused to being at the mercy of so many things—the jungle, the animals and insects, hunger, thirst, and the fatigue of a long, drawn-out hike. I remained positive. This had become my way of life, and I could not fathom what he would face at first. You see, I did not comprehend yet what I myself had experienced over the past three years. Not until decades later did I realize that I had walked over three thousand miles during the three years I lived with the Sateré nation.

Daniel was about twenty-three, a year or two older than I was, very light skinned, and he had a grim case of acne on his face. Now after days of hiking outside he had a terrific sunburn. Somehow, we finally arrived at the place where I would show him this people whom he had wanted so much to know as I did. Before we entered the village, we saw some of our scouts. I told them that I had brought my friend Daniel. Of course, there had been no way to advise them that I was bringing him. It was definitely a surprise visit. I asked them to tell everyone that I had brought a man with me and that I had brought some other things too. They went ahead of us to announce our arrival to Tuxaua.

As we rested, waiting for tribesmen to reappear, I thought about what was in our heavy packs: enough supplies for three months and something for a couple dozen tribesmen. I had never brought anything to give to the tribesmen before. I had not been sure what was good for them. Those who were close to me already used my stuff when they wanted. So, I chose to bring them what they already knew, things we had shared. I wished it could be more because I would be leaving for good and I wanted to be remembered. I brought a new rede for Kaúnã. I was happy with that gift. But I could not carry twenty hammocks through the rainforest.

Out of the more than two hundred people in the tribe, I had relationships with about twenty-five. Except Pajé, who made it clear, I never really knew who didn't like me or accept me. Those who never wanted me in the tribe and those who feared, perhaps hated, me and dreaded my return each time kept their distance. I only saw them at dances or rituals and never closely enough to recognize their outright disapproval. I was deeply thankful for the great benefit of knowing a few dozen in a deeper way than I knew even my own family.

This last trip back to the tribe, I finally decided on gifts to bring to the leaders and to those who were closest to me. For the leaders I brought a mirror, a comb, a toothbrush, and toothpaste. I brought the others just one of these things. I had pondered too long about what and how many to bring to the others. It turned out it didn't matter what I had chosen to give to those twenty-five or so who were close to me, because I had brought Daniel. Daniel was enough to delight the whole village. When we arrived, the people gathered around and looked at him, voicing their predictable curiosity.

"WehPeeeeeh! WehPeeeh!"

Daniel was upset with these high sounds the people were making. He couldn't know he himself was a good reason for o Povo to make such a commotion. We both looked strange to them, wearing so much clothing and carrying so much stuff. I was dressed in a t-shirt, a sweatshirt, jeans, socks, and shoes. This was more than I usually wore, and I had brought extra in my backpack to give away too.

My pack was holding sixty kilos, which was too heavy for me. Because of the weight, we had traveled more slowly, and so the hike in through the forest was longer and harder. Since we had been wearing the same clothes for more than a week, Daniel had decided to change into some red nylon shorts that he had taken out of his backpack. When we entered the village, the people gathered around, unable to contain their enchantment with Daniel's red shorts.

"Peeeeeeeeeh! Wehpeeeeeeeeh!"

Everyone sounded off in their shrillest voices as they pointed at Daniel from all directions. They pointed at his shorts. They pointed at his sunburn, then at the blemishes and freckles on his skin and face. Then they squealed with glee.

"Peeeeeeeeeh! Weh Peeeeeeeh! Peeeeeeeeeh!" they serenaded together like a chorus of Xingu screech owls. I had long forgotten many of my first impressions and theirs of me until I brought Daniel. I almost enjoyed their pointing out the oddness of my poor friend. I even agreed with their impressions and got a good laugh. *Desculpe*, sorry, Daniel.

Daniel was mortified. He had just endured the most grueling seven-day hike of his life and now found his trials had only just begun. His exhaustion, his stress, and his fear made him glow red. As the people inspected him, he blushed redder and redder.

"Peeeeeeeeh! Weh Peeeeeeeeh!"

"What are they saying? Justino, what are they going to do to me? What are they pointing at? What are they going to do with me?"

"*Nada*, Daniel. They are just curious. *Fique tranquilo*. Calm down. *Calma*, Daniel. It's okay."

"Justino, don't leave me! Stay close to me, Justino!" Daniel cried, moving closer.

That evening, when it was time to join the community evening bath, I suggested that he be left alone to rest. They didn't bother him. Still, that night, exhausted Daniel could not sleep at all. So just before daybreak when they came to get us for the morning swim, I told them again not to bother him.

"*Deixa ele.* Just let him be," I told them. I hoped he would rest and adjust.

Then, when the call for the bath rang out the next morning, I insisted that Daniel join us.

"You need to go with us now. It's time to join the people in the things they do."

When he started to get soap and toothpaste out, I tried to advise him again.

"Daniel, don't bring anything. They will just take it and use it up, and then you won't have any. Just come as you are."

Daniel had put on his red nylon shorts again, which were going to get a reaction. At first, I decided not to say anything. But when I saw that he intended to enter the water with the shorts on, I cautioned him.

"Daniel, take off those shorts. They will just draw attention to you. Trust me, you need to take off the shorts."

"No, I'm not going nude! I'm keeping my shorts on."

"Look around. Everyone is naked. No one has any clothes on. You need to get rid of the shorts."

Poor Daniel remained strong in his convictions and went into the river with the shorts on, and they would not leave him alone. They followed him wherever he went, in and out of the water—making fun of him.

"Peeeeeeeeeeeeeh Weh Peeeeeeeeeeee!" they repeated with great excitement, young and old.

They pressed close and studied his arms and face and bent down to look closely at his legs. They pointed, almost touching him, at all the many interesting parts of his body, especially the shorts. He looked at me in desperation. I had not expected them to enjoy him so much. I shook my head. He had invited their harassment by ignoring my warnings.

"Daniel, as long as you have those silly shorts on, they will never leave you in peace! Why don't you just take them off?" I sighed, powerless to help him.

Then he took off the shorts. Now, I am much lighter skinned than o Povo, but I am so very much darker than Daniel. Even I was surprised at his naked, lily-white lower parts! When they viewed the paleness of his newly exposed nude body, they became manic. The crowd lost control.

"Weh??? Peeeeeeeeeeeeh!" they yowled, walking in circles around him and laughing hysterically. It was just too much for them. The entertainment, the sheer delight—they were beside themselves.

That first week, over and over, I had to convince Daniel not to run away. He wanted to try to escape into the forest and just disappear. He was overwhelmed with terror that they would decide to do something terrible to him. I told him that his novelty would pass and he would adjust to their ways and they to his. But he wasn't trusting of my advice. He had no knowledge, empathy, or respect for the way of o Povo and no trust in me to teach him. From the beginning, when we had hiked for ten days to the village, he had not listened to me. Now, I only hoped that the memory of that grueling journey together had convinced him he might not survive an escape.

Daniel endured the trauma of his adjustment and did his best to adapt. He had brought his guitar, and in the evenings he sang beautiful songs and wept with homesickness. He truly believed he would never see his parents, his loved ones, and a saner life again.

Of course, the guitar was another thing that I had begged him not to bring. Just as I predicted, every person in the tribe wanted to play with his guitar day and night. It was a constant struggle to decide how to protect the guitar and whose turn it was and what to do about it. I wasn't very patient about things like this. But Daniel had insisted on bringing it, and they certainly loved it. The índios made flutes from the jungle reeds, and many played exquisite music too. I never really learned their melodies, but their ageless music was soothing to hear in the forest. It carried me away up over the treetops and the water.

I felt Daniel's sorrow as he wept through the words of his favorite songs of *saudades*, longing. Every evening around the fire he sang as the unstoppable tears streamed down his face. Many times, the tribe's musicians joined him with their flutes. Their accompaniment to Daniel's tearful guitar music, echoing back his refrains, was amazing to hear. It pierced the soul. *Ai! Foi bom, mas muito bom!* Ah, this was so good, so very good to hear!

This mixture of praise and longing drew out my own feelings from the depths of my heart. This may have redeemed every regret for my bringing him. We were there with the tribe about two months. However long it seemed to Daniel, it went very quickly for me. Very quickly. If I had realized how difficult it was going to be for my friend to make this trip with me or what challenges I would face in looking after him, I may not have brought him. But I rethought my regrets.

After I reviewed the situation, I realized that Daniel had good reason to fear. He didn't swim well, he couldn't navigate in the jungle, he was not of a flexible or easygoing disposition, and he wasn't accustomed to so many things that had become second nature to me. He feared the very people that were sustaining him. He didn't take to heart any of my warnings of the actual dangers and challenges ahead of him. They were unimaginable to him. And then when they were upon us, I made light of them to preserve his peace. I had remained too positive, as if that was the only view of things. I had lost track over time of what the real consequences of jungle living were for me and would be for him. And now he showed me with clarity that it was something to reckon with. I was forced to face up to this because his being with me was a real hardship for both of us. I should have better prepared him.

Looking back, I see now that Daniel taught me some important things. He gave me a fresh frame of reference, a context from which to view and value my experience with the tribe as it was coming to a close. And he had unforgettable experiences as he participated with me in the meetings with the believers in Jesus during which we sang together as he played his guitar. He accompanied us as we sang "Jesus Loves Me" in their language, and the men loved to sing with Daniel, believing those words. They had no Bible yet, but they had heard many of the stories of Jesus and believed He was near to each of them. Daniel made me a better witness to the incredible things I had learned and experienced in the previous three years of my life with o Povo, a tribe that had existed for eons.

When I told Kaúnã that I would not come back again, he was very disappointed and downcast in his appearance.

"You are my brother. My brother cannot go," said Kaúnã in his frustration with me.

"Kaúnã, I am your brother, yes. I am your older brother. Take me to Tuxaua," I said to my younger brother, using the authority he had given over to me. I could not see Chief Tuxaua without a prearrangement.

"Kaúnã, I must tell Tuxaua that I am leaving now. I cannot be here anymore. You remember I told you this when there was a woman in my hammock. Tuxaua must know this now, as you do."

In only a day Kaúnã had arranged a meeting with both the chief of our tribe and the Storyteller. He had the respect of the leaders, not because of his relationship with me, but because he was an excellent hunter. He took me to Tuxaua near his house, where we had been together more than once. There was a gathering of tribesmen there, most of whom I knew well. "Maybe the Storyteller plans to give us a lesson," I thought. I approached Tuxaua and told him I would not come back to the tribe again and wished him everything good. I thanked him for allowing me to be with his people. Kaúnã helped them understand by elaborating loudly after each of the sentences I spoke in their language. Everything Kaúnã said was better than my words and just what I had on my heart. He spoke as my brother.

I could see in the face of those who gathered with us a great frustration. They didn't want me to leave and didn't want to say goodbye. Some who were closest to me showed sadness, but o Povo don't cry. I held myself together and didn't cry, either. Daniel was not with me but waited for me. Tuxaua accepted my words of farewell kindly. Without festivity but with honor he gave me many gifts that I still have today: a thatched hammock, handmade boots, a knife, and a machete. Others gave me paintings, bow and arrows, and crowns of ornaments to wear made of colorful feathers. I thanked them all, choking back tears. I packed their gifts in my bag but only after I had emptied it of everything I had brought for them and much more. I left with only the clothes on my body and the gifts they gave me. In my casa I had left for Kaúnã all my belongings, my clothing, a new hammock, and my blanket.

I left the tribe and the Amazon region on November 7, 1972. At this writing, I've never been back. Two years later, in 1974, word was sent from the tribe to the Posto FUNAI requesting that I return. I heard about this sometime later as this request made its way to the Wycliffe Institute in Brasília, the Federal Capital of Brazil. Wycliffe was kind enough to make a radio announcement as well as send a letter to me in Goiânia telling me the tribe requested my return. I was greatly moved by this contact from them. Since I could not go, I believe Wycliffe sent another missionary to work with o Povo, Kaúnã's very tribe.

CHAPTER 28

AFTER AMAZONAS

After I left the tribe, I attended another Wycliffe linguistics course in Brasília, and sometime late into the course I discovered I was not feeling well. I tried to push through, which was my way. I was still undecided about where I was going to live after the course was over. A pastor in Anápolis had suggested that I study at the ICEC, Institute of Christian Education and Culture, in Goiânia. I hoped to stay connected with the Churches of Christ in Goiânia because this is where I sensed that my experience with the tribe and with my teammates would be best understood and accepted. With these two things in mind, I personally visited with the director of the school, Pastor Medes, in Goiânia to introduce myself and discuss admission to the college.

Pastor Medes received me with a warm welcome. As was usually the case, I had not a centavo for tuition! No longer working as a missionary, I didn't really have a church or a church's support, my family was not able to help me, I had no money saved, and I was unemployed. Pastor Medes had said to come to Goiânia anyway and something could be worked out.

When I arrived, I had three shirts and three pairs of pants in my suitcase. The director looked around me for more baggage and asked if I had anything to unpack for my room such as kitchen supplies, dishes, a pillow or blanket, or books. The answer was no.

"*Então, você vai morar em minha casa.* Then you will live at my house," he said.

This Pastor Medes had a wife named Leda who took charge of me.

With the responsibility of her two children, she treated me as if I were her third. I had no notebook, no pen or pencil, and no paper, so she went out and bought school supplies for me.

I had only brought my Bíblia, given to me by the wife of David Cooper, and I still have it today. Leda gave to me, as gifts, a concordance and a biblical encyclopedia to go with my Bible and told me I would be needing them daily. The school dorm was set up in a communal way where the cost of water, electricity, food, transportation, and all necessities were divided equally among the students. I had no way of paying for any of this. She said this is why I was so fortunate to be living in the house of the director. It seemed I was all set and ready to attend seminary.

But then I began to turn yellow. My skin was yellow, head to toe. Even the whites of my eyes were yellow. Everyone thought I had hepatitis. The director was afraid that I might be infecting his family, especially his children. He moved me to the dormitory at the school. At first, I attended class and took care of myself. But soon I was so sick I was confined to my bed.

When the fever spiked, I became delirious and violent with muscle spasms and convulsions. The other students said I broke everything around me until the fever crisis was over. One of the professors, also a missionary, took me to the hospital and stayed with me there.

In this era, in rural Brazil, the local hospital was a hostel and clinic where you received medical attention, but daily care was given by your relatives or friends. There wasn't a cafeteria for meals or sufficient nursing staff to bathe or feed patients. During my stay, my teachers and fellow students were my visiting nurses.

The school had a little red Fusca, a VW Bug, that they used to cart me back and forth from the school to the hospital when I was having a bad time. The staff tested my blood at the hospital more than once to see if I had hepatitis or malaria, and the results were negative for both diseases. Still, everyone believed I had hepatitis.

Zé Carlos, a young man who worked in the lab at the hospital and also attended the Igreja de Cristo, Church of Christ, offered to come and get blood samples from me at the school dormitory rather than wait for them to bring me in the Fusca. The doctors had said my blood needed to be drawn in the midst of a fever crisis in order to get a good sample. When Zé Carlos first arrived at the school during one of my crises, there was no way to draw my blood because I was hallucinating with the fever. They said that I was too violent and crazy. They tied me down so that I wouldn't hurt anyone but still could not get a needle in me. Though I weighed only forty-nine kilos—one hundred eight pounds—I had destroyed everything in the room during so many crises of the fever.

After twenty-four days there, with continuous bouts of fever, the doctors were convinced there was no hope for me. One doctor who attended me interviewed me in detail to see if there was any more *informações* I could give to help them. He had diagnosed me with malaria when I was taken back to the hospital to stay for treatment. I explained to him that I had lived in the Amazon region for three years and that I had taken medication every day to avoid getting malaria. Of my team I was the only one who escaped the disease while living there.

While in Manaus, we heard that if you take the malaria pills faithfully once a week, you will not come down with it. I bought them and took them every week after that, and I never got it while living in the Amazon region. But every one of my teammates did get malaria in spite of using the antimalarial medication.

"Em realidade, você pegou malaria," said the doctor with finality. "In reality, you did catch malaria, and it's been incubating for years in your liver."

The other doctors did not think I would survive. They were stumped. They admitted they didn't know what to do for me. *"Não sabemos como tratar o organismo.* We really don't know how to treat the disease now that it has become so resistant to medication."

For years, I had gone without intense treatment when I needed it. The plasmodium parasite that causes malaria had localized in my liver, and now the doctors thought it might not be treatable. Malaria multiplies in red blood cells of humans, and these single-celled parasites had taken up residence in my liver. The hospital and school contacted missionary groups in Asia and Africa and other places to try different medications for me. The medications arrived, I took them, but nothing cured my malaria.

While I was in the hospital, I received a visit from a group of five people—three men and two women from Goiânia. They presented themselves to me and said they had heard of me and had come to invite me to be the pastor of their church. I was very surprised.

"But, you realize I am sick," I said. "I'm very bad off, and I don't even know yet if I am going to live."

Strangely enough, they still wanted me to be their pastor. As soon as I was discharged from the hospital, greatly in need of a job, and still unsure of my health, I accepted their offer. I didn't really have any options, and they apparently didn't, either. Zé Carlos, the man who worked in the hospital lab and who had come to the school to take my blood samples, attended this church too. He was part of the group that had come to visit me in the hospital and probably the one who had first recommended me.

I attended their church, the Igreja de Cristo, on Sunday and counted eleven people there for the worship. Five of them had visited me in the hospital, so I already knew half the attendees. It was the end of March of 1973 when they showed me the little room in the church where I would live as the pastor. I was to receive a salary of 240 *cruzeiros*, or about $80.00 per month. I chuckle at this amount now, the legal minimum wage of the time, but it was such a blessing! Without that salary, I would have had no money at all. Twenty-five dollars of this wage was needed to cover utilities, and the rest would have to cover my food and schooling. I had my first paying job, a place to live, and a position as a full-time student. Now, if I could just survive a mysterious strain of malaria.

CHAPTER 29

DORMANT AND DEADLY

With my new job as pastor, I moved my living quarters to the little office offered to me at the church. It was eight kilometers between the school and the church. I couldn't afford the ônibus. I had to walk the eight kilometers, almost five miles, to school to arrive in time to have *café de manhã*, breakfast, at the school cafeteria before my first class started at 7:00 a.m. This breakfast was a piece of bread with butter and a cup of coffee with milk. No matter! The malaria had damaged my liver so much that I could digest very little else. I took classes until noon and then enjoyed a small lunch at the school as well.

Every day I had spells of muscular cramping and fever from the malaria. These spells seemed to come on in the afternoon or evening. Often the episodes developed as I was walking between school and the church. I would begin to perspire and feel first hot and then cold as I shuddered and convulsed almost as if in an epileptic seizure. I looked for a bench to sit on as I shook for thirty or forty minutes, feeling my muscles tighten and turn to ice. This piercing cold attacked every muscle in my body from head to toe. Wherever I was, there was no way to calm myself or control my limbs. My arms struck out, my legs kicked, I trembled and shook and I hurt all over with unspeakable pain. If I could not find a place to sit, I often fell down with these spasms, sometimes even gratefully fainting. When I did fall, I lay feebly on the ground, my muscles too weak, spastic, or uncoordinated to get me up again for some time. When I recovered enough to get up and walk, my clothing was completely soaked in sweat and I was *absolutamente* exhausted.

People looked away as they passed by me. They didn't know how to help me or what I needed. I felt ashamed and deeply despondent. This was a profoundly desperate and lonely time in my life. I couldn't stop these malaria spells from happening, and so I continued to push hard to carry on through them. I knew myself to be a sort of obstinate, determined person. I liked a challenge, to work hard, and so I cast these personal attributes of mine into play. With passion, I resolved to improve myself. I would grind hard as a student through the sickness. I would tough it out this way with my warrior mentality.

I met a woman from the Baptist church at a house church meeting who told me her son owned a private high school. In a casual conversation with her, I candidly confided that I had only completed the fourth grade. I confessed that I was currently studying at seminary and the road was tough. She was immediately concerned that I might be denied the certificate of graduation I earned from the seminary if I didn't have a grade school diploma.

"I want to talk to my son about you," she told me.

Soon I received a letter from her telling me that she had set up a consultation with her son at the high school he directed. I met with him and he interviewed me to learn my story.

"I'm going to give you a scholarship to my school," he said. This was a fantastic opportunity for me. *Maraviloso!* In this way I also began studying for my *Primeira Grao* diploma, my grade school diploma.

I continued walking the eight kilometers from the church to seminary to have my breakfast and attend the Bible classes, which lasted until about noon. Then I lunched at the school. I ate quickly so that I could lie down on the floor for fifteen minutes before my hike to grade school. I ran most of the three kilometers there because classes started at 1:00 in the afternoon. I usually arrived late, slid into a desk, and listened to the classes until about 5:20.

By 5:30 p.m. I was on my way to church to lead worship. This is the time of day that I was most susceptible to a crisis of fever from the malaria. There were days I could keep this schedule and days when I just couldn't. We had worship for young people and the congregation on Wednesday, Friday, and Saturday nights and Sunday morning and evening. After worship, I studied for both seminary and my grade school diploma. I was making up for the four years of elementary school that I had missed when I had lived in Paraná. Many nights I *estudava muito*, studied a lot! I crammed until dawn. Without a doubt, this was one of the most difficult periods in my life. Not only was I sick, I was not feeling well on the medication I was prescribed. I wonder now how I studied until late at night, walked to seminary in the morning and to school in the afternoon, preached and led worship at night, and endured the daily regimen of harsh medications and debilitating fevers.

One day I became so exhausted and dehydrated that I called my friend Litemar to my room to take my blood that day for diagnosis. I simply could not get myself to the clinic. Litemar decided to look after me by hooking me up to IV fluids in my little room at the church whenever I was too weak to go to the hospital. This frequent hydration helped me with my nausea. I was able to continue with seminary, school, and my job, but still I was losing weight and appetite and strength as the days passed. Some days when Litemar came, I lay down on my bed, too feeble even to talk to him. I was very grateful to have him hook me up with that glucose and fluids tube right there in my room. To eat or drink would have meant lifting my arms and moving my head, and I didn't have that much energy left in me.

One Wednesday night it was time for a prayer service at the church. I was arriving to do what I could. I was the pastor of this church, and it was full even though I could hardly do a thing to lead them. At seminary in the morning, school in the afternoon, taking IV fluids and studying at night—I would not be preaching a very long sermon. It was a miracle the church had been growing. This was a lesson I was learning—that its growth wasn't my doing. I dragged myself into the service and stood in weakness and preached the Word of God. What did I preach? The same thing that I preach today: That the Lord frees us from the evil one and from the bondage of sin and invites us into the kingdom of God. The Lord Jesus takes our sin away, changes us, heals us, and gives us purpose and new life with access to Him. The Lord turns curses to blessings and redeems every moment of our lives. I needed to listen to the truth of the message I preached. I was a picture of desperation and despair.

CHAPTER 30

WHEN I AM WEAK

On a Wednesday night prayer *reunião*, meeting, a woman named Auserite came to our church for the very first time. Both her mother-in-law and her husband, Guilherme, had brought her to receive prayer for her infirmities.

This woman was very bad off. She was a *Mãe de Santo*, a *macumbeiro* saint. This means that she was a priestess in the practice of the knowledge and traditions of the spirits of Macumba, a popular Afro-Brazilian spiritist religion. Her religious specialties included leading prayer services; making sacrifices; leading celebrations, healing ceremonies, and invocations; counseling; serving the community; and interpreting and obeying the commands of the spirits of Macumba. Her duties required her to essentially practice a Voodoo-like spirit possession and magic combined with the sacraments of local, mainstream Brazilian religions. As a type of shaman, she entered a trance to become a conduit for the spirit world. She conjured and invited the spirits into control over every part of the macumbeiro's life, administering the will of the spirits. The Macumba followers looked to the spirits for guidance and prosperity in their jobs, their finances, their health, and in their relationships with others.

The spirits that Guilherme's wife had received were using her life and her body and causing her great suffering. Her family had brought her to the church for prayer because her terrible nightmares had become unendurable. Auserite was terrified that someone was going to kill her children, Jumar and Juliane. At last, she was willing to come to the church because of her growing panic and distress for her children.

That night I was too sick to lead worship, and so I had asked our people to go ahead with the service without me. When the worship began, I was lying down taking IV fluids in my room arranged by my friend Litemar. The prayer service began normally, with praying and singing. I was too weak to get up, but I could hear them from my room.

Then, I could hear the disturbances coming from a woman as they prayed for her. The demons were making themselves known. Demonic manifestations are not always so obvious as they were with this poor woman. She was moaning loudly and speaking in frightening voices. I could hear her screaming in pain or fear. Her violent shouting got louder, and the commotion got worse. She was soon moving about the room in ways that endangered those who were in prayer for her. I called out from my room for someone to come because I felt I should try to help out in some way.

Zé Carlos showed up in my doorway and agreed to help me walk to the worship area. The woman, Auserite, was really in a very bad way—her face contorted, flinging her limbs spastically while they prayed for her. Zé brought my bottle of glucose as he walked with me, steadying me. As we joined them, Auserite was grabbing the hardwood church pews and moving these long, heavy bancos around the church with inhuman strength. She became so violent, it seemed she could shift around four or five of those big, heavy pews at once. Everyone was distressed and afraid since it was so difficult to keep her from hurting herself or those who were trying to help her. This was a horrific thing to see. It had become so out of control, most of the worshipers became upset or fearful and left. A few remained to pray Auserite through this terrible spell of demonic abuse with us. Like Zé Carlos, they were committed to praying through the night, if need be.

After I joined them, we continued together in fervent prayer. In time the woman quieted. And it wasn't long before Auserite was freed from the demons. *Livre!* Free! The spirits had left her and left that place. The people still at the service were astonished by God's answers to their prayers. I was too. I acknowledged that Jesus' power is made strong in our weakness. I was physically so broken, so feeble, that I had to hold on to Zé Carlos. Because I was weak, my prayers—all of our prayers—were made strong. Why? Because we have no power of our own!

This was in October, springtime in Brazil. Every day I had been getting weaker. The daily medicine I took was not working and was probably making me worse. My first crisis had begun in April, and now, after seven months, I was losing my will to go on. I asked my doctor what to do, and he said that I had to learn to live with my situation. I had to somehow ride out the episodes and endure the side effects of the medicine since they could do nothing more for me.

In every way I was fragile—physically and emotionally and spiritually. I was exhausted and downhearted. I began to ask God why He had sent me to the Amazonas only to return to die. In my despondence, sometimes I doubted that God had ever spoken to me at all. As I doubted God's love and care for me, my belief was being tested that He could be trusted to care for others. I was really beginning to crumble into despair.

"Why have you abandoned me?" I asked. "Are you there? Were you really there in the beginning when I believed you were? Did I imagine all the works I witnessed? Were they not miracles but only my imagination?"

I felt completely alone. Emotionally, I was too unstable to fight the lies of the enemy. In November, the doctor decided to increase my medicine dose to four pills a day. Though I took the dose he prescribed, I still did not get better. I hopelessly became convinced that I would die. It was the first time that I really believed I would die, and I was truly afraid of death then. I didn't want to face death in such a bad state of mind, so full of fear and despair. Everything hurt in me—my mind, my soul, my head, my gut. My liver was very bad, sore to touch, continually aching. My skin hurt. I came to the realization that I had finally given up. Given up on everything—on God, on life, on me. I was approaching the lowest point of my life.

When I awoke one morning, I decided I would not go to school. It was pointless. I couldn't even get up, anyway. I lay in bed all day. In the afternoon, I stumbled, my legs very weak, out of my room and laid myself down on one of the benches in the church. I just stayed there, too faint to move, as the afternoon drifted into evening. I felt a heavy darkness fall on me, and I waited for the familiar bout of fever to come back all over again. Lightning-sharp pains and spasms had begun. They spread from my legs up through my body and stabbed into my head. Freezing chills, the awful headache, joint aches, muscles jerking and cramping, my body sweating and shaking—I would lose control of my movements, my mental state. The intense and enduring pain made me wish for death so that this sickness could be over once and for all. Yes, this is what I hoped for.

"Today I will endure my last crisis," I said to myself. "*Hoje vou morrer. Today I will die.*"

I didn't want to die alone. My parents and family were living in Paraná, and here I lay helpless in Goiás, so far from them. I teared at the thought of the distance of my family. The malaria fever descended over me as I lay on the wooden church pew. The church *zelador*, housekeeper, Orvalina, who lived in a tiny house behind the church, came through the sala where I lay.

I pleaded in a whisper, "Orvalina, I am getting the fever now, and I am very bad off today. Will you stay near me until the crisis is over?"

The sweating and the shakes were overwhelming. Orvalina brought Isalina, a friend who was staying with her, and they helped me from the church bench to my room. After I lay down in my bed, they stayed near, sitting on the little stools at the table by the stove in order to pray me through the crisis. The tremors took over and I gave in to them, sadly confident that I would only have to lose control of my muscles and limbs one last time.

I remember that I sang the hymn that had come to my mind while they prayed for me. It was a song about taking the Lord's hand during torment and danger and weakness. They probably couldn't hear my song, but it came up from my heart, and I know God heard it as I sang, "Lord, I only want to be with you."

When the fever was at its worst and my bed was shaking with my tremors, I saw a light come in through the door. It was blue and green and like a flame as it spread over my room. After that I saw nothing else. I must have lost consciousness.

Certain that I was breathing and covered properly for the night, my gentle *irmãs*, sisters, left my room to tend to their own families. Orvalina was well aware I was getting worse and worse. She had looked in on me more than once, living so near and being the compassionate and caring person that she was.

The next morning, I awakened in the early light feeling strong and happy. Gone was my fear and dread. I hadn't been hungry in months, but I was famished that morning. I imagined the taste of fresh milk and *pão francês*, French bread, with butter. I got up and walked down to the *padaria*, neighborhood corner store, and bought those hot, petite, crusty loaves of bread and fresh milk that I had been dreaming about.

Orvalina came to see if I had gotten up for school and met me coming in. She took a look at me with a raised eyebrow. Something was different. My frame was very thin and frail-looking, my skin and eyes still yellow. I had not been able to eat eggs or take milk for a long time due to the state of my liver. Yet after a terrible night, here I was up and dressed and had already ambled out to the padaria and bought breakfast.

"You must be hungry, Pastor Justino!" Orvalina smiled her approval.

She heated the milk to pour into my café and buttered the warm pãozinhos and soon waved me off to school. Orvalina and her friend Isalina had cared for me like two angels sent by God.

CHAPTER 31

CRAMMING

My step was light. I felt good. The day wore on, and my morning classes turned to lunch and then seminary and then supper and then evening worship, and I didn't have a single symptom of malaria that day. I gradually comprehended that I had endured my very last fever crisis the night before. Never again did I suffer another one. Oh, what God had done!

In less than a year I caught up on the four years of class time and home study for my grammar school diploma. I passed the exams for those classes, and now it was time to enter high school. The director of the school said he would have liked to have given me a free high school education as well, but it wasn't possible to do this. In a consultation with me he explained that I couldn't attend his school as a student anymore. There were government requirements, which were not as stringent in grade school, that had to be met with high school credits.

"I want you to attend our courses, and yet you won't really be enrolled in the classes. You won't be a student of the school now and, therefore, cannot take any of the exams. But you can prove you know the material by taking the government exams on the subjects at the end of the courses."

This was an amazing gift. I knew very little arithmetic. I was twenty-two and I had never read a book from beginning to end. I was about to be introduced to classical literature, humanities, philosophies, higher mathematics, languages, sciences, and histories I had never even heard of.

I would be allowed to audit any and all of the courses in this expensive private school and then take the free government exams provided by Brazil's Department of Education to earn my high school diploma.

This kind educator led me to a class that was just beginning and had me sit where I could hear the lecture. This was in a large classroom where students came to take exams. Despite my poverty of origin, my meager finances, and my humble background, I was to be given an exceptional education. This is how God took care of me.

These were difficult courses, and I had to *estudar muito*, study hard. Day and night I read the texts. It wasn't that I loved learning; I was determined to do it. I was driven by acute embarrassment regarding my lack of culture and knowledge. I was a poor boy. I felt ignorant, backward, and stupid through and through. *Bobo*, as we say. Even when working with my ministry team, I felt ashamed of my telltale dialect and poor grammar. I was embarrassed just buying food at the market because of my illiteracy and lack of math skills. I felt people had good reason to look down on me, because I looked down on myself. This spurred me on to study hard.

When I was in the Amazonas, I visited the home of a family who had a little girl of about nine years old. As I sat talking with her and her parents, the little girl pointed out my poor Portuguese.

"*Você é muito bobo!* You are very slow [silly, stupid]!"

The truth of these words stung me deeply then, and they have echoed back to me over the years. I hated the constant reminder that I appeared simpleminded and ill-spoken even to elementary school children. I hoped to change my social appearance with an education, and I worked diligently with that purpose in mind. Sometimes I still feel that I am bobo. Dumb. I confess that I still carry this inferiority complex as a thorn in the flesh underneath my still incorrect speech and humble upbringing. "*Você é muito bobo*" still hurts. But God's grace sustains me!

There was a certain math professor who was very kind to me. He was teaching algebra to the class and wrote with his chalk on the board: X = -1. I was instantly thrilled to know the answer to the variable X. I was so untaught that I believed that the value of X was always going to be -1 in every equation ahead of me. "How great to know that," I thought, appreciating the good of knowing the answer to X. The math professor recognized my error and took me aside to teach me many possible variations in value for the variable X.

This sensitive teacher was careful not to embarrass me. He recognized my desperate need to catch up and delighted in coaching me. After two weeks of practice, I had completed the algebra course. The teacher, although I was auditing, gave me private tutoring at his own home. He invited me to join his other tutoring sessions, and at his home I learned physics, math, and chemistry. When new students came to his courses, he then asked me to teach them what I knew. I practiced first- and second-year algebra equations with new students to bring them up to par. I discovered I was very good at doing this, having learned firsthand what steps were needed to catch up when behind. What better teacher than a remedial student.

At the end of two years, I completed all my courses and passed all the high school government exams except for two—in mathematics and science. The next semester I passed those two exams and became a high school graduate. I was ecstatic with this achievement because in my formative years I had been so ashamed of my lack of education. God had taken away my lack and made me adequate. He met my need to better myself, and He led me into opportunities to study and improve my self-esteem. He is so good! My identity in Him as a messenger of His was strengthened as He continued to lead me down the path He had laid out for me.

CHAPTER 32

DESTINATION ARGENTINA

Sebastião and Gerson were two young men who visited me at the school of theology where I was completing seminary. Sebastião was from Brasília, and Gerson was from São Paulo, and they both had also spent time in the Amazonas during the time I was there. They hoped to return to the Amazon region one day and hoped I would go with them.

These two guys were so great to talk to. They understood what it felt like to have lived in the Amazonas and be changed by the experience. I had recently been wishing I had someone to to talk to about my beloved Povo, Kaúnã's tribe. I told Sebastião and Gerson that I had left the tribe and the Amazon region in the spring of 1972 and had not been back. Now, after two years, I had gotten word from them, all the way from the Amazon rainforest.

"How could that be? How could news from your tribe even get to you, Justino? Did someone come all the way here?" asked Gerson, incredulous.

"Someone took a message from the tribe to the Posto FUNAI," I said. "Then somehow the message made its way to the Wycliffe Institute in Brasília, and Wycliffe made a radio announcement and then sent a letter to me here in Goiânia."

"Incredible. What was the message?" asked Gerson, his eyes wide. "The tribe wants you to come back?"

I nodded, my eyes burning with saudades. I had received the letter several weeks earlier.

"Wow, Kaúnã's very tribe sending word for you to return," said Gerson. "That's communication from another world, isn't it?"

"That must have made your head spin," said Sebastião. "What are you going to do?"

"I've hardly had a chance to think about it."

I explained to them I'd been very busy pastoring my church, earning diplomas from grade school through high school, and getting my seminary degree. I was greatly moved by the contact from the tribe, but I didn't see how I could go. I wasn't sure that's what God wanted me to do.

"Wycliffe has probably sent another missionary by now to work with the tribe anyway," I said.

So much had happened since living in the Amazonas, and it was good to catch up with Gerson and Sebastião. When I last saw them, I didn't really have a church or a church's support, my family was not able to help me, I had no money saved, and I was unemployed. Pastor Medes had said to come to Goiânia anyway and something could be worked out. God had always been working in my life. Now, I wondered if He was doing something new as I visited with Gerson and Sebastião.

"Justino, we've both been thinking about you. It's really not the right time for us to go back to Amazonas, either. We actually came here to ask you to come with us to work in Argentina leading a youth evangelism team under JOCUM (Youth With A Mission) there," said Gerson, Sebastião smiling in agreement.

They told me more of their plans, and I began to contemplate my options, realizing that this invitation had come at an interesting time. I had been working really hard and had completed a great deal in school, and I was approaching the end of my seminary courses. My church had grown from just a handful to seventy-eight people. I thought long and hard about this offer from Sebastião and Gerson to go to Argentina. Yes, it had come at just the right time.

The very next church meeting I told my congregation that I would be leaving and that I had been invited to help lead a missionary team in Argentina. Within a few weeks I would be returning to my life as an adventurer. I was again a missionário voluntário. Of course, this meant I was without a salary again. Some of the more affluent members from the church were happy to support me in a personal way and financed my trip home to Paraná. This gave me a chance to spend some time with my parents and brothers and sisters before joining my colleagues in Argentina.

When I arrived at my parents' town, Assis Chateaubriand, I was welcomed with open arms and a festa. It was attended by not only my family but also many of the members of my father's Presbyterian church. It was a very joyful party intended to commemorate my graduation from seminary, and I was deeply moved by this show of approval and support from my own family and friends. Now that I had essentially grown up, I was better able to appreciate this shower of unexpected respect and affection. They wanted me to stay and work with their church and offered me a job on the spot. I wept! To be valued, even honored, by these friends and family was an emotional experience for me.

But I knew I couldn't accept this offer. My father had surely known since I first came home from the Amazonas that I could not serve as a minister in his church. He had accepted this. I had become too independent as a missionary to be subject to the Presbyterian organization though I had been part of it all my life. I resolved to try to talk to Pai more about our differences, our experiences with God, and my future while I was here in Paraná with the family. I would tell him how I was approaching new crossroads in my life. Hopefully he would understand my view of things and not be disappointed.

That evening I looked for a chance get my father alone. This was never easy with such a big family. Even my married brothers and sisters and their children were here to see me. I saw Pai exit the porch door towards the *campos*, fields, just after sunset. I handed Mamãe a grandbaby and extricated myself from playful *caratê* with my nephews. I hurried after Pai, hoping we could talk before dinner.

Bearing in mind I was unemployed, I prompted myself to tell Pai first thing how I appreciated the offer to work as a pastor in his church. But I'd remind him I couldn't accept. I wanted to tell Pai about the request the tribe had sent to Wycliffe for me to come back to them. That had really stayed on my mind though I did suppose it was saudades, as I was profoundly missing them. I believed I should continue to advance my schooling, but I wanted to do something besides study right now. I was almost certain I would be going to Argentina as a missionary with Sebastião and Gerson. I had never felt so free and yet so pulled in so many directions.

"Good, I hoped you would come out and walk with me, filho," Pai said, hearing me behind him and slowing his pace. My heart beat like I had been running hard. "Justino, I already know you can't be a pastor here in Paraná," he said. "Don't worry about that. I wasn't counting on it. They wanted to ask you, and that made me happy. I am very proud of you."

"*Isso significa muito para mim, Pai.* That means a lot to me, Pai. I really don't like to disappoint you."

These words he spoke to me really steadied me. I was reminded that he had said he was proud of me after my first seven months with the tribe. While tears ran down his cheeks, he had asked me to forgive him for doubting me and not supporting me in the beginning. Now, as I walked with my father in his fields, I felt I could tell him anything and everything that was on my mind. I didn't bring up the differences we had because they didn't seem important at all. As he listened to me, nodding his support, I told him of the opportunities I had in front of me.

"Filho, you have many options, and that is very good. I would remain optimistic if I were you. I'm so glad you are here for a few days. You need some time with your family, first." Then he told me he would pray for God to light the way for me just as he had been praying since I had left home at sixteen.

"Pai, I was seventeen."

"You were a boy. Now you are a man."

That night, I reflected on my Pai and his father, my Avô. They were cultural and religious minorities, pioneers of their lands and communities, and reformers in the practice of their Protestant faith. I had received so much from them on the road they had charted before me. I was twenty-four and so wanted to honor them even as I also struggled to walk my own divergent path with God.

A few days later I had a dream.

I was a soldier. I was in my uniform, wearing boots, a helmet, and a bow and arrow strapped on my back. I was walking in a field toward a mountain ahead of me. I began to climb up the mountain. As I ascended, I saw that there was a rope that extended from the top of the mountain above my head all the way to another mountain. So, I crossed over from one mountain to the other by traveling arm over arm along the rope. When I got to the other mountain, I saw my two colleagues, Gerson and Sebastião. They were in trouble. A huge serpent coiled near them, ready to strike.

"Deixa comigo, que eu sei matar este cobra! Leave this to me—I know how to kill this snake!" I called to them.

The young men waited as I placed an arrow in my bow and took aim. My arrow was right on. The serpent took the fatal shot and collapsed, dead.

I believed the dream was God's confirmation that I was to go to Argentina. I made up my mind to talk to Pai and Mamãe and make the preparations.

Soon, my very first passport was delivered. I said goodbye to my family and left for Argentina by bus. *No meu íntimo*, in my core, was the idea that I should try to find Sebastião and Gerson at Iguaçu Falls. This had not been agreed upon before, but I felt sure I would see them there. The Iguaçu waterfalls are on the border of the state of Paraná, Brazil, and part of the Iguazu River, which borders both Brazil and Argentina at the falls. The Iguazu River flows into Brazil, but the falls are on the Argentine side. It's the largest waterfall system in the world and just three hours away from my parents' town. There was going to be a leadership course given by JCOV (Spanish JOCUM, the extension of YWAM) in Buenos Aires, and I had been invited to attend this course by a letter I had been sent.

I had some spiritual and biblical convictions that were different from the JCOV group, and I hoped this would not cause conflicts in our goals and practices. I was purposely not affiliated with any established churches, and I wanted to continue to worship and serve God as freely as I had for my years in the Amazon forest and pastoring my own congregation in Goiânia.

Even though I recognized the difference between my father and mother's more traditional faith and mine, I was still ignorant of some of the theological forces pushing different perspectives of the faith in the world and in my own country. All I knew was that I was still personally experiencing in my own life that God speaks, heals, liberates, and gives a resurrected life to those who believe and are willing to receive it.

I became a reader to better inform myself about culture and the people around me. In class as a seminary student, I had heard the lecturer refer to the Brazilian novelist and poet Machado de Assis, born in Rio de Janeiro in 1864. I had never read or even heard of his poems or stories. I had no knowledge of romanticism or realism.

I wanted to change this about myself. "A pastor or a missionary should not be ignorant," I thought. Soon after that I saw a young man in the street selling books by Machado de Assis. Delighted that he had eleven books to sell, I bought them all.

In four months, I had read them all. I still have them today. That year I read everything by Machado de Assis, and through this author I was exposed to other classic writers such as Voltaire, Shakespeare, Milton, and

Edgar Allan Poe. This intellectual growth inspired me. I was a man open to ideas and learning. Having this stronger and more confident identity helped me to accept the challenges ahead as my destiny.

Just as I had felt I would, when I arrived at Iguaçu Falls, I encountered Sebastião and Gerson as if it were a divine appointment. I had not been sure it was God's leading, but seeing them affirmed that I was on the right track in timing and in preparation. When it came time to take that course with the JCOV group, I felt competent to express my ideas. I realized I had overcome much of my insecurity. The education God had provided for me enabled me to voice my opinions about how our evangelism team might be formed. JCOV accepted me as a planner and a leader.

Whether in Argentina or in Brazil, I understood that my educational growth was God's intellectual and emotional blessing. Better informed, I was better equipped to find my path among other opportunities that were presented to me. I was asked to work with the Bethania Bible Church of Brazil with Sebastião after he was finished with his seminary training. I ultimately decided to stay and work with JCOV in Argentina until Sebastião finished seminary in Brazil and could join us. Gerson had finished his seminary training and stayed in Argentina with me.

While awaiting Sebastião's return to Argentina, Gerson and I formed two teams. Gerson's team would go to the south while I would take my team to the north. Soon we would meet the young people who would join us, see the places God would show us from north to south, and experience what God had planned for us as witnesses of His love and mercy. We were both full of hope and expectation.

CHAPTER 33

GOD AND GUERILLAS

Our mission target city was Tucumán, the capital of the Province of Tucumán in Argentina, and we were all in agreement that the Holy Spirit was taking us there. We were Glória, Elizabethe, Jorje, Adriana, Lori, and I. From Buenos Aires it was a two-day trip—over twenty hours on the train.

We had been given information about a pastor we were to contact in Tucumán when we arrived there. We soon found the house of the pastor, but he was away, and no one else was home. None of our group knew anyone else in the city. So, we went to a nice little *parque* in the center of the city to inquire of God what He would have us do. It was a wonderful time of prayer. While we prayed together, there was a word that came to my heart: *rioseco*. Also, while we were praying, one of the girls had a vision of the mountains. She described for us how the mountains opened and a river entered between them and then dried up. When she told us about it, we discussed it, but none of us understood what she had seen or what the word that had come to me meant.

Now this was the middle of the day, and we had been traveling for two days. We were very hungry. So, we walked together to a place where we could buy something to eat. There, the first person we talked to was able to tell us where we could find some mountains where the river was dried up. He told us that we must be looking for the town of Rio Seco, Dry River.

"Take the train north about thirty minutes, and you can get off at Rio Seco."

He also warned us that the area was full of guerillas, so we needed to be watchful of violence. Were we alarmed? No, we were elated that God had answered our prayers for direction, and we had no fear of what awaited us. We had asked first, "Lord, where shall we go?" And then we had asked, "Lord, what is 'rioseco'?" Together, we had recognized His guidance.

When we arrived at Rio Seco, we inquired around to locate a church or someone to whom we could talk. There was no known church, but the name of a known *seguidor de Jesus*, follower of Jesus, was given to us: Tio Sousa. We got directions to the house of Tio Sousa and went there. He was not at home, but his wife and daughter invited us in. We were very grateful since the group of us were dead on our feet. Talking with his wife, we came to know a bit more about the dangerous situation there.

The wife of Tio Sousa explained that he had a jeep that he used to drive people up into the mountains as his occupation. Señora Sousa told us the village was surrounded by hills and mountains, and it was a center for the local underground resistance to the repressive new government. We soon learned more accurately that it was the stronghold and hiding place of the current guerrilla movement, which we'd been warned of earlier by the person who directed us to Rio Seco.

These guerrillas were part of a freedom movement seeking democratic reform and social justice. The current regime in Argentina was now led by Jorge Rafael Videla, who had very recently directed a military coup that deposed Isabel Martinez De Perón. Under the new regime, an estimated 15,000–30,000 political dissidents and many of their families would vanish. Kidnappings, thefts, illegal adoptions of babies, torture, mass executions, and concentration camps would all become day-to-day operations for Videla's junta army. The Argentine people's resistance to the dictator was forced to go underground in guerrilla warfare against the government.

We missionaries had arrived in Argentina right after the coup, into a country undergoing revolution. We had a superficial level of awareness that the Argentine government had a history of instability but were unprepared for how unstable and chaotic the situation really was.

At nightfall, Tio Sousa finally came home. Tio and his wife and two children were a simple, humble family. They fed us and made room for the six of us in their house. Their one-room wooden house hardly had enough space for sitting, let alone sleeping. We shared stories with each other about our lives until late in the evening. Then Tio said we would all be sleeping there with his family. The little they had they were willing to share, and six guests, exhausted from travel, were grateful to receive it. Jorje and I slept in the kitchen area, the Sousa family slept on the bed, and the four girls slept on the floor in the front room.

There wasn't a toilet in the house, only a little outhouse outside. It was a hole in the ground. This was roughing it for our team—Glória, Elizabethe, Jorje, Lori, Adriana, and myself. After camping in their tiny sala for a week, Tio found a solution to our cramped living quarters. He knew a family who hosted a house church, and they offered us space in their home.

Our team moved to the house church rather than crowd Tio's family any longer. We would be able to do our outreach into the neighborhood around the church and have a local place to meet and pray and introduce people to the love of Christ. We told Tio that we would lead services in the evenings and take care of his ministry tasks while we were there since there were six of us. Tio Sousa said he was happy for the ministry help, and his invitation to have us stay seemed to be respected by the local villagers.

"*Ustedes foram embiados por Dios.* You were sent by God," he said. "We have few believers in this city. My wife and I worship together with our children, and we invite others, but we are actually the only regular members of our church." Our team was happy to know we were in a place where God was at work.

There was a young woman Tio knew who had been injured in the recent bombing of a train. Two of the guerrillas who had attacked the train had escaped, and this injured woman from Rio Seco was actually one of them. Tio Sousa apparently knew this when he took us to pray with her. Many people had been injured in that explosion, and so this female guerrilla had been able to blend in with all the injured at the hospital. Since she was the daughter of someone known in Rio Seco, it was assumed she was just a passenger on the train recovering from her injuries, not a guerrilla fighter. While we were walking near the hospital, we saw her mother.

"My daughter is very bad," she told us. She knew that her daughter was a dissident and had been the cause of her own injury and many others, but she also wanted us to visit her and pray for her. These things shocked us. But we were not there to take a side in the war. We went to her bedside and prayed for her and tried to comfort her.

There at the hospital we learned that this female soldier was part of the freedom movement for Argentina. Her grave injuries revealed her dangerous life. Because of her commitment and sacrifice for this cause, she had seen and taken part in some horrific acts of war. We told her that if she cared about freedom, she needed to be free herself before she could free anyone else. We told her of the freedom from the prison of guilt and death that the Lord Jesus offers and of His love for her. We told her she could have freedom and forgiveness for the sins she had committed in a cause that could not bring peace or power or change like Jesus brings. She was the first person who believed in Jesus during our time in Rio Seco. She was the beginning for us. After she accepted Jesus, she urged us to meet with other fighters in her group.

I went with Jorje and Adriana to see the soldier's companions up in the mountains, but we were not well received. We didn't go back after this, not surprised at their hostility and mistrust of us. They had just lost a brave soldier from their group to another cause, the cause of Jesus Christ. The girl's family, though, was grateful that their daughter had become a believer in Jesus. This would take her out of the war, at least for now. Just a couple weeks later, a relative of their family was killed fighting for freedom in the same guerrilla warfare. It seemed there was violence everywhere around us.

This consistent support from Tio gave us a foot in the door of local villagers. Whenever we invited them, the people came. Jorje and I preached most of the time, and Lori and Adriana were good teachers. Elizabethe knew the Bible very well and could also preach. I, as the coordinator or facilitator of the missionary team, did whatever they needed me to do. They were teenagers, and I was twenty-four.

After a couple of weeks, the pastor we were looking for in Tucumán had arrived home from his trip, and he invited us to come to his city to work with him. So, we moved to work in the city of Tucumán, doing the same sorts of ministry there as we had in Rio Seco. One day in Tucumán, Jorje, Adriana, and I went to the post office to send out our mail. While we were in the building, we saw a group of men with guns on the street passing by. Suddenly, the guns were pointing our way, and a roar of machine gun bullets shattered the glass on the building front. Three people in line with us were shot down and killed right in front of us. By instinct, everyone went down with them. Blood was everywhere. As we picked ourselves up from the floor, we were amazed that the three of us were unharmed.

Though we were not hurt, we were deeply traumatized. I wanted to leave the country. I didn't want to expose my team to the dangers of ministry in a land of violence and death. In this case, the attack on the post office, a federal building, was a blatant anti-government protest. We were there as representatives of a government, a kingdom that was of a different realm. Where we stood, we tried to keep ourselves from value judgments against anyone. Being Brazilian, we respected our police state and recognized the security in a stable government that represented law and order to us. But we kept ourselves from political leanings in Argentina.

We discussed our options as a team. We believed as a team that God had brought us there. He had spoken to each of us separately as well as together. Our group decision was to stay for the time being under God's protection and not seek our personal security in any government. Except for Adriana, we stayed for another three months. At her parents' request, Adriana returned to Buenos Aires to study. Her parents said it was not because of the revolution.

After the post office shooting, we received a letter from a Pastor Garcia inviting us to his village in the far north, close to the border of Bolivia. We considered this an action of God's Spirit and accepted the invitation to move farther north in the province of Tucumán and began work with Pastor Garcia. We stayed at his home, which gave us space and comfort for our team. There were five of us now that Adriana had gone home to school. This pastor's Baptist church had existed for over thirty-five years and yet did not have more than thirty members. There didn't seem to be a good reason for this since it was well situated near a crowded residential area.

Our team of five prayed together for Pastor Garcia's neighborhood, and then we walked together praying for salvation and new life with Jesus for each household, *casa por casa*, house by house. In sixty days, we were thrilled with forty-two new people in the church. These people were brought by God's hand reaching out to everyone.

Working with Pastor Garcia's church was a very good experience for me. It was very traditional when we arrived. And when they saw that we were different in our approach—more expectant of God and more expressive in our worship—they were a little annoyed with us. At first, Pastor Garcia was even reluctant to let me preach. He thought we were too "Pentecostal" and that we would drive off his flock. I told him I didn't have a Pentecostal background; I was just not as traditional as he was used to.

"Well, what are you planning to preach on?" he asked me. He didn't want any surprises.

"I would like to preach on Isaiah 53, on Jesus the suffering servant."

Pastor Garcia thought that would be okay, and he agreed to let me preach. I was to preach at the church the following Sunday night, and many people were coming to hear me.

I prepared well for my sermon—a prophecy of Jesus' suffering when He comes to free us from sin and death and take our suffering upon Himself.

But it was our sins...that ripped and tore and crushed him—our sins! He took the punishment, and that made us whole. Through his bruises we get healed. -ISAIAH 53 (MSG)

I felt full of fervor and passion for that night. I really wanted to be bold for the Lord and in the strength of His might, not my own. I felt I was where He had put me, in that suffering, war-torn country.

That evening I was preaching my sermon, and all seemed to be going well. I suddenly saw what appeared to be a stream of fire reach out from the pulpit to a woman in the congregation. I will never forget it. I had never seen anything like this before. The woman cried out in what seemed to be pain. I stopped my preaching and spoke to her.

"Señora," I said, "*Está bien?* Are you okay? Can you come here to me?"

She came to me, and I asked her to tell me what happened. The woman began to cry. She said that she had felt a burning, and she loosened her blouse from her skirt to show a place of redness on her back. She had felt the fire come from the pulpit to her abdomen and out through her back. She explained that she was scheduled to have kidney surgery the following week. Her husband stood near her in shock.

Later we were told that her husband was the previous pastor of the congregation. His wife was scheduled to have surgery to resolve her kidney problem and to possibly even remove her kidney. It was soon revealed that she did not need the surgery they were planning after all. Her bloodwork showed that her kidney problem was already resolved. The woman was healed during the worship just as if she had received a new kidney. She had received *a cura*, the cure, that evening from Jesus himself! It was thrilling for all of us there. It was the first miracle that we experienced in our seventy days with the little church.

We felt God's presence in a very profound way. Pastor Garcia said he felt that his church had caught on fire too. He said God had used our little group to change their perspective and their way of life. He wrote those thoughts in a Bible that he gave to me, which I keep with thanksgiving for the revival that came to us and to Igreja de San Salvador del Jujuy, Tucumán.

So much happened at that little church that word got around. My colleague Gerson, who had taken his team to the south of Argentina, later met me for a talk in Buenos Aires. He pulled me aside with a somber face.

"Justino, I've been wanting to talk to you. I've been concerned about you. I've heard different things about the church you are working with up in the north—about healings and demons being cast out and things like this."

"Gerson, if this is something I was doing, you might have reason to be concerned," I answered. "But you don't need to worry. I'm not worried. This is not something that I am doing. It is what God is doing. When God is doing something, we have nothing to worry about."

"Well, be careful, Justino," warned Gerson, shaking his head. "Be careful of what you are getting into. Do you understand?"

"Be careful of what? Be careful of God?" I replied. "I have learned to be careful to follow God."

I knew Gerson's intentions were honest and kind. But this was something he didn't understand because he had not been a witness to God's recent marvelous works among us. I shrugged my shoulders and let his comments go without protesting. I was learning a lot, myself. I was an eyewitness to what the Lord was doing, but it was really too *increível*, incredible, for me to explain. I had seen God's miracles, but I was no less amazed by what God did. I was as surprised and speechless as anyone. But I didn't feel I needed to defend it. This wasn't what I was used to, either. But there was just no going back to "business as usual." I was seeing and learning and expecting more now. I understood Gerson's apprehension, but I wouldn't be able to make his questions or concerns go away.

"Since it is God who is doing this, I will move with Him. I will keep going with His leading," I said.

How could I stop what God was doing? I knew that if my ministry got me into trouble, it would be the kind of trouble that God intended to take me through. He would take care of us. Gerson is still my very dear friend today and serves the Lord in Miami, Florida.

For the Iglesia de San Salvador de Jujuy there had been more growth in the past two months than there had been in thirty years. No wonder word had gotten around about that little church. There were about thirty people when we arrived and more than eighty when we left. It was a blessing being there, a marvelous growing experience for all of us. And it was a place of peace and healing right in the middle of an area of fear and violence.

CHAPTER 34

DESPONDENT DAUGHTERS

It was soon after my talk with Gerson that our team met Luite Lemos in Santiago del Estero, which is the capital of a province in northern Argentina. He helped pastor a church there. Spending time in Luite's home and at his church, we got to know his family. Luite had a beautiful teenage daughter who seemed depressed. She had been fighting with her mother and father and had been disillusioned with life for some time, and this was no secret at home or at work. She worked with her parents in their family business, which was a local department store franchise.

One day I sat down to talk to the young lady while I was visiting their home. When I asked her if I could pray with her, she said yes. During the prayer, she opened her heart up to Jesus. She asked God for forgiveness for her sins. That very day she received new life—a new life with Jesus Christ. She had a change of heart about everything in her life. Right away, she went to her father's store and told him that she felt happy and close to God. There was another lady at Luite's store who heard about this and said that her own daughter was very rebellious and certainly unhappy too. She wondered if, like Luite's daughter, I could pray and ask God for help for her daughter. Luite promised the woman he would bring me to her house.

Luite came and picked me up by car and took me to this woman's home to pray with her daughter. When we walked in, I was amazed at the lovely furnishings and décor of this very beautiful home. That first visit, the woman's daughter wasn't even home. So, they arranged for me to come again another time when I could talk with the daughter. The parents were separated, and her father lived in a hotel.

When I visited this young lady, she was also responsive to God's love. In the same way as Luite's daughter, she accepted Jesus as King over her life, and her life was changed. After her father learned that I had something to do with the transformation of his daughter, he wanted to meet me. He came to see me. I was surprised by the demeanor of importance he carried.

"Are you Justino?" he boomed.

"Yes, Señor. I'm Justino."

"It was you who was in the house of Luite Lemos?"

"Yes, Señor. That was me," I said respectfully.

"Was that you who prayed with Felina?" continued the man.

"Your daughter, Felina? Yes, that was me who prayed with her."

"Then, you are the one who changed the life of my daughter?"

"No, Señor. That was not me."

"You said you prayed for her!" he interrupted.

"Señor, I prayed with her, but it was not me, but Jesus, who changed her life. I cannot change anyone's life."

"Yes, well, you were the one who prayed for her. And her life is suddenly different. She is very well now. And I want to thank you in a special way for what you did for her and for all of us by changing her life."

"Señor, it was not I who changed her life. It was the Lord Jesus Christ. Please understand that it is God who did this work, not me."

"Yes, yes. I know what you are saying, but we are so happy that our daughter is well again. I want to do something to thank you, and I have thought of something that would help you. I will introduce you here."

"What do you mean, sir?"

"Listen, I own some shops, the radio station, and the television station here. I'll take you down to one of my shops and dress you with class. You will look very sharp in a fine new suit. Then we will put you on the radio and the television to talk about Jesus."

"Sir, I don't need any of this."

"Don't you see, you could make a lot of money with these gifts that you have from God. You could be famous."

"No, no thank you, Señor!" I protested.

"Why not? Then what do you want?"

"Señor, I want to stay like I am. You have already made me very happy with the news of your daughter. I don't want fame. I don't want money. I don't need any of this, and I thank you for your kind offer. I want to stay with my Lord Jesus, just as I am."

The wealthy businessman left, unsatisfied, to go see Luite Lemos. Soon after that I got a call from Luite. Luite Lemos tried to convince me to accept the radio and television offer, saying that I would not be the only beneficiary, but Luite himself would also be a participant, as my manager. This could help not only his family business but also many people. I felt bad. They were not able to understand how easy this proposal was to turn down.

"I'm sorry, Luite. This doesn't attract me in any way. I appreciate your kindness, but it is not what I want for my life. And what is more important—this is not what God has called me to do here. I am certain that this is not what God wants for me."

"We can buy you a car, Justino. I can be your driver."

"No, Luite. You see, it's not up to me, anyway. It's up to God. He decides my life."

The phone calls continued along the same lines from Luite and Felina's father.

"Justino, let me take you down to my store and pick out some nice new clothes for you."

The offers never stopped until our team moved to another city.

CHAPTER 35

A DREAM DEFERRED

I n those months in Argentina, we traveled from Buenos Aires to
Cordoba through many beautiful mountain cities of the north. The
view of the countryside was breathtaking. The missionary work had
been thrilling and challenging. I saw snow fall to the ground for the first
time in my life and felt blessed to see it!

I was in a great state of joy at this time. I was especially excited about
my plans to go to Philadelphia and celebrate the United States
Bicentennial on July 4, 1976. I was to travel together with other invited
members of JOCUM, the international youth for Christ mission group I
was a part of. Step by step, every detail had been arranged, I believed, by
obvious interventions of God, who was bringing to fruition His plans for
me. In the province of La Cordoba, Argentina, I preached in a little
church about how the Lord had blessed me in organizing everything
about this journey ahead.

After the service, a family took us by van through a scenic, curvy
mountain region into the town of La Falda. We finally arrived at a place to
stay arranged for us by *Irmão*, Brother, Plata. This picturesque lodge was
divided into *chaléts*, rustic mountain cabins. Jorje and I were to share a
room. Jorje went to help the girls carry their bags to their rooms while I
took ours to our room. When I opened the door of our room, *Deus estava
lá*. God was there. It was as if there were a curtain, or veil, and He was
there just behind it.

Within me, He said, "*Você não está falando verdade.* You have not been speaking the truth. *Você está se mentindo.* You are deceiving yourself."

"*Como assim, Senhor?* What do you mean, Lord?"

I had just given my testimony that God had blessed me with the opportunity to go to the United States. In my own possession I had the travel documents, the airline tickets, a letter of invitation to a conference in the United States, and even an invitation to attend a special 1976 Bicentennial Celebration event. I had given all credit to God. I had claimed that all of this had come to me as a gift of God. I had understood this to be different from the generous gifts offered by Luite's friend. I had never doubted that this trip was God's provision and His plan.

"*Você não vai.* You are not going."

This was what God told me. I was incredulous.

"*O que está dizendo, Senhor?* What are you saying, Lord? I am ready to go. I have the airline ticket, I have the visa, I have the money for the trip, I have the invitation from the mission. JOCUM invited me to go with them. How can I not be going?"

"You didn't ask if this is my will for you, if this is my direction for your life. *Isso não é minha vontade para você.* This is not my will for you."

"But Lord, you let me receive the invitation to go and directed every *passo*, footstep, after that. I thought you gave me all of these things—the vision, the money, the airfare. Everything came from you."

"*Isso não é minha vontade para você.* This is not my will for you."

My mind held tightly to visions of La Falda, Valle Hermosa, Huerta Grande, the beautiful places where we had traveled before preparing to leave the country. The snow that we saw for the first time in our lives felt to all of us like an affirmation from heaven. Having been personally invited by JOCUM of Argentina to go to Montreal in 1976, I was also greatly looking forward to stopping first in Philadelphia to see the commemorations of the 200th birthday of the United States of America. From there we were to go on to Quebec and Montreal in Canada. I was ready and lacking nothing, not even money! I had my passport, visa, and even American dollars to spend. I kept going over it in my head. The airline tickets were bought, and I was staying tonight near where I was soon to fly out to North America.

I struggled to believe otherwise, but God's voice had clearly said to me, "You are not going to the United States or Canada."

Even as I pleaded, God made me to understand within me that it was not *His* will and that I simply was not going. I was very disappointed and angry. I argued and grieved over this, but I perceived without a doubt that God was saying no to my plans. My trip to the United States and Canada did not fit His plan for me, and so now I had to cancel my trip. I was not going.

CHAPTER 36

THE GIFT OF LITEMAR

The experience with God's inner voice in that room in La Falda, Cordoba, continued to come back to me until I had changed all my plans. I was to return to Brazil, be reunited with my parents, and go back to school. God was steering me in another direction. His plan was clearly not the fulfillment of my *sonho*, dream, to go to the United States.

That night I didn't sleep. I just couldn't believe it. How had everything come to me so perfectly? How could I not interpret those open doors as God's will for me? It was so hard to open my hand and let it go like this was nothing. The state of my life had, in every way, appeared to be God's plan for me, the way every detail had been worked out and everything was seeming to come together. I had never been more certain that I was right in the center of God's will. How could I have thought otherwise? How could all this have come to me without God's intervention?

I had believed that this trip was a culmination of God's restoring and remaking me. Me—a penniless farm boy with a fourth-grade education, redeemed, called and sent to an Amazonian tribe, given seminary training, given a church to pastor, given a private education all the way from grade school through high school, then given the leadership of a missionary team to Argentina. It seemed just part of my journey with Jesus to be invited by JOCUM, to be given this amazing trip to participate in the bicentennial celebration in Philadelphia.

Pastors and missionaries working with JOCUM and YWAM were coming together at a worldwide meeting of *jovens*, youth, for Christ, and I had been *included* in their number. This was something the rich, the famous, or the educated might be able to do, but not *me*. How I struggled with letting go of that happy ending! I had believed that this trip was the icing on the cake of how God was using my weakness, my deficiency, and my roots of poverty to teach me about His strength and blessing in my life. I had proclaimed my realization of this blessing and this truth in my testimonies. And now I found that this wasn't even true! How could I have gotten so far off course? I didn't plan this trip. It had simply fallen into my lap! *E, eu queria tanto ir!* And, I so badly wanted to go!

Hector, the man who had invited me, was the director of JOCUM in Argentina. The next day I wrote a letter to Hector to explain that he should take all the documents out of my name and present them to another person. I was not able to go after all. Hector was as surprised as I was and called me at the La Falda lodge asking why I had canceled.

"I don't understand!" Hector had replied.

"I guess it's not for us to understand God, but to hear Him and obey Him," I responded numbly, still stunned, myself. It was scarcely sinking in that it wasn't God's will for me to go. I didn't understand how I had misread my own will for His.

On my way out of Cordoba, I made a stop in Buenos Aires at the home of teammate Adriana. She was *tão bonita, inteligente*, so pretty, smart, and I had wondered at times if she may have felt attracted to me as I was to her. We were not permitted to *namorar*, to pursue romantic relationships, while in missionary service, and both of us had been true to this discipline. We talked and enjoyed a nice weekend together with her parents. At the end, we mutually agreed we didn't share the same goals for the future. After all, she was enrolled in school in Argentina, and I was leaving. It was good to have some closure between us; it was not my way to leave anything unresolved. But my heart was heavy with loss. We said a fond goodbye, and I never saw or heard from her again.

Right after my return to Brazil, I saw my friend Litemar from Goiânia. He wanted to study for the Vestibular, which is the test that gives you the opportunity to attend university in Brazil. Few passed this test without private instruction, and Litemar wanted to have someone to study with him for practical and moral support.

"Justino, I really want to go to college, but I can't do it alone. I have a proposal. You do this with me! I'll give you everything you need to study for the three-month prep course and the exam."

Litemar was the young medic who had arranged for the IV treatments that had sustained me during my many months with malaria. I already owed so much to him, but he was very persistent. I agreed. I wanted to study too.

I was to return to Brazil, be reunited with my parents, and go back to school. How I hoped this offer from Litemar was to be God's will. It appeared to be. I was wary that it was too good to be true. Since I wanted it so much, maybe it was off the table. Litemar had a little room at the back of his house where I could stay, and we would begin our three-month course together. Another friend, Vilmar, got me a job at a *loja de parafuso*, which makes me laugh now. This is a parts store where you can buy all kinds of fuses. I was of little help to them, but they hired me, incredibly, and even paid me.

October, November, December passed by, and Litemar and I had completed our course of study. Exam week arrived—the week of the Vestibular. The college entrance exam was upon us. This was a big deal. This college entrance exam impacted young people for the rest of their lives. They needed to remove every complication in their lives and buckle down and study for these brutal *exames*. They did this knowing few of their number would be selected. We registered and received our exam times.

I had recently moved to the house of another friend, Augustinho, and his wife Terezinha. Their house was at the other end of the city, a long way away from the testing site. Since I had no car, there was potentially going to be some difficulty in getting across the city to the exam. There were three days of exames—Friday night, Saturday night, and Sunday morning. Litemar and I were booked to test together. In fact, the first exam night I saw him sitting in the seat right in front of mine.

After Saturday's exam, I told Litemar I was planning to attend an all-night prayer vigil at Agripina's house that night.

"Should I pick you up there?"

"No," I assured him. "I'll just stay there and take the bus from Agripina's. See you in the morning."

I did sleep a little while on a couch after the vigil ended, in my clothes, at the house where the prayer meeting was held. Agripina awakened me to let me know it was 5:30 a.m. I hurried out just before daybreak to wait for a bus. When I tried to get on the bus, I found I didn't have any money in my pocket! My bus money must have fallen out at Agripina's house. I ran back to look for it, but the front gate had locked behind me so I couldn't knock on the door to rouse Agripina. All the family were probably asleep, not having slept all night with the vigil at their home. I would have to make my way by foot.

Mortified, I shot out at a fast trot. Terrified I would miss the exam, I stepped up into a higher gear. It was a five-kilometer distance, but I ran all the way! Arriving absolutely drenched and gasping for air, I reached the testing site gate just before it was shut and locked. I slid into my seat, seconds before the exam began.

"*O que foi! Que passou?* What happened! Where were you?" came Litemar's shouted whisper.

"*Tranquilo. Relaxe.* Everything's cool. Relax," I choked out, in honest relief.

We took the all-day test and went out to dinner. Then two weeks later, the results of the one hundred of us who tested were sent to the newspapers and local media. Litemar bought a newspaper with the scores and called me.

"*Justino, está sabendo as noticias? Você passou!* Have you heard the news? You passed! Yeah, you're number 42."

"I passed? You're kidding! What about you?"

"I didn't pass."

"You've got to be joking! You didn't pass?"

"*Não!*"

This was a heavy blow for Litemar, but it was no shame. Neither of us really expected to pass the first time around. In those days, hardly anyone did. The Vestibular in Brazil was very difficult and very competitive. There were only so many seats at university and many hundreds who tried for them.

After that, the day arrived to register for college classes. Litemar called me up to

remind me. "*Justino, hoje é dia de matrícula!* Justino, today is registration day!" I didn't have a good job. I had barely enough money to live on, much less pay for books, materials, and college living expenses. I explained to Litemar that I couldn't register yet. I just wouldn't be attending that semester. I needed to work full-time.

"*Não, Justino. Eu vou pagar.* I will pay for you. You are going. You will work at my office. I'll give you bus money and help you with food and rent. I already planned to pay for college and books for you."

This was a private college—expensive. This was so much to take from anyone. I knew that God's provision is more than we can ask or imagine, but I already owed my life to Litemar. He insisted. He would not receive a *no* answer from me. Litemar's generosity sent me to *faculdade*, college, in 1977 to pursue a degree in law.

CHAPTER 37

WRESTLING WITH GOD

The Vestibular was a community event: the yearly college entrance exams were on everyone's minds. It was a time of gathering for prayer for the students preparing for the exams, for those who passed them, and for the stress and challenge ahead of *universidade*, university. This was the reason I went to the all-night prayer meeting on that Saturday night when I lost my bus money and almost missed my last exam. And, it was there at that prayer vigil that I met Janete.

As I began to see more of Janete, I discovered she was a very accomplished musician. She played violin, accordion, guitar, and piano. She sang too. She and her two sisters, Jane and Giudete, had pooled their talents and created a performing musical group. Soon I was being invited to their family midday meal and became enchanted with the whole family. This was community like I had never known in my own family. Janete and I began to namorar. In time, I believed that she must be the one God had intended for me when he brought me home from Argentina to Brazil.

It was 1977 when I became good friends with a married couple, Pastor Sinomar de Silveira and his wife Elizabethe, a manager of the Banco de Bradesco. Sinomar talked to me about his church, Cristã Evangélica, where he had been pastoring for ten years. Sinomar, as a young pastor of thirty, wanted to focus on reaching his youth. We shared ideas with each other, as he and I had studied under the same professor in seminary. When Sinomar suggested we work together to grow his church, I gladly accepted the opportunity. On Saturdays and Sundays, I worked at Cristã Evangélica, and during the weekdays, I worked at Litemar's office. I attended my classes and studied at night.

On Friday nights, Sinomar and I took all the youth to a vacant gathering place outside the city called Setor Balneário Meia Ponte to pray until morning. Every Friday we prayed through the night for the redemption of souls, for intervention in the lives of the jovens, for Christ's direction and guidance, for healing, and for inner growth. Right away the church began to grow phenomenally. It was clear God was responding to the prayers and faith of these young people. This inspired the whole church to even greater faith. The youth group turned into a *multidão* of young servants of Christ. In 1979 we built a building for five hundred church members. *Maravilha!* It was tremendous!

We felt we were part of a supernatural movement that was reaching youth for Christ and seeing the history of Cristã Evangélica completely transformed. It was an inspiring time for Janete and me as we worked as partners in this ministry. We began to see ourselves as partners in life too. We decided to marry, and she wore the engagement ring I had given her. Soon we were happily choosing furniture for our first home.

I have to say, if it is not already clear, that in that *época*, era, of my life, I was an intensely serious man. All my difficult and life-changing experiences had probably made me too intense. After returning to Brazil, I should have begun to take myself less seriously and maintained a broader outlook. Maybe it was the constant studying. Maybe I was missing my old life of excitement and adventure. But in those days, I became even more single-minded, decisive, unwavering, and very introspective. I was rather grave, actually. But I was *fiel a Deus, firme com Deus*, resolute and loyal to God. I assumed Janete appreciated my serious nature, as I did her more sanguine approach to life. Janete and I had planned our wedding for January 1978, and it was already November. Only God in heaven could change my mind about those wedding plans.

I had gotten home late from a night class. By the time I was finished studying, it was almost midnight. When I entered my room, I was reminded of when God spoke to my heart in La Falda, Argentina, abruptly changing the course of my life by telling me that I was to return to Brazil rather than go to the United States. Just as in La Falda, God's voice came to me that night in my room.

As I entered my room, I knew with clarity that it was God. It was as if

I heard His voice, but it was inside me. I can still see my twin bed by the wall, a curtain, a little table and chair, a small stove in my simple quarters. I was arrested from my thoughts of school and my course work and my wedding plans by this divine visit deep within my heart. Like last time, it was as if He spoke from behind the curtain, where my eyes looked. But He spoke within me.

"*Janete não é a mulher que vai se casar.* Janete isn't the woman you will marry. This marriage is not my plan for your life."

Oh no, not again! How do I quiet my thoughts when I know God hears them? I was in turmoil again. The very thing that was everything to me was being blocked from my path. How could my God deprive me of the wife I had chosen, whom He had put on my path? But I knew I had to obey God in whatever He was saying and whatever He was doing! "Pay attention, Justino," I said to myself. My first concern was how to tell her parents. I thought of their disappointment, knowing how parents regarded themselves as protectors of their daughters. I understood this would greatly disappoint them, and it felt more than uncomfortable to consider telling them.

"Meu Deus, I understand you, and I am ready to obey—but I don't know how to speak to Dona Iracema and Senhor Francisco! ... And Lord, I don't know how to break up with Janete."

I continued on in openness before the Lord, knowing that I could not stray from His will but struggling as He made His intentions for me perfectly clear. I did not know how to do this. It was something so far from who I was: set in my ways.

"*Não sei como cancelar isso.* How do I abandon this commitment to her and her family? I don't have it in me to do it. I don't know how to call this off."

I understood that I must trust God's will rather than my own. The fact that His will was so crystal clear did not help me to obey it. I pleaded with God to accomplish His will on my behalf.

"Lord, I don't want to disobey you, but things have gone too far for me to do this. I have made so many commitments that have brought us to this point."

I carried on during the next two weeks in stunned disbelief. Everything looked the same, but all had changed, and still nothing happened. Then God's presence and word came again in the same way, in the same place in my room.

"*Justino, você deve cancelar esses planos que você fez.* You must break these plans that you have made, Justino."

This was unthinkable for me. How could I present my face to Janete's family and tell them, *em nome de Deus,* in the name of God, I was breaking off the marriage plans? I wrestled with God's direction, not knowing how to obey God and obey my conscience. How could the two be opposed? I believed God's command to be right, but I didn't have the strength to carry it out. It seemed impossible to follow my conscience and disobey God. I couldn't navigate this sea of conflict in my soul. I acknowledged my helplessness before God to do His will with my own efforts. I cried out in my mind to God.

"Please, Lord, out of obedience to you, I ask you to bring about your will in my life and Janete's. I ask you to create the conditions to end this relationship with Janete and her family and to cancel the wedding plans. This is the only way I know how to obey you. You know how I feel about her. You know how I want to obey your will rather than my own—but cannot. Your will over mine. I submit my life to you completely. Please take this love and this commitment toward Janete from me and do what your will is for me."

After that, I hoped I was in a state of surrender that would satisfy God's command. I had tried to change my heart and mind and will to obey Him. Another week passed. I hadn't gone to Janete's house to see her. I had been very busy with schoolwork as it was November and near the semester's end. Another few days passed, and I got an early morning call from Janete's sister, Jane, who lived in Goiânia.

"*Justino, venha almoçar comigo.* Come have lunch with me."

In Brazil, generally almoço, taken at midday, is the most substantial meal of the day. We don't really have a "bite to eat" for lunch in Brazil. A sandwich isn't lunch; it's a snack. Jane was inviting me to come to dinner, but at the lunch hour.

"Jane, I would like to come, but today I can't. I am swamped here at work, and I have class tonight."

Janete's sister knew that it would take me some time to get to her house by bus and then back again during my midday break from work.

"*É urgente.* It's urgent. You'd better get a taxi, Justino. I need to speak with you right away."

I sensed something was happening that God had engineered, and so I took a taxi to Jane's house. My mind raced with doubts that God would make this easier than if I did it myself. Did they hear something or suspect me? I felt both hope and dread. As soon as I arrived and she let me in the door, she started to cry.

"I feel so embarrassed and so ashamed to talk to you about this, Justino. I don't know how to tell you."

"What is it, Jane?" I asked.

"*Vamos almoçar*. Let's eat now," she said, grabbing a tissue as she set about putting the meal on the table. "I don't know how to tell you, but I will not hide anything from you," she added.

Jane's husband and children arrived from work and school, and we all sat down to luncheon. After the family had eaten and left, Jane told me what she had to say.

"Janete has met someone! She went out with him on Saturday night. She really likes this *cara*, guy. I just can't believe it. I can't believe she would do this to you or to all of us. I can't understand it."

Jane was shaking her head. She was dumbfounded. I very much wanted to help her, but I was speechless.

"Justino, truthfully, she is completely *in love* with this man."

She left no questions in the air.

"I feel so bad telling you this, but it's true. I'm so sorry, so embarrassed, but I thought you should know."

"Jane, *não se preocupe*, don't worry. *Deus está neste negócio.* God is in this. He is working this out, taking care of this. He is in control. I am okay. I will be fine. I know that God is in this."

I went back to work full of shock, pain, loss, relief, comfort, peace. I loved this whole family, and they loved me.

"*Obrigado, meu Deus, meu Pai.* Thank you, my God, my Father. You are taking care of my life. You know I want your will, not mine. Thank you, Father."

My eyes filled with tears. He would let me feel this betrayal rather than them, and He would sustain me.

That night I had class and study. The next week I had college exams. I was very stressed, but God surely sustained me. It wasn't over yet, but I knew that He was taking care of all of us. Every Saturday all the family got together for a midday dinner. I was always invited, and this time I knew I shouldn't miss. I had had no contact with Janete, and I was nervous about seeing her.

I picked up Janete and took her to her parents' house, where we all had luncheon together with the rest of the family. Everything seemed normal but surreal to me. Then I took her home and went to a class. Then I picked up Janete for church that Saturday night, as was our custom. Nothing was ever mentioned regarding our relationship, and I was resolved not to bring it up.

Another week passed, and Jane invited me to luncheon again. I went to her house, and it was the same story.

"I hoped that this would pass and everything would work out, Justino. But Janete and this young man have been seeing each other often. It's really getting serious. I don't understand why she hasn't talked to you. I feel so very bad for you, Justino. And I feel for her too."

I was able to rest more easily in God's care at this point. I was firmer, more at peace.

"Jane, God is taking care of everything. He is at work, and He is in control of our lives. Don't worry. He is taking care of me. You can count on it."

I did my best to reassure her, but there was so much that I felt I should not say, yet. I had chosen to leave it up to God, hadn't I? The next Saturday, I was back having the usual meal with the entire family at Janete's parents' house once again. All at once, my heart began to pound in my ears. It didn't seem right and honest to keep quiet any longer. So, I addressed Janete's parents together at the table when everyone was sitting down.

"I have discovered that Janete has been seeing someone else and cares for him," I blurted out quickly, steadied by this reality expressed, finally.

"*O que?* What??" All eyes at the table gazed at Janete, except her parents. They were too shocked to believe it. They only looked at me, questioning, until Janete began to weep. I continued speaking.

"I'm so sorry you weren't aware. But I wanted you to know why this is the last time I will share this meal with you as part of the family. I wanted to say goodbye and tell you how much I care for all of you and thank you for all that you have done for me. I want Janete to know that I think she is a wonderful girl, an incredible person, and that while my feelings are tender, they are not bitter. I truly believe that all that has happened recently has been God's will for both of us. And God will continue to bring about His will in all of our lives. I will always remember the love I received from your family and how you made me feel like I belonged."

I asked Janete for my engagement ring, which she still had on her finger. She took it off, sobbing, and gave it to me. We finally were able to look at each other.

"Can you ever forgive me?" she asked. *"Eu sinto muito. Você não mereceu isso.* I am so very sorry. You didn't deserve this. You were so good to me, Justino."

She asked the pardon of her parents and sisters. "I am so ashamed of myself," she said.

I knew that things were going on in her heart that she didn't know how to explain. She had added so much to my life in the past two years. Surprisingly, I realized I held nothing against her and felt only fondness and compassion for her. I wondered why I didn't tell her that. That would have been a more compassionate way. We should have had a talk together many days ago, but I was too stubborn. And hurt.

I went home grieved for the loss of the future I thought *we* had planned and frustrated with the burden of disassembling it financially as well as emotionally. How I would miss them all, having joined their lives with mine. What should I do with the furniture she had chosen for the home we would live in? We had a bed, table, couch, many things that she had chosen—each item representing an aching memory. I had even bought a piano for Janete. She seemed so happy with it. But she was not happy with me, I guess. Our wedding was a month away.

Janete suffered too. The opinion of many church members turned against her. I never wanted her to be hurt. But the entire youth group was upset with her and ostracized her for her betrayal. I wanted people to understand, but there was so much that could not be explained. Words are volatile, misleading, misunderstood, or repeated wrong. All explanations are suspect. How impossible it is at times to explain the hand of God. The what and why He does or doesn't do is mystifying. We just had to let God carry us through. And He did.

CHAPTER 38

TEREZINHA'S HEART

Augustinho and Terezinha became like family to me during this time of my life. By trade, Augustinho was a painter of houses. Terezinha was the *zeladora* of the church, and this meant that she was the housekeeper and janitor. She cleaned the church, inside and out, and even did some gardening. The couple had four children, two girls and two boys, and lived in a little house next to the church. Terezinha also prepared food for pastors and leaders of the church. Now that I was no longer taking meals with Janete's family, I was back to eating her lunch at the church.

Working through my heartbreak over Janete was a bitter process, and I didn't want to brood in public. I felt God had taken from me things that were very precious, and I was counting them up. Not only was there the loss of Janete and our life together but also the loss of her family. I sort of disappeared in my misery and solitude and found myself so depressed and dehydrated that I needed to go to the hospital. There it was decided I should stay for testing, and I was *internado*, admitted. The attending doctor wanted to make sure I had not had another attack of malaria. I was found to be completely clear of malaria. "Even pastors and missionaries need to take care of their minds and bodies," the nurse said with the pursed lips of a mother. I was kept for a few days of rest and consultation about self-care and the effects of stress.

Augustinho and Terezinha had moved their family from the little house on the church grounds to a larger home, which had an extra bedroom to rent. I agreed to rent the room from them, and Terezinha happily took care of me along with all the family. It was Terezinha who helped me most during this confusing and unhappy time. Her busy and complicated life took my eyes off myself. When I was feeling down and unable to pick myself up, I learned how to face up to my sense of loss and express my sorrow to her. She made me some tea and steered me back into daily life and work. She prepared the meals, washed and ironed our clothes, and kindly treated me in every way as a younger brother and friend.

As a ministry offering, it was Terezinha who brought meals and cleaned up after the young people who gathered for discipling at the church. In meetings with leaders or visiting pastors, she brought in *cafézinho*, coffee and refreshments, and gave faithful support as a loving mother to the church. These extra things she cheerfully did as ministry to God because she already had a job as zeladora for the church. She was a compassionate and generous saint.

Her husband, Augustinho, was generally a good man, but he had a worsening gambling problem. He worked hard all week but struggled to control his betting addiction on the weekends. Countless nights Terezinha and I searched all over for him in the local neighborhoods of Goiânia. We often found Augustinho playing snooker in some pool hall and rarely with any money left. He consistently disappeared on Friday nights after work and didn't come home on his own until Sunday, his weekly paycheck spent. I could barely help the family with what little money I put together from my job selling medicines and my job at the church. After I subtracted food, omnibus, books, and college classes, there was little left to share with them besides the rent I paid.

Meanwhile, the church was growing, and the work with young people had increased with scores of new jovens coming every month. Many were coming into the kingdom of God through faith in Jesus. One of the new believers in the youth group was a young man named Marcelo. He became very involved.

One day Terezinha told us something we could never have expected. She confessed she was pregnant and Marcelo was the father of her baby. Here she was, in her later thirties, married to a troubled husband, with four children and now expecting another child with barely an adequate income to take care of them all. The boys were young adolescents now. The girls were still little. Though this was a terribly complicated and problematic time, this would not change my fondness and respect for her as a person. She was the kindest, most giving person I had ever known. Yet incredibly, she had become pregnant by a boy half her age. It was certainly hard to believe.

Augustinho left her. Marcelo left too. Alone, pregnant, and with four children to raise, she discovered her grace-giving church to be remarkably generous in their support of her. For a time, they withdrew from her socially, but they still looked after her financially and spiritually. They prayed for her and became Jesus to her, physically helping her family during their time of brokenness and poverty.

Marcelo's father had a trucking business. The next year his father allowed him to take a cargo far north into the remote Amazonas when he was short a driver. Marcelo never returned from that trip. Many months later, the truck was discovered robbed of its cargo. Marcelo's body was found buried in a grave near the highway.

Marcelo's distraught and brokenhearted parents transferred the bitterness of their grief to Terezinha. As they became consumed with hatred, they regarded Terezinha as completely evil. They saw her as the cause of his death and could not forgive her. When they lost their son Marcelo, they said that nothing could possibly free them from their animosity. This tragedy was too much for them to bear. I knew that forgiveness is not a feeling and there are layers of things to forgive when people are grieving. I was in a period of reckoning with this surrender of each of those layers, myself.

I worship God and love Him with all my heart, but many times I do not understand what He is doing. I only know that He is surely doing something, and it's beyond my comprehension. He will bring something out of brokenness. He had taught me to reserve judgment, for we are weaker than we know and often helpless to make the right choices. When we are not strong, when we are hurt, the conditions exist for God to complete a work of transformation in us. It doesn't mean His work is over. When life is incomprehensible, we remember that God loves us in spite of our lack of faith. When we are ready, He will supply the forgiveness we lack.

Marcelo's tragic death brought his parents such unbearable pain that Terezinha felt she should respond to it. She decided to let them raise the baby as a gift of God to them. Terezinha publicly presented the child of Marcelo to them in order to comfort them in their suffering. It was a very beautiful and healing sacrifice that must have been indescribably difficult for her. Because of their little grandchild, Marcelo's parents found that they were able to forgive Terezinha. As the time of her healing and restoration passed, Terezinha again enjoyed fellowship with everyone in the church and grew to be loved and respected as *a pastora*, the pastor— the devout woman of God that she is today.

CHAPTER 39

THE CHEMICAL COMPANY

Percival was a man I knew from the pharmacy where I worked selling medicines who became a looming personality in my life. He was an expert chemist and a gifted and intelligent man with four children.

I was just on my way to the house of Percival on a Sunday morning when I saw his wife, Gina, coming down the sidewalk toward me. I actually did not know Gina yet. I had intended to pass by the pharmacy after leaving the church on my way to Percival's house. He and I had been working on something for church that evening that we were to discuss. Seeing that this woman and her daughters were near the pharmacy and appeared very upset, I stopped to inquire.

"Is everything alright? *O que foi?* What happened?"

"My husband wants to commit suicide!" Gina said. "He works here at the pharmacy, and he has made up some poison to drink!"

"Oh no—it must be Percival! Is it Percival?"

She nodded wide-eyed as I stepped past her and her daughters. I rushed into the pharmacy and called out his name. There he sat at a table with a glass in front of him. I calculated that the glass contained the concoction he intended to drink. Sitting down at the table, I bumped the glass with my hand, and the liquid spilled out on the table. When I asked him why he wanted to die, he began to talk. He opened up his heart and told me of his pain as I listened. After he calmed down, he decided he did not really want to die. We gathered his wife and daughters, and I went with them to his house.

I stayed with his family for the rest of the day, taking the noon meal with them, and they all came to church with me that evening. That night Percival believed in Jesus and accepted Him into his life. Percival's wife and daughters were baptized in the church soon after that. It seemed to me they were becoming a happy family as I observed their kind interactions and teamwork. Of course, I was not an expert on family dynamics, having experienced my worst years living with my own family. At that time, I couldn't have imagined the huge impact Percival was to have on his family, our church, and on me in the coming months.

Percival was a chemical practitioner. He had worked his whole life in pharmacies and laboratories. He knew how to combine and manage chemical compounds for all kinds of uses—home, hospital, farm, or business. He prepared various types of solutions, from mercury for thermometers to hydrochloric acid for cleaning bathrooms. He was very knowledgeable, sort of a walking encyclopedia, and could make what we consider simple things sound complex.

"Percival, could you give me some Mercurochrome for this cut on my hand?"

"You know, Justino, Mercurochrome is just a little merbromin—actually 2% mercury bromine—and 98% alcohol or water. It's an organomercuric disodium salt compound and a fluorescein."

"Is that so? Could you mix some up for me? I just want it for this little slash I have on my finger."

I recently learned on my own that the Mercurochrome we used for cuts and scrapes is no longer sold in some countries because of its mercury content. From him I learned that with just a few chemical compounds, if you have a good understanding of their functions and properties, you can produce products that are marketable for antimalarials, chemotherapy, and countless medicines, antiseptics, cosmetics, and cleaners. Percival was full of plans and ideas, and one that was prominent in his mind was to form a chemical company with me. He was serious about the two of us becoming partners in this start-up.

"But I don't have any money to put into it," I said. "Besides, I'm studying to be a lawyer, and I'm a pastor. Why would I want to get involved with the chemical industry?"

"Because it's something that makes money. There is a good market," persuaded Percival. "Just put in what money you have, and you will get a great return."

I explained to Percival that I had no real capital that I could invest into a business. He said I surely had something to sell!

"Well, I have nothing of value but my old *fusquinha*, little VW Bug. I guess I could sell that."

Now, I was not much of a skeptic anymore. I had become more open and relational with people. With more of his persuasion, I resolved to sell the bedroom furniture and the piano I had bought for my ex-fiancée, along with the fusquinha. I quit my part-time job at the pharmacy and put that time into working with Percival. We started our business in the chemical industry in Percival's home.

Percival happened to be an extraordinary salesman. He was trusted and well known in Goiânia for his products in all the pharmacies there. He made hydrogen peroxide, purified and distilled waters, Mercurochrome, paregoric liquid, and various other solutions commonly found in products used by Brazilian consumers.

One day, Percival said, *"Justino, vamos ao São Paulo. Let's go to São Paulo to buy glass bottles."*

He wanted containers for our products at a cheaper price. So, together we left Goiânia for São Paulo, a thousand kilometres away, to find glass bottles for our chemicals. After about eighteen hours on the ônibus, we arrived in São Paulo and found a hotel to spend the night.

There I was the next day, a farm boy walking around for the first time in my life in the vast, lively city of São Paulo, at that time a city of five million people. My head was spinning all around. Percival had the addresses of some businesses where he intended to make inquiries—Santa Marina, Wheaton Brazil, Polifarma, and some others that supplied stoppers and caps for the bottles we needed. What a picture we made— two simple, unassuming men, one the elder, one much younger, from the interior of Brazil, about to do some business deals in the big city with multinational companies! We hoped to present ourselves well, so we bought ready-made suits of clothing for each of us before going to the offices. Percival selected good shoes, socks, and ties with these dress suits for us. More experienced, he knew better how to look professional, and I followed.

The first problem we encountered was that we had no planned agenda. We had arrived by bus, we had no telephone, and we certainly were on no one's schedule at Wheaton Brazil or Santa Marina.

"Look, we've got two men here from Goiânia. They say they have no appointment and they don't know who they need to talk to but insist they need to see someone here in this building." The Wheaton employee at the reception desk frowned at us through his spectacles.

"Specifically, they would like a meeting with the director of glass supplies sales."

At this first business we visited, we sat down and waited only an hour before we were politely attended to. We were brought into a fine-looking office and seated in comfortable, orange-cushioned chairs. After the introductions were made, the man behind the desk asked the reason for our visit.

"What can I do for you? What is it you are looking for, gentlemen?"

"We have a business in the city of Goiânia, and we are needing glass supplies to contain the chemicals and solutions we produce," spoke Percival in his educated tone.

"Hmm. We really don't supply glass containers in your area of the country." When he looked at the inventory we needed, he said, "Besides, this is a very small quantity for the volume we deal with." The sight of our fallen faces may have compelled him to add, "I tell you what, could you come back tomorrow and see me again? I will investigate this matter and see if we can do anything for you."

Suddenly encouraged, we assured this department director that we would be back the next day to meet with him at the given appointment time. After that, we were back out on the streets of São Paulo catching buses to two other offices, Brasma and then Polifarma. We never got to Santa Marina. We returned the next day in a taxi to make our 10:00 a.m. appointment at Wheaton Brazil.

As we listened in amazement, the man explained to us what he could, in fact, do for us. He was willing to sell us such and such sizes of glass bottles in such and such quantities. When the package was added up, it was about three times as many bottles as we could possibly fill with products for our limited local clientele. But the price was right. Percival winked at me and made the deal anyway, and we left the city for our little town of Goiânia.

Sooner than we were even close to ready, a truckload of glassware arrived in Goiânia to be filled and distributed to our stores and pharmacies. Box after box of clinking glass items were unloaded in front of Percival's house, our place of business. His wife, Gina, was the first to ask the question of the year.

"*Ai ai ai! Tantos vidros!* So many bottles! What are we going to do with so many glass bottles?"

Yes, and the next month brought another truckload. And the next month. Percival remained upbeat. He and I had drawn up a business contract between Wheaton Brazil and the two of us.

"*Eu realmente gosto de vocês.* I really like you guys," the magnanimous representative from Wheaton Brazil had said.

From the beginning, we had no idea what this connection with Wheaton Brazil would put into our hands. They had made our corporation a multistate glass supplier for the area of Triângulo Mineiro. This was a triangle of rivers connecting cities in Brazil's northeastern interior. Triângulo Mineiro was becoming one of the most developed regions in all of Brazil. Supplying the area meant we supplied the cities of Minas Gerais, Goiás, Maranhão, Mato Grosso, and Mato Grosso do Sul, who all now wanted to buy from us. Pharmacies, distributors, laboratories, infirmaries, colleges, anyone who needed glass bottles came to us. We became a district glass bottling site that supplied to the entire region of northeast Brazil.

We connected with Brasma as the distributor for the caps to our bottles and with other companies for other materials. When we described ourselves as a concession for bottles, it was unheard of in the region. I well remember the arrival of those trucks and trying to find places for all the bottles. And how to pay for them in the allotted thirty to sixty days before we had any money come in! Pharmacies and laboratories of the region called São Paulo for their glassware, but São Paulo had named us as the distribution site.

"You have to call Goiânia—we no longer take care of that region," they said, giving them our number and address.

Since we were still yet to be discovered, no one knew who we were. And neither did we, for that matter. Percival quickly recognized our need to advertise so that we could be located and contacted. We became Physius Chemica Limitada. Our little company in Goiânia rocketed into sensational prosperity. Over a two-year period, we were forced to learn how to run our business: order, make, and distribute our products; set up workable strategies; hire and train staff; make and manage a good deal of money; and grow our company to meet the demands. It seemed we had outstanding success that only God Himself could have given us.

I was enjoying having money to spend on the people I loved. I could now build a new house for my parents and was able to increase my rent to help support the family of Terezinha, where I was living. Things were going so well with the business that it was hard to foresee that this dream could still become a nightmare. But, after a couple of years, things began to happen to complicate our lives.

Now that I had my own car, had built a house, was a pastor, was a graduate of seminary and college, and could support myself and a family, there seemed to be more expectations of me than when I was in my less affluent state. I was sought after to answer everyone's need at church, at home, and in the business. I was finally more stable and at ease with myself and enjoying the blessings of God in my life, but I found myself at a loss to deal patiently with the thorny problems of others. And now Percival, who was twenty years my senior, my business partner and advisor, who had been a great help to me, became my biggest complication.

Whether it was the grind of long work hours, the toxic effects of high stress, or the allure of instant success, something corrupted Percival's commitment to his family, to sobriety, to his church, and to God. The situation deteriorated quickly. I wondered if he had inhaled too many of his chemical compounds when he appeared to lose his emotional stability. Percival didn't come to church anymore. He went back to heavy drinking. He started spending a lot of money, ending up in debt. He broke the hearts of his wife and his children. His life became chaotic, risky, insane. I couldn't trust him anymore. I had essentially lost my friend, partner, and fellow traveler in quite a novel adventure.

Ultimately, Percival had a complete breakdown. One day, putting liquid Vaseline all over his naked body, he ran outside into the streets. It was impossible for anyone to secure him because he was so slippery. The police had to be called to keep him from hurting himself or someone else.

I realized a hard and crushing truth: it was over. We needed to sell the business, even at a loss. Percival didn't want to sell, but he couldn't carry the load without me, and so he had to agree. We sold it. Without a doubt we lost millions of cruzeiros. It wasn't the loss of the money that hurt so much. It was losing God's blessing in an exciting venture that we believed could have helped many people. What had started out as a journey with God turned to ruins.

Just as Percival had predicted, we certainly did make money. We had worked together in the chemical business in 1978 through 1980. For the first time in my life, I had money to give away and to save for the future. We had bought a new car for me and a new car for him. Our business had thrived under his guidance. In the first two years of our business partnership, when Percival was still connected to the church, he had not had another mental health crisis. But now it seemed the darkness that had nearly led him to suicide a few years earlier had come back to overwhelm his life, affect me, and hurt others in relationship with him. Other family situations grew progressively worse as well. Selling the business and disengaging in every aspect of our partnership took months. Every step in the process was painful, but it had to be done. I stayed connected to the family as long as I could, but finally I knew I had to say goodbye and walk away from it all.

CHAPTER 40

DESTINY

In those last months of shutting down the business, I was ready to make other changes too. I felt a new sense of expectancy—that I was soon to find a place or people to whom God was guiding me. There were some pastors of the Igreja Cristã Evangélica brotherhood who invited me to preach for them at their churches. I was free on Sunday mornings because I worked at my own congregation, Igreja Fama, on Sunday evenings. Pastor Abrão asked me to preach at his church one Sunday when he was to be away later in the month. I had been the pastor at his church, Igreja de Cristo, back in 1973 until October of 1975 while I was in seminary before I left for Argentina.

Many memories of that church swirled around in my head and inspired me to pass by the front of the church before I was to preach there to see if I might see some folks I knew. That day I arrived at just the right time, when the service was finishing and the people were coming out of the building. Loitering there a moment, I thought of the attractive young lady, Maria Lucia, who had shown interest in me back in 1973. Though I liked her, I really wasn't ready to be involved with anyone then. I was committed to leading my first church, finishing my schooling at seminary and my secondary education, and soon answering God's call to Argentina. It wasn't the time to even contemplate romance. Just as I was thinking these thoughts, whom should I see coming down the steps of the church but Maria Lucia herself.

Well! At the same time that I recognized Maria Lucia, I couldn't help noticing the very intriguing *moça*, young lady, who was with her—a striking brunette with darker skin, wearing glasses.

I couldn't take my eyes off her.

At this very moment, memories of the Lord's presence in my room came back to me. God had called me to return to Brazil from Argentina, and I was to settle down and form lasting relationships. And then I had become so convinced that Janete was the one for me. At that time, I was not able to see God's hand clearly. I had pushed back and questioned God. I was so sure and so wrong, and now the breakup seemed so long ago.

Now memories of my life with this, my first church, crowded into my mind, colliding with all the events of the past year. I had now terminated my business with Percival and was considering a move away from my current position at Igreja Fama. I was constructing a home for my parents, and they had been living with me in a completed part of the house—the home I believed God had led me to provide for them. They had moved all the way from Paraná to Goiás to be near me.

As I stood there in front of this church I had belonged to, where I had spent nearly three years learning and serving, my mind was filled with the things that God had done to guide my steps. He had shown me the special needs of young people while I unexpectedly grasped that I was one of them. We were stubborn paradoxes learning together that the more difficulties we faced growing up, the more help God made available to us. They put me in touch with moods and emotions I had been oblivious to most of my life. How the young loved to sing and worship together at night, thanking Jesus for His life-giving presence.

Families had come on Sundays and asked me to pray for them with remarkable confidence and trust in my leadership. The Lord answered our prayers and navigated us through many storms. The ministry taught me that God's invisible work was much more important than my visible work. I was a very young pastor, and this was not a seamless ministry, but Jesus grew us up from a handful to a building full.

I studied for my grade school diplomas and attended seminary, and God bought me books and provided my teachers. Many nights I crammed until dawn because I so valued these benefits God rained down on me. God showed me that my personal independence was often a weakness because my greatest strengths came from His hand, not mine. Sick with malaria, I endured the harsh medications and fevers and still led worship services because He sustained me through His people like Orvalina and her friend Isalina. And Litemar looked after me by hooking me up to IV fluids in my little room at the church. God's miracles blessed us all, and my own health was one of those miracles.

These reflections and images in my mind filtered my vision as I saw that very pretty, very interesting, dark-haired girl who wore glasses standing on the stairs beside Maria Lucia.

"Who is that girl?" parroted in my head like an echo in the forest. God had said that I would meet another girl who was the one He had chosen for me. I had not dated another girl since Janete, in November of 1977. I had become cautious in these matters. Today, I felt freedom.

After I preached at the church that evening, I returned home and called my friend Guilherme. I wanted to know if he knew the dark-haired girl I had seen with Maria Lucia. Guilherme and his wife, Auserite, would know. Auserite was the one who had been healed from demonic oppression one night through the fervent prayers of the congregation. This couple had become a *bênção*, blessing, to the believers there. So, I knew they'd be the ones to ask.

"Guilherme," I said, "I saw a girl on the steps of the church with Maria Lucia, and I would like to meet her." I described her and asked him if he knew who she was.

"If this is who I think it is, it's Alcione, Justino. She's been at the church only a short time. She works at the bank, Caixa Económico da Estado de Goiás."

Guilherme gave me the location of the office where she worked. The next day I went to the bank where she worked to see what I could see. There Alcione was at work—the very person I had described to Guilherme—striking, attractive, long dark hair, and dark eyes. I left before she could see me. Next, I asked Guilherme where she lived. This is embarrassing to confess. I began to drive by her house when I was in the area and even when I wasn't in the area at all. I hoped to eventually get up the nerve to call and introduce myself. Finally, I called her at work.

"Hello, Alcione? This is Moacir Rosa."

I told her I had seen her at the church and had asked Guilherme about her. I don't know why I didn't use my first name. Instead, I used my middle name, Moacir. That wasn't smart. I told her I would like to get to know her.

Alcione said that she had recently been through a breakup with a boyfriend and wasn't really interested in dating anyone. I tried to make a date with her anyway. It didn't materialize. I called a few other times and nothing came of my pursuits. But I couldn't get her out of my mind.

One day, weeks later, there was a young people's retreat given at the Presbyterian Retreat Center in Goiás. It was something you wouldn't want to miss. In my courtship with Janete, I had written a few songs, and she, a musician, had put my music into notation. I had submitted my songs to the Festival of Music in Anápolis, Brazil, and one had taken second place at the festival.

When I arrived at the camp where the retreat was held, some of the girls with Alcione said, "Look, Pastor Justino is here!"

This was a better introduction than I could have given myself. I was so relieved that someone knew of me and was glad I had come. Though Alcione had probably seen me drive by her house a couple of times, she didn't recognize I was that guy.

Next thing I heard was Gilberto, the worship leader at the retreat, calling out my name.

"We are very glad to have you here with us, Pastor Justino, since we are going to sing the song you wrote!"

Then they proceeded to sing my winning song with instrumental accompaniment! Getting this recognition at the camp was so gratifying. Hearing my name and my song gave me some confidence and helped me navigate the setback I had given myself by using my middle name and trying to get Alcione's interest with awkward phone calls. Now that we had been sort of reintroduced, I hoped we might be able to talk to each other face to face.

Feeling less of a trespasser, I watched for a chance to talk to her. It was so easy to spot her the way she stood out—her dark eyes bright and her smile so big. If only she were looking at me!

It was Saturday night, and the camp retreat was to end at noon on Sunday, and she didn't seem to even notice I was there. Finally, I walked up and asked Alcione if I could see her at her church for the service that was coming Sunday night. She agreed! She even smiled, and I did, too, at the thought of having a date with this beautiful girl!

It was finally Sunday night. I dressed in something casual with dress shoes and was on my way out the door when, unexpectedly, my parents brought in some friends to see their nearly finished house. They wanted to show them around and have a bite to eat and hoped I would give them the tour. These friends were from out of town and were to be houseguests that evening. I could not get away without hurting their feelings or being rude to my parents. There was still no telephone installed in the house, so I couldn't advise Alcione.

Our first date was foiled. She would surely be upset with me for standing her up! I hoped she would understand that the wait time for a new telephone was six months. Surely, she would appreciate why I couldn't call her. She didn't. Weeks passed by, and there was nothing I could do to break the chill.

Now April 28 was approaching, and Zé Carlos was getting married and had asked me to be a groomsman at his wedding. I really didn't want to attend his wedding alone. Zé was the medic from the hospital who had set up those home intravenous treatments for me when I was sick with malaria. I wondered if enough time had passed since I stood Alcione up that we might be on friendlier terms. Or was it still too soon to ask her out again?

The wedding was to be held at the very church where I had first seen her on the steps—my old church! I decided to call her up and flat out ask her if she would accompany me to the wedding. Hopefully she would find compassion in her heart since I was to be a groomsman and I had no one to go with me. And she knew the bride and groom. I called and asked her all of that.

"Zé Carlos?" she said, pausing to think about my question. "*Tudo bem*. Okay."

She agreed!

CHAPTER 41

JUSTINO AND ALCIONE

The wedding of Zé Carlos was missing an important element. The one who was to play the wedding march had not appeared even an hour after all the guests were seated. Zé Carlos came over to where Alcione and I were seated and asked me if I would fill in for the missing piano player.

"No, no, Zé. I can only play piano like a *papagaio,* parrot, you know. You will have to find somebody else!"

When someone was finally found to play the keyboard, our friends Zé and Helida were married. After the wedding, everyone gathered at Helida's parents' home for the reception. At long last, I had a private moment with Alcione.

"Alcione," I said to her. "Would you like to go out with me to dinner?"

"Now?"

She had seemed to be looking down and around and at everything other than at me. I wondered what was making her so uncomfortable. I had thought that I looked good wearing my favorite clothes—a beige pair of plaid dress pants and a bright, wine-colored shirt with black stripes. I guess the squares and the stripes were not going to set any new trends. *Chocante,* shocking, was how she described my outfit later; she had apparently agreed to go out to dinner with me to hide me from the looks of her friends. A smile of relief shone on her face when I took my suit jacket out of the car and put it on. It had seemed too hot to wear my jacket at the wedding while we fanned ourselves through the two-hour wait for the piano man.

Off to the best restaurant in Goiânia we went. It was a *churrascaria*, a place where the meat is cooked on a spit over fire. At this churrascaria, twenty or more kinds of meat were grilled or roasted and brought to our table on skewers. The waiters were very attentive. At every assenting nod of our heads another sizzling morsel, fresh from the fire, was sliced onto our plates. Side dishes of rice, beans, tomato *vinegrete*, hot vegetables, salads, fruits, french fries, fried manioc root, crusty French bread, cheese bread, fried bananas, and grilled pineapple were spread about the table. The peaches with cream, my favorite *sobremesa*, dessert, was the most delicious thing I ever remember eating.

That first night out together, I learned that Alcione loved to eat. I was amazed at how much she could get down. I watched her, very grateful that she was just a bit *encantado*, enchanted, with me because I had found us some great food. I enjoyed that very much. That was our first date. I hoped for another.

"Alcione, would you like to spend the day together so we can talk and get to know each other better?"

Coming up, there was a *feriado*, holiday, on the first of May. Thank goodness she accepted, because I had already planned the next outing for us. This time we had the whole day to spend hours together talking, sharing with each other our stories and our dreams for the future. I discovered Alcione to be a person who knew her own mind. I was likewise very direct and goal-oriented. She liked my name, Justino Moacir, after the grandfather and father who named me. I enjoyed the music of her voice and her vibrant and comprehensive way of telling me about herself while seeing me hang on every word. She was not embarrassed. And she was as interested as she was interesting. I was sure we were a good match. When it was time to take Alcione home, I asked her if she felt there was a good reason for us to continue seeing one another.

"Alcione, I'm at the time of my life when I am ready to get married. I have lived on my own for eleven years, and now I am living with my parents once again. I've moved them into a new house that I built for them, and now we are one too many in the house. I want to build a new place for myself and my wife."

I told her how I had caused my parents to suffer when I had moved away and that now my parents wanted to make up for the years they felt we had lost. With all good intentions, they were smothering me. I just couldn't take living with them much longer. But I couldn't rent a place outside of their home without hurting their feelings. They would only understand my moving away from them if it was for a good reason.

Alcione seemed to follow, even identify, with my story. I told her how I had been an angry, alienated, aggressive youth and a very unorthodox teenager, leaving home without their support or understanding. I had not fully come to terms with their disappointment in me or mine in them. I wanted to see if I could address the hollow place between us. To them, my life in the Amazon was a dangerous, selfish adventure. My missionary service in Argentina was another adventure of the same type. At one time they had thought of me as a runaway. Things were much better now. But it was time to show them some special consideration and help them know the son they had with them while they could.

Alcione listened intently to all that I said. Then she talked about her own upbringing too. We talked for hours. Her way of recounting her many stories with such honesty and objectivity and buoyant self-confidence made me fall in love with her. With her melodious voice and flashing, dark eyes, she openly told the solemn truth about herself, about me, and about personal, spiritual matters without trying to impress, flatter, or judge. She didn't soft-pedal anything. She was just straightforward, and her authenticity was sweet music to me. As a pastor, I had seen and heard a lot of persuasion and drama. Here before me was beautiful Alcione—a real woman with a strong identity. And her way of seeing things made me smile. I couldn't help it. She boosted and softened my rather solemn outlook.

After explaining my family situation to Alcione, she had not been put off. She reflected back to me her wish to love her family in a deeper way too. She seemed to accept how serious I was and to not be brought down by it. Near the end of our day together I could hardly find the words to draw our time to a close. I was just really serious about life. And I was serious about her. She had been frank with me—transparent, genuine, and blunt. Sometimes the things she said ruffled my feathers because she so obviously was *not* trying to make me feel secure or make herself look good. She laughed easily. At herself and at me.

"If you think we have a future together, then I would like to know today. I don't want to waste your time or mine," I told her.

Eu sei, I know, this was probably a little too soon to drop this on her.

It was only our first full day together. I had already accumulated an assortment of errors in pursuing her. However, I believed that Alcione was the one for me, and I wanted to know right away if I was on the wrong track. This was more than a matter of compatibility. It was a matter of finding out if we were meant for each other by God's design. I believed she was God's choice for me and wanted to know how she saw us.

"*Se não da, fale.*" I urged her. "If you think this won't work out, speak up. Tell me."

I wasn't interested in dating. I didn't care about having fun. I wanted to begin a new life with my wife. I didn't feel it should take a long time to find out if we shared perspectives as long as we were open and honest. And that's how Alcione was. Open and honest. To a fault! Her truthfulness was a marvelous trait to me.

Alcione gave me a fair answer. She said she wasn't ready to call it quits. She was not opposed to spending more time with me. Ouch, that hurt a little! Not quite what I hoped to hear. But at least she was wanting to continue. So, as we said goodnight to each other and to the end of that feriado, we had both agreed, *vamos indo.* Let's keep going.

I drove home dazzled that Alcione had agreed we should see each other more. We had learned that we were quite different in our families, our upbringing, and even physically. I thought she might not think we were good for each other or that the adjustment might be too hard. We had both been hurt before in romance, and so we knew there was great risk in two strong personalities moving ahead too fast. What enchanted me most about her was her guileless outspokenness. She said it had gotten her into trouble with people. For me, this weakness she confessed prevailed because it prepared me to fall in love with her. I trusted her. Never had I met someone so sincere and straight with me. Alcione was the real thing. She was who I had been waiting for.

Orvalina, one of the women who looked after me when I was very sick with malaria, had a daughter named Ana Maria, who was engaged to be married to Maurice, who was the son of the other woman, Isalina. Two friends were to be mothers-in-law of the same family! The *namorados*, fiancés, Ana Maria and Maurice, were to be married on Dia dos Namorados, the Brazilian Valentine's Day, June 12, 1980. Alcione and I were both invited to this church wedding at the Primeira Igreja Cristã Evangélica of Goiânia.

Before this wedding, I went to a jewelry store, by myself, and bought wedding rings. On the evening of June 12, I passed by and picked up Alcione so that we could attend the wedding together. When we got out of the car, there on the street, I took the rings out of my pocket. Looking around, I noticed we were on a very pretty street in front of a very pretty church. And I was with a stunning young lady.

"*Alcione, olha*—I showed her the rings. *Você aceita casar comigo?* Will you marry me?"

I could hardly believe that I had just asked her to marry me!

"*Aceito,*" was Alcione's answer. "I accept. I will."

We were engaged! We put our rings on our fingers there in front of the church. When she smiled at me, my heart was made new and happy. Then we went into the wedding of Ana Maria and Maurice as *noivos*, fiancés! After just six weeks of getting to know one another, we were engaged to be married. For both of us, it was the perfect amount of time. I felt we were made for each other. She said out loud that we were, and that thrilled me.

After the wedding of Maurice and Ana Maria, we went to see our parents to announce our engagement. I remember that my father hadn't really liked the idea of my marrying Alcione! He still had his heart set on my marrying his own favorite prospect. People in the church began to show sympathy for my father because of the way I was disappointing him. Another man in our church had wanted me to marry his daughter. He took me aside to ask if I was absolutely sure I was making the right choice. This hardly bothered us; it was all so ridiculous. We shook off the unwanted opinions and, of course, we were not influenced even a little bit.

Matchmaking was everybody's business in those days. No one had the independence or privacy in personal or family matters that they wished for. My father was only wanting the best for me and was still thinking I was young and impetuous. He did not yet know Alcione and assumed that I did not know her, either. Alcione and I endured the interrogations and stayed strong for each other. We were very happy and knew we were doing the right thing. I was so impressed with Alcione's confidence. The strength of my bride-to-be shone out to me as she held strong opinions about many things but didn't impose them on others. She refused to harbor anger or waver in doubt because of these pressures put on us by the church people and even my father. It was unacceptable, and yet we could hardly do anything but come together in solidarity with each other against the whole lot of them. Joyfully, we set our wedding date for

October 4, 1980, less than four months from our engagement day. It couldn't come fast enough! How thrilled we were when that day finally arrived and we were married!

Now, I had built a house for my parents, and they had been living there during its construction. I had always wanted to build a house for my mother and dad to live in until the end of their days. When I visited them in Paraná in 1979, my father asked me for help. My brothers Gerci and Jesus were not ready to move, but Pai wanted to move away from Paraná to where the climate was warmer. He asked me if I could help him move Mamãe and my little sisters Neida and Luzineide.

I asked him if he would accept coming to live in Goiânia, Goiás. His face brightened, and he called my mother into the room to ask her if she would like to live near her son Justino in Goiânia. She was so ready that she packed many boxes as well as suitcases and sent my sisters home with me! Within three months, my mother and father were living with my sisters and me too. My Pai would now have a house with no mortgage to take care of—an inheritance he and Mãe could leave to their family. It was a great pleasure to have my family near me, often even attending church services where I was leading. Even Pai enjoyed moving away from some of his traditions. In the coming years, many of the Rosa family would move to the state of Goiás not far from us.

When Alcione and I married, I moved out of that house into a *casinha*, small house, I rented for us. At first, we had almost no furniture or appliances, but little by little we bought together what we needed. We soon furnished our own living room, bedroom, and kitchen. We were both very busy working full-time, and I studied during much of our free time. I was to be graduated from university on December 22, and this was a very exciting time for me! How thrilled I was to be able to show my father my degree in *teologia* and make him proud of me.

All the things I believed the Lord had guided me in I was seeing come together. Daily I thanked God for His hand on my life. Alcione and I thanked Him together. Even though we did not always or immediately understand His purposes, we knew we must carefully obey His will rather than our own. When we did this, we recognized that there were incredible benefits.

It was my tendency to overplan and overwork. I would get overinvolved in a project because it was the Lord's work. But the Lord always brought me back. His work wasn't my project. It was His. I had the most wonderful partner in Alcione, who often saw things from a different perspective than I did and said so. She had a deep relationship with Jesus and a love of prayer. Now the two of us were walking hand in hand. She had a way of breaking through my resigned stoicism and getting me to talk about things that were stressful. Before her, I had made it a practice to pray and put things out of my mind that I couldn't control. She said that, realistically, that could mean putting her out of my mind. She liked to talk about everything, even the negative, hurtful, or frustrating things that I might rather ignore or forget for my own peace of mind. Alcione kept me in touch with the people around me, even my family. This wonderful girl helped me to find new joy in knowing and being known. She was a gift from heaven.

When I was invited to return to the Igreja de Cristo to work, Alcione and I considered this together as a couple. It would mean moving away from the church we had been married in. But in the end, we decided this was best. About a month before my *formatura*, graduation, I had a dream that left a very strong impression on me. I felt it was from God.

This dream was so vivid. I was looking at the sky, and suddenly the sky became black. Then I saw jagged rays of lightning strike together across the sky. The black sky broke in the middle, with the lightning cutting the sky into two pieces. Then I heard a voice say, "*Seu Pai...*Your Dad..."

I cried out and Alcione awakened. "*O que passou?* What's wrong?" she asked.

"My father is going to die," I told Alcione. I didn't know why, but I knew God was communicating this to me.

I called all my ten brothers and sisters and arranged for the family to come together so that we could spend time with Papai before he left us. Some said they couldn't come, but I insisted they must. In the end, every child of my father's and every grandchild except one came to be with him during *Natal*, Christmas, just as we planned. This became a time of great joy, *uma festa de Natal*, a Christmas party, in the new house of my parents. Most of my siblings had traveled a good distance with their children to be there. Their parents had moved a long way to be near me. It was grand to see everybody's face, hear of their lives, join our hearts together for our parents' sake. Together we were taking the opportunity that God had prepared for us to honor them.

The men roasted different kinds of choice meats over an outside fire, and the women made the *arroz*, rice, *feijão*, beans, *saladas*, salads, *sopas*, soups, *molhos*, salsas, *frutas*, fruits, and favorite breads and sweets. *Coisas lindas!* Marvelous things! This was a *churrasco,* feast of barbecued meats, which every *família Brasileira,* Brazilian family, loves.

When it was time to eat, I spoke of Natal, the birth of Jesus Christ, and God's love for us. I spoke of our love for each other and read a text from the Bíblia. Then we prayed together and were about to sit down when Papai asked to speak as well. Of course, we were eager to hear him.

"*Eu queria agradecer todos de vocês.* I want to thank each and every one of you for coming this Christmas to be with me. All of my children—my sons and daughters and in-law children, my grandchildren—all of you here with me."

"*Minha única tristeza,* my only sadness, is that this is the last Christmas you will have your Papai. The time of your papa has come to a close. The Lord is calling your daddy."

The sala was quiet but full of *emoção.* We knew that we would not all be together with him like this again. Not on this earth, anyway. Papai looked over at my mother, near him.

"*Almerinda, mi perdoa.* Almerinda, forgive me. I have been a difficult man, irritable, anxious, aggressive, demanding. Forgive me when I have not been as I should be." Then he spoke directly to each of his eleven children, asking forgiveness of each one, expressing thanksgiving for his or her participation in the family and their presence with him that Natal. He looked at each one of us, calling us each by our names first and then "daughter" or "son."

"I know at seventy I am not so old, but my time left here is not long now—*Deus está chamando seu Pai.* The Lord is calling your daddy home. Please, son, forgive your father. Please, daughter, *perdoe o seu Pai.*"

We were all deeply moved. For our Papai to express his remorse and love in this way was not just emotional but very cathartic. We knew our parents were not perfect. They had mirrored the harsh conditions they themselves had been raised in. In many ways they had suffered more than we had. I had fought back harder than my siblings, and I think they wondered why I had been so rebellious. Even I wondered at the intensity and duration of my own defiance. But Alcione had a way of validating my mutiny when she shared her own personal view of this to me. She said that when our own parents are opposed to God's voice in our lives, we are required to resist them. She said she also endured the opposition rather than the support of her folks and maintained there was no other path but resistance for her. She didn't regret it or worry how to make it up to them. She trusted God to do that. How I admired her strength and valued her counsel. I will never forget those new harmonious days we had together with my big family. A certain peace grew between all of us in the family, which remained throughout the years.

Natal acabou. Christmas came to an end. We ate our Christmas feast with our hearts full, experiencing the presence of our family with a greater awareness than we ever had. Some of us had to leave the next day; others were able to stay until the New Year.

On New Year's Day, those of us still together joined the kids playing out in the street. Even Papai came outside and played a little *futebol,* soccer, with his children and grandchildren. One brother was able to stay with us until about January 6. I was so glad for Papai that he had this time with his sons and daughters at the end of his life.

After that, Alcione and I visited with Papai and Mamãe at least one day a week. Sometimes I mentioned my less than idyllic childhood to Alcione to prepare her for being with my family. Immediately, she shook her head and took my side, saying it wasn't my fault, it was my circumstances, and we were to thank Jesus, who redeems all our circumstances. She reminded me none of us had a perfect family, and she refused to harbor resentment over this. I savored the gentleness and genuine love Alcione showed my parents. She always brought something delicious she had cooked for the four of us. She showed affection toward them as if they were her own parents. She saw my childhood rebellion as a natural and important consequence of the dire circumstances I lived in. She even saw this as good and *necessary.*

"This aggression you showed wasn't all your human failing. It was survival. It was a cry for help, and Jesus answered it. You broke the chains for your whole family."

She urged me to be with my parents as much as possible so that they would know me better. I brought this subject up with Papai, and he didn't suddenly go on a walk. He didn't change the subject or get busy with his projects. He looked me in the eye. He addressed the prejudice he endured as a black man and spoke of the community intolerance toward non-Catholics during his life. He admitted he didn't want us to fail at being both minorities and Protestants, because everyone was watching us. His ardent desire, he admitted, was to honor the memory of his father, my grandfather Justino, who had carved out this bold and uncompromising path for us. "*Especially* the child who wore his name should honor his grandfather," he said. He admitted this was an injustice toward me.

"But *filho,* son, you showed me it is God we must honor above all things. Religions and cultures and families will *sempre*, always, have flaws. You did the right thing. You had to give up your own family to follow Jesus. I knew you loved us. You would only leave our church and our family if God told you He had something better for you. I am very happy you changed to the seminary of Igreja de Cristo and that you know how to listen to God in these matters of who you are and what you are about and where you are going. I honestly like to come to your church more than my own even though it's different in so many ways. I'm a Presbyterian minister, but I am glad you are not. Your ways of praying and worshiping have made God more real to me. I wouldn't have the faith I have in God now if I hadn't watched you live out your life with God, trying to find out His will for you. And if you hadn't left my church, you wouldn't know God like you do today. And neither would I." This sincerity of my father made him so dear to me that I vowed to have that kind of honesty with my own children if Alcione and I had them.

I often came around in the afternoons to take Papai out for a café and *pão de queijo*, cheese bread, at a special little shop he loved. During one of those times *tomando café*, going for coffee, with him, he reminded me again that our time was short.

"*Filho, Deus está me chamando.* Son, God is calling me. *Meu tempo é curto.* My time is short. It's time to start preparing for this."

I protested, but I knew he was serious and it was true. God was speaking to our hearts together. I thought a gathering of friends would comfort and encourage Mamãe and Papai, so I planned a *feijoada* for his birthday, January 18. A *feijoada* is a national meal of Portuguese and African origin made in a large pot to share with a gathering of loved ones. The big pot is filled with a stew made up of pork and beef with seasonings and black beans and is served with typical Brazilian side dishes such as turnip greens and orange slices. This historical meal has been shared for centuries by all Brasileiros to commemorate every feasible occasion. Most people believe feijoada was invented by Brazilian slaves, who combined scraps of meat they received from their owners with their plentiful black beans. In Brazil, that huge pot of feijoada is shared in the same way cake commemorates weddings, holidays, graduations, baptisms, or birthday parties. Since Papai was having his birthday on a Sunday, we invited friends to join our family for the feijoada meal for Papai's birthday.

Saturday morning the telephone rang. It was Mãe. It was a new sound to hear my mother's voice on the phone since we had just recently put the telephone in her home.

"*Seu pai não está bem.* Your dad is not well. He passed a very bad night," my mother told me.

"*Estou indo, Mãe.* I'm on my way," I told my mother.

We left in a hurry, Alcione and I, driving as fast as we could. When we arrived at my parents' house, my father could not lie down or sit up. He was so agitated he doubled over when we propped him up with pillows. He said his head was burning on one side, and he moaned in his suffering.

"*Pai, vamos para o hospital.* Pai, let's go to the hospital," I said.

"*Não, filho.* No, son, open the Bible and let's pray."

I read a piece of Scripture, and then he asked us to sing his favorite *canticos da igreja*, church hymns. We started with a special favorite of his.

After we sang another hymn, Papai agreed to go to the hospital.

"*Cuide de sua Mãe pra mim, filho. Cuide de seus irmãos.* Take care of your mother for me, son. Take care of your brothers and sisters."

I promised I would, and I meant it with my heart and soul. I looked at my mother at his side. And I still had an unmarried brother and two little sisters whom my father was concerned about. I put him in my car and took him to the hospital. When I got to the hospital, I realized I did not have my wallet with me. Dr. Sebastião was the attending physician at the hospital in Goiânia, and he knew me. They let me go home to get my *carteira*, billfold, while they took my father right into care. Alcione, my mother, and my brother were there by my father's side while I went home.

As I was in the hallway of my home, approaching the place where my billfold and checkbook lay, I sensed the Lord speaking to me.

God spoke this to my mind: "*Alcione está gravida—un menino chamado Samuel!* Alcione is pregnant—a boy called Samuel!"

I felt a rush of joy. It still brings tears to my eyes. Alcione and I did not know we were expecting a child! It was precious news to have at this moment of loss. And it was good for me to know I must look out for her too. She was a strong woman and would not take attention away from my mother and dad. I believe God wanted to strengthen my faith in Him so that I would rest in Him during these challenging times ahead. Our Lord God does not want our hearts to be troubled or afraid. He wants to bring peace to our inner being every day.

My brother Jesus stayed the night with my father, all of us hoping Papai would make it through the night for his seventieth birthday. And he did!

We went to the hospital early in the morning to find him awake and alert. Family came from everywhere to spend his birthday with him. The room was crowded with loved ones, and he spoke to Mamãe and all of his children, grandchildren, nephews, and nieces with a delight that was very much like that of Christmas. We sang his favorite songs and passed the day with one another just as if it were the birthday *feijoada* we had planned. I don't think any of us were afraid of his passing. Because of God, we were completely prepared, and so was he. Pai knew our faces and spoke to each of us one by one. He was talking with my brother Jesus before he called me over next.

"*Tininho, vem aqui!* Tininho, come here!" he said to me, using his pet name for me, which means "little Justino." I drew near to his bed awed at how well he looked with the nice shave they had given him.

"Tininho, I thought you might pass by the little house where we always have *café e pão de queijo,* coffee and cheese bread, and bring me something to eat."

"Sure, Pai. I will go there and get you something, if you like," I beamed, pleased to be asked.

Papai looked so satisfied, so happy. He smiled a big, radiant smile. And then he was gone. Just like that, *Papai morreu.* We closed his eyes for him and sat down all around his bed, comforted by the gentle way he had gone. It was January 18, *anniversario dele,* his birthday. I remembered the dream with the lightning cutting across the blackened sky. It was God's chosen timing. I was steadied and in complete peace. We all were.

Alcione soon made an appointment with the doctor and discovered she was pregnant. When our baby was born, we named him Samuel Moacir Rosa after my father. That some of these events were shown to me by God in order to direct my life may seem incomprehensible to many. Maybe I have needed more reassurance and guidance than is common. All I know is that this is how my life unfolded, and this is how the Lord dealt with me and cared for me.

O Fim, The End

EPILOGUE

When Justino arrived in the spring of 1994 to take leadership of our Communidade de Cristo church in Campinas, Brazil, those on our team were elated. We had heard him speak at a mini-retreat in Campinas in the late 1980s, and it was a watershed time for us. He gave us a picture of what God was doing in Brazil and what could be possible in the future. Three of our missionary team, Jim Gullett, Jeff Greene, and Chip Stauffer, met with him in the state of Minas Gerais in 1990. His ministry was then a key part of a large network of Brazilian Christian churches that were emerging and flourishing in central Brazil. We sought to learn from this Brazilian leader who led churches and also taught at the seminary in the capital, Brasília.

In that central part of Brazil, Justino had planted and developed seven churches in addition to practicing law. We were incredibly impressed with his love of God and how he had been used to build and lead churches in the past decade. God eventually led our team to approach him about moving south to Campinas where we had planted a church. We believed the time and place was ripe for Brazilian leadership, which could greatly expand the church in a very metropolitan area in the state of São Paulo. So, we met with him again and also invited him to Campinas to see our work. After discussions, mutual dreaming, and much prayer, Justino agreed to move his family and take over leadership of our Communidade de Cristo in Campinas.

What a great move that proved to be. As a dirt-poor farm boy of nineteen with only a fourth-grade education, he had lived as a missionary with an undiscovered tribe deep in the Amazon territory. Later, he traveled to Argentina in the middle of a revolution to minister in various regions of the country. After then returning to central Brazil, he pursued a comprehensive education, became an attorney, and planted a network of seven churches. He then agreed to move his family to Campinas, near São Paulo, where he grew the church we planted and soon established other satellite campuses. Justino Rosa is a testimony to God's unfathomable design and power.

Justino's story has rendered in me a new openness to the stories of others and a deeper contemplation of the one I am living. His faith has profoundly raised my own expectations of life lived under God's reign and in His company. As I often watched Justino wipe the tears from his eyes and cheeks when he shared his story with me, I experienced the words of Jesus—"Whoever believes in me...'Out of his heart will flow rivers of living water'" (John 7:38 ESV). I learned that if we listen for God's guidance, He will indeed speak to our hearts.

Justino's children, Samuel, Thiago, and Miryam, each are involved in ministry today having been greatly influenced by their father's experience with God. Today, Justino's son Thiago is pastoring our dear Campinas church in Brazil, now called Comunidade Betesda–Igreja de Cristo. Miryam became Mimi (and part of our family) when she stayed with us for a season as a teenager. She fell in love with Arizona and also with her best American friend, who later became her husband, Jake. Their family is now serving as missionaries in Thailand. Justino's eldest son, Samuel, an American pastor in Delaware, Ohio, echoes his dad's life sermon, saying, "Never doubt God's absolute, infinite, and eternal love for you when troubles come! These tests are precisely what we need to pass our way through in order to be fully prepared to take on the life assignments God has set aside for us!"

Justino's story tells how God responded to his cry for help and changed his life. As we see how God takes him on assignments of mercy into a hurting world, Justino's faith challenges us to expect miracles from God like he does. This is Justino Rosa's account of how God enables him to transcend his personal constraints of spiritual oppression, fear of society, abject poverty, humble education, and the paradoxical religious, political, and social norms of his era wherever he travels. It is an exciting living testimony that God is just as near to His children today as He was two thousand years ago when He came and walked with us. He calls us to walk with Him today, helping us find our way through our rebellion, anger, and hurt to a life in Him.

With this testimony of Justino's life in mind, we can easily imagine how friendship with God deepens the meaning and value of life on earth, on this first interval of our journey with Him. I'm grateful Justino has given his story to us. Its actualities, its many distant backdrops, and its marvelous events transport us to a vantage point where we can glimpse God's majestic hand over all of us in all the world for all time.

ACKNOWLEDGMENTS

Some of the most treasured hours of my life have been spent listening to Justino recount his adventures while I put everything down in English. Justino's wife, Alcione, told me she discovered more about Justino's early life this way. Justino's daughter, Miryam, learned English while staying in the US with Chip and me for a summer. She became the person who translated the manuscript back to Portuguese for Justino's review numerous times. Her brothers Samuel and Thiago helped.

LeRoy Lawson, even while busy composing his own new manuscripts, surprised me by reading the manuscript in a weekend. Thank you, Roy, my mentor, pastor, and friend.

Paige, Charley, and Holly, our children, supported my writing in many ways. One bought me a new computer. One helped with liberal cheerful perspective. One kept urging me, "Mom, you must get this published. I'm behind you one hundred percent."

Mick Silva was a champion for me. He accepted the manuscript and, enduring a barrage of emails from me for months, carefully sculpted it, as content editors must do. His continued guidance has been invaluable.

Carol Wagner read Justino's story and loved it first, when it was a box of papers. I am thankful for all my readers who encouraged me by describing the impact Justino's story had on them—Darien Keane, Christy Lowry, Tom Eaton, Steve and Mary Wilson, Larry Daily, Louie Matta, Cindy Cameron, Trevor and Greg Hutchins, Terry Willey, Kristin Funston, and Aunt Nancy. Many thanks to Savannah, Roy, Dr. Barro, Bryan, Dave, and Bob, who wrote brilliant words from their hearts that belong in big letters.

We will always be grateful for our CMF teammates who worked closely with us and with Justino in Southeast Brazil—especially Jeff and Patty Greene and Jim and Holly Gullett.

Finally, I want to thank Dave Sheets and his staff at BelieversBookServices for producing a beautiful book. I truly appreciate the second mile you have run for me, editors Roberta Nichols, Dr. Mark Tuggle, and Penny Tuggle.

I thank God for the gift of this story, the assignment, the trust, the joy in writing it. My husband Chip has always backed it, delighted in it, and let me read it to him for years.

ABOUT THE AUTHOR

Ann T. Stauffer studied at Abilene Christian University and Ottawa University. She earned a BA in English Education and has experience in high school teaching and administration. Ann spent several years in Brazil with her husband and family working with a team of families to establish communities of Christ. She enjoys sailing, art, music, travel, and spending time with family and friends.